UNFAIR TRADING PRACTICES IN THE FOOD SUPPLY CHAIN

UNFAIR TRADING PRACTICES IN THE FOOD SUPPLY CHAIN

Implications of Directive (EU) 2019/633

Bert Keirsbilck
Evelyne Terryn
(eds.)

INTERSENTIA

Cambridge – Antwerp – Chicago

Intersentia Ltd
8 Wellington Street
Cambridge | CB1 1HW | United Kingdom
Tel.: +44 1223 736 170 | Fax: +44 1223 736 169
Email: mail@intersentia.co.uk
www.intersentia.com | www.intersentia.co.uk

Distribution for the UK and Ireland:
NBN International
Airport Business Centre, 10 Thornbury Road
Plymouth, PL6 7 PP
United Kingdom
Tel.: +44 1752 202 301 | Fax: +44 1752 202 331
Email: orders@nbninternational.com

Distribution for Europe and all other countries:
Intersentia Publishing nv
Groenstraat 31
2640 Mortsel
Belgium
Tel.: +32 3 680 15 50 | Fax: +32 3 658 71 21
Email: mail@intersentia.be

Distribution for the USA and Canada:
Independent Publishers Group
Order Department
814 North Franklin Street
Chicago, IL60610
USA
Tel.: +1 800 888 4741 (toll free) | Fax: +1312 337 5985
Email: orders@ipgbook.com

Unfair trading practices in the food supply chain. Implications of Directive (EU) 2019/633
Bert Keirsbilck and Evelyne Terryn (eds.)

ISBN: 978-1-78068-980-7 (hardcover)
ISBN: 978-1-78068-999-9 (pdf)
D/2020/7849/39
NUR 822

British Library Cataloguing in Publication Data. A catalogue record for this book is available from the British Library.

CONTENTS

CHAPTER 1

RUN-UP, LEGAL BASIS AND SCOPE OF APPLICATION

Elisa Paredis
PhD candidate, Consumer Competition Market, KU Leuven

Bert Keirsbilck
Associate professor, Consumer Competition Market, KU Leuven

1. INTRODUCTION

1. On 17 April 2019, the European Parliament and Council adopted *Directive 2019/633 on unfair trading practices in business-to-business relationships in the agricultural and food supply chain* ("UTPD"). This Directive is aimed to counteract certain unfair trading practices ("UTPs") that result from an abuse of the imbalance of bargaining power by buyers towards suppliers of agricultural and food products.[1]

According to the European legislator, structural changes in the (agricultural and food) supply chain, such as vertical integration and concentration of large retailers, have placed many buyers in a strong bargaining position vis-à-vis their suppliers. This position enables them to unilaterally impose contract terms on their weaker counterpart and to shape the business relationship exclusively to their own economic interests, which may not coincide with the most efficient outcome.[2] Just like consumers[3], the weaker counterparty may not be in the

1 *Proposal for a Directive on unfair trading practices in business-to-business relationships in the food supply chain*, 12 April 2018, Explanatory Memorandum, COM(2018) 173 final, 1; Commission Staff Working Document, *Impact assessment accompanying the document Proposal for a Directive on unfair trading practices in business-to-business relationships in the food supply chain*, 12 April 2018, SWD(2018) 92 final, 20–21.

2 Commission Staff Working Document, *Impact Assessment*, 11 and 20–21.

3 *Proposal for a Directive on unfair trading practices in business-to-business relationships in the food supply chain*, 12 April 2018, Explanatory Memorandum, COM(2018) 173 final, 3: *"Regulatory divergence and under-protection of kinds similar to UTPs have given rise to EU initiatives in the area of business-to-consumer protection. (…) The conceptual approach under the EU's business-to-consumer rules indeed shares relevant characteristics with Member States'*

position to actually individually negotiate terms or refuse the offer of its stronger counterparty, and thus does not enjoy 'genuine' freedom to contract.[4] Since alternative trading partners are limited (due to increased concentration) and switching costs may be high, the weaker counterparty will simply accept the unbeneficial terms out of fear of losing the contract and potentially go out of business ('fear factor').[5] Adding to this significant price pressure from consumers and the more market-oriented *Common Agricultural Policy* ("CAP") increasing their vulnerability for price movements, farmers and small suppliers are considered particularly vulnerable to such UTPs stemming from the buyer-side.

On the basis of this reasoning, the UTPD puts in place – in a somewhat similar way as in B2C relationships[6] – a protective regime for the 'weaker' party in the vertical B2B relationship. Yet, the UTPD regime focuses on the contractual relationship between buyers and suppliers of agricultural and food products only. With the justification that such practices stemming from the buyer-side are likely to have a negative impact on the 'standard of living' of the agricultural community, the legal basis chosen for the UTPD is that of Article 43 TFEU.

2. In this first chapter, we will discuss and critically assess the chosen legal basis (Section 3) and scope of application of UTPD (Section 4). Before doing so, we will first map out the developments in the food supply chain and the evolutionary perspectives on the role of freedom of contract in B2C and B2C relations leading up to the creation of the UTPD (Section 2). Eventually, we will come to a conclusion (section 5). One of the general themes of this chapter is that the creation of the UTPD may perhaps be a first step in slowly breaking down the wall between the regulatory approach towards B2C and B2B (contractual) relations.

existing UTP rules governing business-to-business transactions, namely the focus on relatively weaker parties to commercial transactions."

4 EUROPEAN COMMISSION, *Green paper on unfair trading practices in the business-to-business food and non-food supply chain in Europe*, 31 January 2013, COM(2013) 37 final, 6; EUROPEAN ECONOMIC AND SOCIAL COMMITTEE, *Opinion on the Report from the Commission to the European Parliament and the Council on unfair business-to-business trading practices in the food supply chain*, 19 October 2016, *OJ* C34/130, 3.5.4: *"There are some area of food production and manufacturing where contractual freedom no longer exists."*

5 EUROPEAN COMMISSION, *Green paper*, 2013, 6.

6 Explanatory memorandum UTP Proposal, 3.

2. THE RUN-UP TO THE UTPD

2.1. INFORMATIONAL ASYMMETRIES AND IMBALANCES IN BARGAINING POWER – FROM PROTECTION OFFERED IN B2C RELATIONS TO B2B RELATIONS?

3. In EU private law, a sheer contrast exists between B2C and B2B (contractual) relationships.

4. The EU consumer *acquis* offers substantial protection to consumers in their dealings with businesses.

The main *horizontal* consumer protection instruments – that apply across the board to the (promotion of) any sales and service contracts – are the *Unfair Commercial Practices Directive 2005/29/EC* ("UCPD")[7], the *Consumer Rights Directive 2011/83* ("CRD")[8] and the *Unfair Contract Terms Directive 93/13/EC* ("UCTD").[9]

The consumer *acquis* basically follows three 'strategies' of consumer protection:

1. imposing mandatory pre-contractual information requirements (e.g. Article 7 UCPD and Articles 5 and following of the CRD);
2. granting a right of withdrawal in certain situations (such as distance contracts[10] or contracts concluded outside of the business premises as regulated in the CRD);
3. regulating the content of a contract (negatively, e.g. through a prohibition of unfair terms as set out in the UCTD, and positively, e.g. through mandatory rules on conformity as set out in the *Consumer Sales Directive 1999/44/EC*[11]).

---

7 Directive 2005/29/EC of 11 May 2005 concerning unfair business-to-consumer commercial practices in the internal market, *OJ* L 149/22–39. See EUROPEAN COMMISSION, *Guidance on the implementation/application of Directive 2005/29/EC on unfair commercial practices*, SWD/2016/0163 final.

8 Directive 2011/83/EU of 25 October 2011 on consumer rights, *OJ* L 304/64–88.

9 Directive 93/13/EC of 5 April 1993 on unfair terms in consumer contracts, *OJ* L 95/29–34. See also Commission notice, *Guidance on the interpretation and application of Council Directive 93/13/EEC on unfair terms in consumer contracts*, OJ C 323, 27.9.2019, 4–92.

10 As regards the right of withdrawal set out in the CRD for distance contracts, the Court has ruled that "*the right of withdrawal is therefore intended to offset the disadvantage for the consumer resulting from a distance contract by granting him an appropriate period for reflection during which he can examine and test the goods acquired*" See CJEU 23 January 2019 C-430/17 (*Walbusch Walter Busch*), EU:C:2019:47, para 45.

11 Directive 1999/44/EC of the European Parliament and of the Council of 25 May 1999 on certain aspects of the sale of consumer goods and associated guarantees, *OJ* L 171/12–16. From 1 January 2022, the Consumer Sales and Guarantees Directive will be repealed and replaced by Directive (EU) 2019/771of 20 May 2019 on certain aspects concerning contracts for the sale of goods, *OJ* L 136/28–50.

According to the Court of Justice, the UCPD "*relies on the assumption that, in relation to a trader, the consumer is in a weaker position, in that the consumer must be considered to be economically weaker and less experienced in legal matters than the other party to the contract*".[12] Moreover, "*the information provided, before a contract is concluded, on the terms of the contract and the consequences of concluding it, is of fundamental importance for a consumer. It is on the basis of that information that the consumer decides whether he wishes to be contractually bound to the trader.*"[13]

As regards the UCTD, the Court has ruled that "*the system of protection introduced by the directive is based on the idea that the consumer is in a weak position vis-à-vis the seller or supplier, as regards both his bargaining power and his level of knowledge. This leads to the consumer agreeing to terms drawn up in advance by the seller or supplier without being able to influence the content of those terms.*"[14]

5. However, the relationships between businesses (B2B) have largely been left to their own freedom to contract and freedom to compete. Backed with expertise in the commercial field and knowingly and willingly accepting the risk of business life, each business may freely determine its own market strategies and design contracts that best suit their needs – at least so long as these choices do not create anti-competitive effects. Indeed, inequality in business relations is – or was – in general only tackled when the party with a dominant position abuses this position *and* thereby distorts competition on the relevant market. Albeit the prohibition on an abuse of a dominant position in competition law might also outlaw unfair practices, tackling such unfairness is at most a subsidiary, but certainly not its primary aim.[15]

6. In the absence of such an anti-competitive effect on the market – and consequently outside the reach of (EU) competition law – the fair or unfair character of commercial conduct has as a general rule – with a number of exceptions – remained outside the reach of EU commercial and contract law. These 'exceptions' consist of specific interventions with a limited scope, mostly targeting a particular practice (or a number of practices), and/or solely apply in a certain sector or in a particular type of contractual relationship.

12 See CJEU 3 October 2013, C-59/12 (*Zentrale zur Bekämpfung unlauteren Wettbewerbs*), EU:C:2013:634, para 35; CJEU 16 March 2015, C-388/13 (*UPC*), EU:C:2015:225, para 53; CJEU 13 September 2018, C-54/17 (*Wind Tre*), EU:C:2018:710, para 54; CJEU 12 June 2019, C-388/13 (*Orange Polska*), EU:C:2019:480, para 36.

13 CJEU 13 September 2018, C-54/17 and C-55/17 (*Wind Tre*), EU:C:2018:710, para 46; CJEU 23 January 2019 C-430/17 (*Walbusch Walter Busch*), EU:C:2019:47, para 36.

14 See CJEU 9 November 2010, C-137/08 (*VB Pénzügyi Lízing*), EU:C:2010:659, para 46.

15 EUROPEAN COMMISSION, *Green paper on unfair trading practices in the business-to-business food and non-food supply chain in Europe*, 31 January 2013, COM(2013) 37 final, 10 and 12.

Cross-sectoral and in the field of marketing, *Directive 2006/114/EC on misleading and comparative advertising* ("MCAD") installs protection to consumers and businesses (primarily horizontally, vis-à-vis competitors) by imposing certain conditions on comparative advertising and outlawing misleading advertisement.[16] *Directive 86/653/EEC* specifically protects self-employed commercial agents vis-à-vis principals in agency agreements.[17] *Directive 2011/7/EU* specifically combats the issue of late payment in commercial transactions between undertakings.[18] Moreover, in terms of sectors, principles of fairness have been introduced in contractual relations in the milk/dairy sector and the sugar sector, mostly aimed at enhancing transparency by prescribing mandatory written contract and listing a number of elements (e.g. price) that must be determined in the contract.[19]

7. Nonetheless, despite the rather limited regulatory protection offered, the issue of fairness in B2B relations has not remained undiscussed at the EU level, and even has been attracting more and more attention in the last 10–15 years.[20] The realization that, just like consumers, certain – often smaller – businesses may also suffer from an informational asymmetry and find themselves in a weaker bargaining position, unable to fully utilize their economic freedom, thus has already made its entrance within the EU institutions for a number of years.

At one point in time, the possible expansion of the MCAD to better protect businesses (especially SMEs) against unfair commercial practices impairing their ability to make informed choices[21] – thus primarily tackling unfairness in the pre-contractual phase – was put on the table. Concretely, the Commission envisaged to extend the scope of this instrument so as to cover all (misleading) B2B marketing practices as well as to introduce a black-list with certain specific and most harmful B2B misleading marketing practices (e.g. disguising a commercial communication as an invoice or concealing the commercial intent of a communication). Yet, eventually, the MCAD has not been amended.

---

16 Directive 2006/114/EC concerning misleading and comparative advertising, *OJ* L 376/21–27.

17 Directive 86/653/EC of 18 December 1986 on the coordination of the laws of the Member States relating to self-employed commercial agents, *OJ* L 382/17–21.

18 Directive 2011/7/EU of 16 February 2011 on combating late payment in commercial transactions, *OJ* L 48/1–10.

19 Regulation 1308/2013 of 17 December 2013 establishing a common organisation of the markets in agricultural products: Art. 125 (sugar sector), Art. 148 (milk/dairy sector) and Art. 168 (voluntary provision for other sectors) *juncto* recital 13; EUROPEAN COMMISSION, *Green Paper,* 2013, 13.

20 S. DE POURCQ, *Oneerlijke handelspraktijken en bedingen in contracten tussen ondernemingen,* Antwerpen, Intersentia, 2019, 15.

21 EUROPEAN COMMISSION, *Review of the "Small Business Act" for Europe,* 23 February 2011, COM(2011) 78 final, 12; EUROPEAN COMMISSION, *Protecting businesses against misleading market practices and ensuring effective enforcement – Review of Directive 2006/114/ EC concerning,* 27 November 2011, COM(2012) 702 final.

Likewise, the extension of the scope of the UCPD to all B2B commercial practices has been advocated in the past, at least as far as practices at the pre-contractual stage are concerned.[22] Although the UCPD currently applies only to B2C commercial practices, recital 8 nevertheless already admits that "*there are other commercial practices which, although not harming consumers, may hurt competitors and business customers. The Commission should carefully examine the need for Community action in the field of unfair competition beyond the remit of this Directive and, if necessary, make a legislative proposal to cover these other aspects of unfair competition*". Yet, no extension of the UCPD to B2B commercial practices will take place in the near future.

As regards the scope of the UCTD, nothing will change either.[23] Importantly, the amendments by the *Directive (EU) 2019/2161 as regards the better enforcement and modernisation of Union consumer protection rules*[24] – building on a number of recommendations in the so-called *Fitness Check of EU consumer and marketing law*[25] – will not entail any change to the scopes of the UCPD and the UCTD.

8. Nevertheless holding on to the distinction between business-to-consumer and business-to-business regulation, various initiatives, studies and reports did start to pop-up in recent years addressing the matter of inequality in business relations. Perhaps not directly interfering in the (contractual) relations of SMEs, various action plans have been taken at the EU level to help SMEs overcome various hurdles such as lack of information or finance and to improve their access to markets, competitiveness and business environment in general. On top of this, the limits of freedom of contract became apparent in vertical B2B (predominantly contractual) relations as well. The issue of "fairness" in vertical supply chains was first discussed in the food sector, but later on became a topic of discussion in relation to supply chains in general.

---

22 See B. KEIRSBILCK, "Which way forward for the new European law of unfair commercial practices?", *REDC* 2013, 2, (233) 253–254; B. KEIRSBILCK, *The new European law of unfair commercial practices and competition law*, Oxford, Hart Publishing, 2011, 256–257 and 558–559.

23 See M. SCHILLIG, "Inequality of bargaining power versus market for lemons: legal paradigm change and the Court of Justice's jurisprudence on directive 93/13 on unfair contract terms", *European Law Review* 2008, 336–358; H. SCHULTE-NÖLKE, "No market for 'lemons': on the reasons for a judicial unfairness test for B2B contracts", *European Review of Private Law* 2015, 195–216.

24 Directive (EU) 2019/2161 of the European Parliament and of the Council of 27 November 2019 amending Council Directive 93/13/EEC and Directives 98/6/EC, 2005/29/EC and 2011/83/EU of the European Parliament and of the Council as regards the better enforcement and modernisation of Union consumer protection rules, *OJ* L 328/7-28.

25 Among stakeholders insufficient support existed to extend the scope of Directive 2005/29 on unfair business-to-consumer commercial practices and Directive 93/13/EC on unfair terms in consumer contracts to cover business-to-business relations as well, see: CIVIC CONSULTING (prepared for DG JUST), *Study for the Fitness Check of EU consumer and marketing law*, Final report part 1 – Main report, 202–205 and 207 and 272; *Commission Staff Working Document – Report on the Fitness Check*, SWD(2015) 209 final, 128.

2.2. IMBALANCES IN BARGAINING POWER IN B2B VERTICAL SUPPLY CHAINS

9. The first trace on the issue of UTPs in the B2B food supply chain at the EU level can be found in an opinion by the European Economic and Social Committee ("EESC") in 2005 (*The large retail sector – trends and impacts on farmers and consumers*).[26] Although not explicitly mentioning the term "unfair trading practices" – which were, according to the EESC, at that time still a "taboo" due to the unquestioned contractual freedom of undertakings[27] – the EESC in its 2005 opinion did already draw attention to the rise of large retailers due to increasing concentration in the retail food market and the severe price pressure put on these retailers by consumers. A study conducted between 1993 and 2002 indicated that the market share of the top five retailers at that moment had increased up to an average of 69,2% in the then 15 Member States of the EU.[28] Although the opinion points out the benefits of such superstores and hypermarkets for consumers – a large range and variety of food products under one roof at competitive prices –[29], it highlights certain negative consequences of such consolidation and price pressure for certain suppliers as well. Reasonable profit for farmers is put under pressure, threats of delisting are used to achieve better prices or contract terms, buyer power manifests itself in certain contractual obligations such as unjustified high contribution to promotion costs and payments are being delayed.[30] In addition, the EESC calls attention to the specific situation of farmers: due to the reform of the CAP focused on becoming more market-oriented, intervention by providing the same floor price for farm produce to sustain producer prices and ensure proper living conditions has been reduced, making farmers more vulnerable for fluctuation of food prices in line with supply and demand.[31] Nonetheless, the EESC emphasized as well that the degree and nature of the market concentration varies considerably from one Member State to the next and that this element must be taken into

---

26 EUROPEAN ECONOMIC AND SOCIAL COMMITTEE, *Opinion on The large retail sector – trends and impacts on farmers and consumers*, 7 April 2005, C 255/44–49.

27 EUROPEAN ECONOMIC AND SOCIAL COMMITTEE, *Opinion on the Green Paper on unfair trading practices in the business-to-business food and non-food supply chain in Europe*, 11 July 2013, 2.4: *"As early as 2005, however, the European Economic and Social Committee issued an important opinion which – at the time when the question of UTPs was still a taboo – highlighted and criticized a number of negative aspects of the behavior of retail chains"* and 3.1.1: *"So far, no doubt has officially been cast upon the existence of contractual freedom in commercial relations (…). Until recently, this freedom was one of the main arguments not only of the supermarkets, but also public authorities, against the regulation of UTPs, which would allegedly have curtailed such freedom."*

28 EUROPEAN ECONOMIC AND SOCIAL COMMITTEE, *Opinion on the large retail sector*, 2005, 46.

29 *Ibid*, 44.

30 *Ibid*, 47.

31 *Ibid*, 49.

consideration when analysing retailers' behaviour towards suppliers. Indeed, in some Member States the buying and selling side of the market tend to be equally concentrated, and large retailers have even encouraged consolidation among product suppliers.[32]

10. In 2009, the European Commission for the first time addressed these practices in the food sector (*A better functioning food supply chain in Europe*), and explicitly branded them "UTPs", when serious price fluctuations occurred along the food supply chain and discrepancies in response between the various actors among the chain mid-2007 to mid-2008 were reported.[33] The lack of market transparency, inequality of bargaining power and anti-competitive practices were said to lead to market distortions with potentially negative effects on the competitiveness of the food supply chain. Emphasizing the need to better understand and examine in depth contractual practices and their link to asymmetries in bargaining power within the food supply chain, the Commission set out to further assess such practices in the Internal Market and propose further actions.

Specific action consisted in setting up an *Expert Platform on B2B Contractual Practices* within the *High Level Forum for a Better Functioning Food Supply Chain* in 2010.[34] Already in 2011 this Expert Platform delivered, on the basis of a multi-stakeholder dialogue, a set of *Principles of Good Practice* including various examples of fair and unfair practices in vertical relations in the food supply chain[35], signed by eleven organizations representative for the different stakeholders in the vertical food supply chain.[36]

11. To promote, implement and enforce these practices in the various Member States, the High Level Forum launched the *Supply Chain Initiative* ("SCI"): a voluntary scheme based on a registration system in which companies commit to integrate the *Principles of Good Practice* in their day-to-day operations, accept a number of dispute resolution options and promote stakeholder dialogue at EU and the national level.[37]

---

32 *Ibid*, 46–47: For instance, in Ireland and the UK the market of bread supplies is now dominated by a few very large bakeries.

33 EUROPEAN COMMISSION, *A better functioning food supply chain in Europe*, 28 October 2009, COM(2009) 591 final, 2.

34 *Commission decision on establishing the High Level Forum for a better functioning food supply chain*, 1 June 2015, C 179/03.

35 *Vertical relationships in the Food Supply Chain: Principles of Good Practice*, 29 November 2011, available at www.supplychaininitiative.eu.

36 AIM, CEJA, CELCAA, CLITRAVI, Copa Cogeca, ERRT, Eurocommerce, Euro Coop, FoodDrinkEurope, AEAPME and UGAL.

37 *The Supply Chain Initiative: Rules of governance and operations*, available at www.supplychaininitiative.eu, 5.

The SCI does not foresee in a specific mechanism for individual disputes, but solely states that they are to be resolved by calling upon the internal dispute resolution mechanism that the company allegedly in breach must install, through mediation or arbitration or any other judicial or administrative option foreseen in national law. The SCI does install a mechanism to deal with aggregated complaints. Aggregated complaints are to be redressed by national dispute resolution platforms which must be specifically established for this purpose, or to the Chair of the SCI if no national platform is available.[38] Such complaints are handled in a confidential manner and guarantee the anonymity of the complainants to meet their fear of retaliation. The SCI does not foresee in any sanctions in case of non-compliance, except the possibility of being excluded from the SCI.[39] However, concerned about the lack of independent and effective enforcement which addresses weaker parties' fear of commercial retaliation, various stakeholders, such as representatives of primary producers (i.e. farmers: Copa Copega), have not signed up to the framework.[40]

In parallel to the SCI, the Commission nevertheless continued examining preferable solutions for UTPs.[41]

12. Although UTPs in vertical relations had originally been raised in the food sector, it quickly became clear that in other sectors UTPs might pose a problem as well.

The Commission's retail market monitoring exercise of 2010 showed that certain trends identified as potentially leading up to UTPs were present in both food and non-food sectors.[42] Horizontal concentration has already been occurring in, for instance, the market of electronics and household applications and the textile and clothing industry. For example, in the UK and the Nordic countries, large clothing retailers already had a combined market share of over 80% in 2007. The decline in share of small and independent retailers was reported to be a common phenomenon across all sectors and vertical integration throughout the supply chain was said to be on the rise.[43] These changes were also said to be at the basis of a number of identified UTPs in the clothing sector in a report on a study of the clothing industry in six Member States.[44] The mentioned UTPs in this sector – automatic charges for promotional costs, imposed

38 *Ibid*, 12–13.

39 *Ibid*.

40 *Report of the High Level Forum for a Better Functioning Food Supply Chain*, 15 October 2014, 13.

41 EUROPEAN COMMISSION, *Green Paper* 2013, 4.

42 Commission Staff Working Document, *Retail services in the Internal Market*, Accompanying document to Report on Retail Market Monitoring: "Towards more efficient and fairer retail services in the Internal Market", 5 July 2011, SEC(2010) 807.

43 *Ibid*, 9–11 (recent trends) and 40–44 (UTPs).

44 *Business relations in the EU clothing chain: from industry to retail and distribution*, Bocconi University, EESEC Business School, Baker & McKenzie, October 2007, 281 p.

return of unsold goods, systematic delays in payments, … – almost completely match those identified in the food sector. Moreover, the vast majority of retail supermarkets or hypermarkets do not only sell food products, but also other products such as cosmetics, detergents, clothing etc. for which the same terms and conditions are applied.[45]

13. Supported by the European Parliament "*to take a broader and horizontal approach, extending the scope beyond the agro-food industry*"[46], the Commission in its 2013 *Green paper on unfair trading practices in the business-to-business food and non-food supply chain in Europe* invited all interested parties to submit their views on UTPs, here broadly defined as existing on any side of the B2B relationship, at any stage of the B2B retail supply chain, at the pre-contractual stage, during the contractual phase and at the post-contractual phase, in both food and non-food sectors.[47]

14. In the meantime, since EU competition law has its limits in addressing UTPs, the majority of Member States started introducing their own specific (contractual) UTP legislation and most of them did so as well on a cross-sectoral basis.

Various approaches are used, ranging from stretching antitrust provisions to also cover an abuse of economic dependence or relative dominance, stretching EU B2C Directives to also cover B2B situations, using so called "unfair competition laws", contract law or tort law, to using a more 'functional' approach or only installing private regulations or a combination of both private and public regulation.[48] The wide variety of legal instruments used results in different enforcement practices as well, ranging from judicial, administrative to private enforcement or a combination thereof, with little coordination within and between national enforcers.[49] Moreover, the coverage of prohibited UTPs and the effectiveness of the legal rules differ significantly between Member States. This fragmentation in the legal landscape can ultimately lead to barriers to cross-border trade, which according to some constituted a reason for harmonizing EU rules.[50]

---

45 *Ibid*, 29–30; EUROPEAN COMMISSION, *Green Paper*, 2013, 4–5.

46 EUROPEAN PARLIAMENT, *A more efficient and fairer retail market*, 5 July 2011, A7-0217/2011, para. 36; see also EUROPEAN PARLIAMENT, *Unfair trading practices in the food supply chain*, 7 June 2016, A8-0173/2016, O.: "*whereas UTPs do not only take place in the food supply chain, but just as often in non-food supply chains such as those of the garment industry and the automotive industry.*"

47 EUROPEAN COMMISSION, *Green Paper*, 2013, 6.

48 A. RENDA et al., *Study on the legal framework covering business-to-business unfair trading practices in the retail supply chain*, 26 February 2014, DOI: 10.2780/91447.

49 *Ibid*, 17.

50 EUROPEAN ECONOMIC AND SOCIAL COMMITTEE, *The current state of commercial relations between food suppliers and the large retail sector*, own-initiative opinion, 9 May 2013,

15. Nevertheless, instead of envisaging to introduce binding UTP legislation at the EU level, the European Commission initially resisted succumbing to external pressure and decided to focus on strengthening the voluntary SCI and promoting solutions on the national level.[51] In addition, despite the fact that national UTP rules mostly apply cross-sectoral, the Commission in its 2014 *Communication* (*Tackling unfair trading practices in the business-to-business food supply chain*) decided to narrow the scope back to the food supply chain only on the basis of the responses by stakeholders to their 2013 *Green Paper*.[52]

Voluntary schemes were considered a more effective way to deal with UTPs, as they help to create the right mindsets, and foster an environment of commitment, trust and cooperation to find a mutually beneficial solution, instead of reducing the conflict to a zero-sum game. The Commission thus focused on improving awareness of the SCI, especially among SMEs, actively promoting it and facilitating the creation of national platforms.[53]

Furthermore, binding measures were left up to the Member States, who were encouraged to examine whether their current national regulatory framework, including the enforcement, was appropriate. In doing so, they were asked to take note of best practices of other Member States.

To address the legal fragmentation, the Commission aimed to foster a common understanding of UTPs as a basis for legal intervention. It did so by referring to the *Principles of Good Practice* and the examples given there of fair and unfair practices, by identifying four 'key' practices ("*a trading partner's retroactive misuse of unspecified, ambiguous or incomplete contract terms; a trading partner's excessive and unpredictable transfer of costs or risks to its counterparty; a trading partner's use of confidential information; the unfair termination or disruption of a commercial relationship*") and by providing a general definition of UTPs. These were broadly defined as "*practices that grossly deviate from good commercial conduct, are contrary to good faith and fair dealing and are unilaterally imposed by one trading partner on another.*"

16. This focus on national solutions and voluntary platforms remained, even after the discussion intensified in light of the 2015 farmer crisis caused by price declines for dairy and pigmeat, aggrevated by the Russian import ban on agricultural products.[54] This market imbalance (i.e. low demand leading to

C 133, 21: "*Yet the only way of overcoming this fragmentation and this incompatibility is to adopt binding European rules. The EESC strongly recommends that the European Commission take the necessary steps in this direction.*"

51 EUROPEAN COMMISSION, *Tackling unfair trading practices in the business-to-business food supply chain*, 15 July 2014, COM(2014) 472 final, 2 and 9–12.

52 *Ibid*, 5: "*While UTPs can, in principle, be present in any sector, stakeholder feedback to the Green Paper suggests that they are particularly problematic in the food supply chain.*"

53 *Ibid*, 9–10.

54 EUROPEAN COMMISSION, *Report on unfair business-to-business trading practices in the food supply chain*, 29 January 2016, COM(2016) 32 final, 2.

falling prices) was said to increase the contractual imbalance (i.e. weakened bargaining position of farmers) even more and consequently made them more vulnerable for UTPs, sparking increased pressure from the Ministers of Agriculture of the Visegrad Group to propose policy initiatives in this field.[55]

In January 2016, to effectively respond to the challenges in the food supply chain ultimately causing crises such as the recent farmer crisis, the *Agricultural Market Task Force* ("AMTF") was set up by Commissioner Hogan for Agriculture and Rural Development to give advice on how to improve the functioning of the chain and farmers' position.

17. In light of the positive cultural change promoted by the SCI and since national measures to combat UTPs had developed significantly in the last years, the Commission (DG Growth) in its *Report on unfair business-to-business trading practices in the food supply chain* (published in January 2016) did not (yet) see the added value of a specific harmonized regulatory approach for UTPs.[56] The Commission nevertheless stated to continue monitoring the situation and reassess the need for EU action.

18. The Commission could however not count on much support of the other EU bodies. Both the EESC and the European Parliament expressed their disagreement and called upon the Commission to reconsider and put forward a legislative proposal for a EU-level framework tackling UTPs in the food supply chain.[57]

2.3. PROTECTION AGAINST ABUSE OF IMBALANCES IN BARGAINING POWER TO ENSURE A FAIR LIVING STANDARD FOR FARMERS?

19. In its report published in December 2016, the AMTF similarly concluded that an EU framework legislation would improve the position of farmers in the food supply chain, not long after which the Agriculture and Fisheries Council followed.[58]

---

55 *Ibid.*

56 *Ibid.*

57 EUROPEAN PARLIAMENT, *Unfair trading practices in the food supply chain*, O, para. 31 and 36; EUROPEAN ECONOMIC AND SOCIAL COMMITTEE, *Opinion on the 'Report from the Commission to the European Parliament and the Council on unfair business-to-business trading practices in the food supply chain'*, October 2016, C34/130–131, 1.5–1.6; see also the call for EU legislation of the Committee on Agriculture and Rural Development ('AGRI'): COMMITTEE ON AGRICULTURE AND RURAL DEVELOPMENT, *Opinion on unfair trading practices in the food supply chain*, 2 March 2016, 2015/2065(INI), para. 31–35.

58 COUNCIL OF THE EUROPEAN UNION (Agricultural and Fisheries Council), *Conclusions on Strengthening farmers' position in the food supply chain and tackling unfair trading*

The point of departure of the AMTF was the continuing trend of market orientation of the CAP and consequently increasing integration in global markets (see also *supra*).[59] The reduction of public intervention necessary to achieve such integration however does imply greater risks of market instability due to price volatility as well as general lower price levels, as seen in the farmer crisis. This may in turn affect farmers' income and economic viability. Since farmers' trading partners both downstream (e.g. processing, retailing) *and* upstream (e.g. fertilisers, seeds) are significantly concentrated and therefore often in a stronger bargaining position than the mostly fragmented farmers, the concern exists that they will form the main shock absorbers in the supply chain of such market risks.

In light of this shift away from (public) market management, the AMTF recommended various measures that could take up their role of protection against market risks, namely a shift towards installing instruments that strengthen the self-help and self-organisation abilities of the sector.[60] Among measures such as increasing market transparency (e.g. to inform farmers of price transmission and formation along the whole chain), providing tools for risk management or strengthening producer organisations, the AMTF thus also proposed to tackle UTPs at the EU level. Hence, in discussing UTPs, the primary aim of the AMTF of regulating UTPs was not necessarily 'fixing' the lack of genuine contractual freedom or preserving the economic freedom of suppliers as such – as usually in discussions on unfair trading/commercial practices in B2C and B2B relations – or resolving barriers to cross-border trade due to various existing legal regimes – as came across in the discussion by DG Growth – but rather to use this banning of UTPs as a means to safeguard farmers' income.

20. Not surprisingly with this shift in the discussion in mind, DG AGRI became the leading DG on the matter. In July 2017, this DG presented the Inception Impact Assessment of their initiative to improve the food supply chain, among which tackling UTPs. Four options were presented:

---

practices; see also the information note of the Bulgarian, Czech, Hungarian, Latvian, Lithuanian, Slovak and Slovenian delegations to the Agricultural and Fisheries Council in support of an EU legislative framework for UTPs in the food supply chain: *Non-Paper – Better functioning of the Food Supply Chain: addressing unfair trade practices (UTPs) and improving the position of farmers*, Annex to the Agriculture and Fisheries Council of 6 March 2017, 6808/17; see also the information note from the Slovak delegation urging the Commission to submit a proposal for UTPs, supported by the Croatian, Cypriot, Czech, Greek, Hungarian, Lithuanian, Polish, Portuguese, Romanian and Slovenian delegations: *Common note on tackling Unfair Trading Practices with a view of achieving a more balanced Food Supply Chain and strengthening farmers' position*, Annex to the Agriculture and Fisheries Council of 11–12 December 2017, 15417/17.

59 AGRICULTURAL MARKET TASK FORCE, *Improving Market Outcomes: Enhancing the position of farmers in the supply chain*, November 2016, 11 (hereinafter: "AMTF report").

60 *Ibid*, 6, 12, 15.

(i) keeping the status quo of national solutions and the SCI;
(ii) EU-wide non-legislative guidelines and recommendations on how to tackle UTPs best;
(iii) EU framework legislation establishing a baseline of protection by introducing a prohibition on specific manifestly unfair practices; and
(iv) EU framework legislation with general criteria for what is to be considered a UTP.[61]

On the basis of the open public consultation, a consultation of the Member States and an academic workshop accompanying the Impact Assessment in August 2017, the third option was chosen which ultimately resulted in the *Commission Proposal of 12 April 2018 for a Directive on unfair trading practices in business-to-business relationships in the food supply chain.*[62]

21. After several rounds of negotiations, the EU institutions reached a trilogue political agreement on 19 December 2018.[63] Under discussion were mostly the scope (who would be covered; what products and services would be covered?) and what type of conduct would be prohibited.

The final text was ultimately adopted on 9 April 2019 and signed a few days later by the presidents of the European Parliament and of the Council: *Directive 2019/633 of 17 April 2019 on unfair trading practices in business-to-business relationships in the agricultural and food supply chain.*[64] The objective of the UTPD is to reduce the occurrence of UTPs in the food supply chain by introducing a minimum common standard across the EU (i.e. minimum harmonization) that consists of specific prohibited practices.

Protection against UTPs is said to be particularly important for agricultural producers, as they are already in a weakened position due to the uncertainty inherent to their production as a result of biological processes and weather conditions, specific time concerns related to the perishable and seasonal nature of the produce and the increased market-orientation of the CAP.[65] Since such UTPs, when occurring, are said to put the profits and margins of smaller agricultural producers under pressure directly or indirectly (see *infra*) and the prohibitions only apply to 'stronger' buyers towards 'weaker' suppliers, the UTPD aims to contribute to a fair living standard of the agricultural community, being

---

61 EUROPEAN COMMISSION (DG AGRI), *Inception impact assessment: Initiative to improve the food supply chain*, 25 July 2017, ARES(2017)3735471, 5–6.

62 *Proposal for a Directive on unfair trading practices in business-to-business relationships in the food supply chain*, 12 April 2018, COM(2018) 173 final.

63 EUROPEAN COMMISSION, "Agreement on unfair trading practices in the food supply chain will protect all EU farmers", Press release, 19 December 2018, available at http://europa.eu/rapid/press-release_IP-18-6790_en.htm.

64 Directive 2019/633 of 17 April 2019 on unfair trading practices in business-to-business relationships in the agricultural and food supply chain, *OJ* L 111/59–72.

65 Recital 6 UTPD.

one of the aims of the CAP thereby forming the **legal basis** for this directive (Article 43(2) TFEU *juncto* Article 39, see *infra*).[66]

An EU legal framework is considered necessary, first, in light of the divergence of Member States' legal rules on UTPs – and the lack or inefficiency thereof in certain Member States –, leading to dissimilar conditions of competition for operators.[67] Whereas in previous EU documents on UTPs this patchwork of rules was considered to potentially lead to barriers to cross-border trade[68], this is now rephrased in light of the chosen legal basis to be "*liable to impair the objective of ensuring a fair living standard for the agricultural community.*"[69]

Second, the Commission recognizes the shortcomings of the SCI in addressing the matter: due to its voluntary character it does not cover all the operators in the food supply chain, enforcement is ineffective, it cannot conduct its own investigations and confidentiality is not at order in one-on-one disputes.[70] Although recommendations to improve these shortcomings on the national level and with the SCI were given by the EC in 2014 and 2016 (see *supra*), these have not been given full effect.[71]

22. In the Commission's Proposal, the **scope** was limited to a relatively limited number of UTPs occurring in relation to the sales of food products by a SME supplier to a non-SME buyer.[72] The Proposal only targeted buyers established in the EU committing UTPs. Whereas the Council mainly agreed with this scope and only proposed to expand the type of products covered to *agricultural and* food products[73], the European Parliament went further and pleaded, among other things, for a significant expansion of the scope to protect all suppliers against the black-listed practices regardless of their or the buyer's size, prohibit the 'grey listed practices' in any case when there is an abuse of economic independence and proposed to introduce other prohibited practices.[74]

66 Explanatory Memorandum UTP Proposal, 3.

67 *Ibid*, 2.

68 EUROPEAN COMMISSION, *Green Paper* 2013, 9; A. RENDA et al., *Study on the legal framework covering business-to-business unfair trading practices in the retail supply chain*, 33 and 84; EUROPEAN ECONOMIC AND SOCIAL COMMITTEE, 2013, 21.

69 Explanatory memorandum UTP Proposal, 4.

70 *Ibid*, 2–3.

71 *Ibid*, 6.

72 UTP Proposal, Art. 1(2).

73 COUNCIL OF THE EUROPEAN UNION, "Better protection for farmers against unfair trading practices: Council agrees its negotiating position", Press release, 1 October 2018, available at https://www.consilium.europa.eu/en/press/press-releases/2018/10/01/better-protection-for-farmers-against-unfair-trading-practices-council-agrees-its-negotiating-position/.

74 EUROPEAN PARLIAMENT (Committee AGRI), *Report on the proposal for a directive of the European Parliament and of the Council on unfair trading practices in business-to-business relationships in the food supply chain*, 10 October 2018, A8–0309/2018: see Proposed Amendment 9–10, 31, 37 for expansion to all suppliers for black-listed practices and Proposed

In the final text the EU institutions compromised to expand the scope beyond SME suppliers to also cover SME suppliers up to an annual turnover of EUR 350 million, whenever they entered into a supply agreement with a buyer in a higher turnover scale, regardless how big or small the difference, and as long as either the supplier or buyer is established in the Union. The list of blacklisted practices was enlarged from four to ten practices, and two practices were added on the grey list. The UTPD now also covers *all* agricultural products (even those not intended for human consumption) and food products.

23. Having thoroughly explained the run-up to and political background of the UTPD, we will now delve deeper into the **legal basis** (3.) and **scope** of application (4.) of the UTPD.

3. LEGAL BASIS

3.1. JUSTIFICATION

24. As mentioned, the legal basis chosen for the UTPD is that of Article 43(2) TFEU, which entrust the European legislator to develop and implement the CAP. Measures based on this legal basis may be taken either to establish the common organization of agricultural markets or if they are necessary *"for the pursuit of the objectives of the common agricultural policy"* as enlisted in Article 39 TFEU. These objectives include increasing agricultural productivity, stabilizing markets, assuring availability of supplies, ensuring reasonable prices for consumers, and, the specific objective on which this Directive is based, ensuring a fair standard of living for the agricultural community by increasing the individual earnings of persons engaged in agriculture.

25. It is argued that UTPs, when occurring, indeed put farmer's margins and profits under pressure either directly or indirectly.[75] For instance, when a farmer is confronted with a unilateral reduction on the contracted quantity or is forced to take back unsold goods, he or she will unexpectedly lose (a part of) the expected income.[76] Moreover, even when such agricultural producers are not directly exposed to UTPs, the additional costs of such UTPs occurring more downstream are said to still be passed back upstream to the weakest link, being the farmer ('cascading effect').[77]

Amendment 14, 35, 38 for application grey listed practices in case of a relation of 'economic dependence'.

75 Recital 7 UTPD.

76 Explanatory memorandum UTP Proposal, 1.

77 Commission Staff Working Document, Impact assessment UTP Proposal, 27.

Furthermore, laying down a common framework to resolve this issue of UTPs is argued to fill a consequential gap in the CAP in relation to common rules on competitive conditions of operators in the EU, which already exist for producer organisations and cooperatives in relation to competition rules or state aid rules.[78] According to Article 43 TFEU the common organization of markets may only replace the national organization of (agricultural) markets if *"such an organization ensures conditions for trade within the Union similar to those existing in a national market"* – and uniform UTP rules are usually expected in a national market but up until now missing in the Common Market.[79]

26. However, it must be noted that the choice for Article 43(2) TFEU as legal basis is contentious to say the least.

First, the scope of the UTPD reaches well beyond the agricultural products and producers thereof for which measures under the CAP may principally be taken and it is doubtful whether the reasons brought forward to justify this expansion hold true (3.2).

Second, questions arise on whether the principle of proportionality and subsidiarity have been respected (3.3).

Third and finally, it may be argued that the choice for a sector-specific basis excludes the possibility of any future expansion of the UTP rules to other parties and sectors in the same Directive (3.4).

3.2. A COMMON *AGRICULTURAL* POLICY FOR *NON-AGRICULTURAL* PRODUCTS AND PRODUCERS?

27. According to Article 38(2) and (3) TFEU, the CAP principally only covers agricultural products as listed in Annex I (i.e. non-processed products). Measures taken to ensure a fair standard of living for the agricultural community thus principally only cover producers of such products in Annex I. As already briefly mentioned, the UTPD nevertheless offers protection in relation to the sale of agricultural *and food* products, being processed agricultural products intended for human consumption not covered by Annex I, by suppliers with a turnover up to EUR 350 million, thereby having an impact on almost the entire food chain.

28. In the Explanatory Memorandum and Staff Working Document added to the Commission's Proposal, the Commission nevertheless refers to case law of the Court of Justice of the EU that explicitly allows the coverage of food products not listed in Annex I if certain conditions are met. Upon closer look at this case

78 *Ibid.*

79 *Ibid*, 26.

law, non-Annex I products may fall under the scope of EU legislation taken on the basis of Article 43 TFEU only if:

(i) the legislation *contributes* to the *achievement* of one or more of the *objectives in Article 39 TFEU* and
(ii) the legislation, in addition to applying *essentially* to products falling within Annex I TFEU, also covers *incidentally* other products not included in that Annex.[80]

Concerning the first criterion, the broader scope of the UTPD offering protection to suppliers of non-agricultural food products is said to contribute to the objective of ensuring a fair standard of living for the agricultural community, first of all, on the basis of the so-called 'cascading effect' as mentioned above. According to the Staff Working Document, *"an approach which protects agricultural producers and their associations (...) also must take into account indirect negative effects they may suffer through UTPs occurring downstream in the food supply chain but being passed – in terms of their negative effect – through to them, i.e. normally by operators who are not agricultural producers but whose weak bargaining position in the chain makes them vulnerable to UTPs."*[81] The limit of 350 000 000 EUR annual turnover has been chosen since *"the cascading effect on agricultural producers appears to be particularly significant for enterprises with an annual turnover of up to EUR 350 000 000."*[82] Furthermore, if the UTPD would only apply to agricultural producers, this could lead to the

80 CJEU 2 July 2009, C-343/07 (*Bavaria v. Bayerischer Brauerbund*), EU:C:2009:415, para. 50–51: *"it must be borne in mind that the Court has already held that legislation which contributes to the achievement of one or more of the objectives mentioned in Article 33 EC must be adopted on the basis of Article 37 EC, even though, in addition to applying essentially to products falling within Annex I of the Treaty, it also covers incidentally other products not included in that annex"*; CJEU 5 May 1998, C-180/96 (*UK v. Commission*), EU:1998:192, para. 134–135: *"The Court has also held that, where a directive constitutes an essential means of increasing agricultural productivity (an objective laid down in Article 39(1)(a) of the Treay), it must be adopted on the basis of Article 43 of the Treaty even though, in addition to applying essentially to products falling within Annex II, it also covers incidentally other products not included in that annex (...) Having regard to the importance of the role played by the free movement of animals, animal products and products of animal origin in achieving the objectives laid down in Article 39(1) of the Treaty, Article 43 of the Treaty must be regarded as constituting the appropriate legal basis for the adoption of Directive 90/425 and 89/662, even though those directives authorize the Commission incidentally to adopt safeguard measures covered 'products of animal origin', 'products derived from those products' and 'products derived' from animals not included in annex II to the Treaty"*; CJEU 16 November 1989, C-11/88, EU:1989:583: *"Although Directive 87/519 amending Directive 74/63 on undesirable substances and products in animal nutrition, may refer incidentally to certain products not included in Annex II, it applies essentially to products within that annex; furthermore, it is an essential factor in increasing agricultural productivity, which is the stated objective of Article 39(1)(a) of the Treaty."*.

81 Commission Staff Working Document, Impact assessment UTP Proposal, 27.

82 Recital 9 UTPD.

unintended negative consequence of trade being diverted away to their small investor-owned competitors e.g. at the processing stage not enjoying such protection, as buyers in relation to such suppliers would not be confronted with the risk of UTP claims.[83]

29. Whether these arguments in fact hold true can however be debated.

First, concerning the second criterion, one may wonder whether the UTPD applies 'essentially' to agricultural products and only 'incidentally' to non-Annex I products.[84] Since protection is offered not only to agricultural producers but to all suppliers of agricultural and food products up to EUR 350 million turnover, one could imagine that a significant part of products covered are not simply agricultural products such as fruits and vegetables, but rather products processed thereof such as yoghurt, sauces, pasta, sweet drinks, beers, chocolate and even frozen fruits and vegetables. After all, more than 70% of agricultural commodities produced in the EU are transformed into manufactured food products[85], thus more than 'incidentally' being covered by the UTPD.[86]

30. Second, some may doubt whether the UTPD, including its broad scope, in fact contributes to or is "*necessary for*" the achievement of the objective in Article 39(a) TFEU to ensure a fair standard of living for the agricultural community. In the Staff Working Document itself it is stated that "*there is little empirical data going beyond a few case studies which makes it difficult to establish the overall harm caused by UTPs.*"[87]

One major issue underpinning the lack of systematic evidence is the problem of attribution: even when certain elements indicating the deterioration of the position of farmers can be empirically confirmed, due to many confounding factors it can often not be substantiated that UTPs, or even just an uneven distribution in bargaining power, are at the cause of it.[88]

---

83 Commission Staff Working Document, Impact assessment UTP Proposal, 27–28; Explanatory memorandum UTP Proposal, 5.

84 INDEPENDENT RETAIL EUROPE, *Unfair trading practices – comments on the legal base – Article 43 TFEU*, 5.

85 Https://ec.europa.eu/growth/sectors/food/processed-agricultural-products/definition_en.

86 According to P. DE CASTRO (vice-chair of the Committee of Agriculture and Rural Development), the UTPD now covers 97% of the agri-food industry, see A. MANCOSU, "MEP De Castro on CAP reform, UTPs and GIs", *IEG Policy – Informa*, 22 February 2019, https://iegpolicy.agribusinessintelligence.informa.com/PL219377/Interview-MEP-De-Castro-on-CAP-reform-UTPs-and-GIs (last accessed 5/7/2019).

87 Commission Staff Working Document, Impact assessment UTP Proposal, 15; see also J. FALKOWSKI, "The economic aspects of unfair trading practices: measures and indicators", *JRC Technical Report: Unfair trading practices in the food supply chain*, 2017, doi: 10.2760/800, p. 21: "*the evidence on the impact of UTPs on farmers is mostly anecdotal and largely based on case studies. More systematic evidence instead is very limited.*"

88 *Ibid*, 24–25.

For instance, according to existing evidence provided for the US (data for the EU does not appear to be provided), the share of farmers in the total added value created in food production is decreasing. However, this may not necessarily be related to the existence of UTPs, but, for example, occur because food is more and more processed.[89] Another illustration is the manner in which prices were transmitted in 2009 (see *supra*), which indicated that price movements threatening the margin of firms being able to exert market power are transmitted relatively fast and farmers reacted more strongly and quickly to these movements than other parts of the food supply chain. This nevertheless does not prove that the transmission of these prices are caused by UTPs or even relate to an uneven distribution of bargaining power, nor that costs caused by UTPs would always be transmitted to a significant extent.[90]

Moreover, in the opinions and reports preceding the final text of the UTPD, no empirical studies have been brought forward to substantiate the claim in recital 9 that "*that the cascading effect appears to be particularly significant for enterprises with an annual turnover up to EUR 350 million*".

31. In conclusion, it is thus doubtful, not only whether tackling UTPs would in fact increase farmers' revenues due to the various other factors influencing the level of their income such as (over)supply and demand[91], but also whether, even if UTPs have a verifiable impact on farmer's income, the negative costs related to UTP truly cascade back to farmers, so that an expansion of the scope of the UTPD to non-agricultural producers is necessary to achieve the objective of Article 39(b) TFEU.[92]

3.3. THE PRINCIPLE OF PROPORTIONALITY AND THE PRINCIPLE OF SUBSIDIARITY

32. Another issue at order is whether the principle of proportionality and subsidiarity have been respected.

33. First, according to Article 5(4) TEU, which enshrines the principle of **proportionality**, the content and form of Union action may not go beyond what

89 *Ibid.*

90 *Ibid*, 25: "*the existing results suggest that the magnitude and speed of price transmission varies considerably across sectors, stages of the agri-food supply chain and countries*"

91 This is even acknowledged in the AMTF report (*supra*, fn. 57, 31): "*We are under no illusion that such legislation will be panacea for imbalances of bargaining power in the supply chain* [referring to various party contributions stressing the impact of other factors such as oversupply and demand on the relative positions of the actors in a given commercial transaction] *There is no silver bullet that will lead to instantly higher prices, perfect price transmission and a more balanced distribution of added value along the chain.*"

92 See in the same sense: H. SCHEBESTA, T. VERDONK, K. PURNHAGEN and B. KEIRSBILCK, "Unfair Trading Practices in the Food Supply Chain: Regulating Right?", *European Journal of Risk Regulation* 2018, 9, (690) 698.

is necessary to achieve the stated objective. This entails that the same goal could not have been achieved with a less far-reaching measure. In this respect, various arguments have been brought forward that suggest that the UTPD is indeed too far-reaching.

In the feedback to the Inception Impact Assessment, various organizations argued that interfering into the contractual relations of the parties as such is not proportionate to the result that will be achieved concerning the living standard of the agricultural community (see *supra* on the questionable impact).[93] After all, the UTPD – the black list especially – severely impairs buyers' freedom to contract, but does not *resolve* the underlying imbalance in bargaining power. Other measures, such as supporting producer organizations, improving market transparency etc., have a much smaller impact on the freedom to contract, but nevertheless may significantly level-out the differences in power, enabling the agricultural community to agree upon mutually beneficial and efficient solutions. These negotiated contractual agreements may then ultimately reduce the current costs induced by UTPs and have a positive impact on farmers' income.

Moreover, if this underlying issue of bargaining power would be improved by such measures, there would also be no need to involve other, non-agricultural suppliers into the protection scheme to reduce the 'cascading effect'.

In addition, even if an interference in the freedom to contract for buyers towards their agricultural suppliers would be proportionate, one can wonder whether even in this case the relation between non-agricultural suppliers up to a turnover of EUR 350 million and buyers in a higher turnover category must be regulated as well. This scope covers a significant part of the entire food supply chain to safeguard the standard of living of the agricultural community only.[94]

Moreover, no (empirical) evidence has been brought forward that underpins this 'cascading claim' up to a turnover of EUR 350 million (see also *supra*).

34. Second, in line with the principle of **subsidiarity** in Article 5(3) TEU, the institutions may only act – when it concerns a shared competence – if and in so far as the objectives of the proposed action cannot be sufficiently achieved by the Member States (i.e. necessity) and if the objectives can better be achieved at EU level (i.e. added value).

---

93 *Ibid;* Feedback EuroCommerce; Feedback LTO Nederland: *"Tackling UTPs is important, but this will not be enough to improve farmers' income. This is based on our experience with the SCI pilot initiative in the Netherlands during 2013–2015 and a farmers' survey we did in 2015. Market transparency needs to be adapted to the needs of the operators."*; Feedback Primary Food Processors: *"PFP considers that unfair trading practices are today a much lesser challenge to our competitiveness than many other regulatory or political issues (such as the importance of maintaining a primary food processing industry in the EU, trade negotiations, plant protection etc.)"*

94 Feedback Confederation of Danish Enterprises to the Initiative to improve the food supply chain, available at https://ec.europa.eu/info/law/better-regulation/initiatives/ares-2017-3735471/feedback_en?p_id=40090.

Concerning the necessity of EU action, it is argued that a situation of under-protection of the most vulnerable operators against UTPs exists in the EU, as certain Member States have no rules on UTPs or, even if they have such rules, lack effective enforcement. The existing voluntary codes – encompassing the SCI – do not effectively replace hard law.[95] Concerning the added value of EU action, the Staff Working Document refers to the inadequate implementation of the Commission's recommendations on improving Member States' legislation regarding UTPs as published in its 2014 Communication and 2016 Report. In the latter report, the Commission argued that EU action was not needed as it expected certain positive developments (introduction of UTP legislation in various Member States and the implementation of the SCI) to continue, for which it suggested a number of recommendations to further improve Member States' regulatory framework with regard to UTPs. However, since Member States did not (all) follow up on most of the Commission's recommendations, it is argued that the situation of under-protection continues to exist and therefore a legislative proposal at EU level implies clear added value.[96]

35. This reasoning raises a number of questions. According to the *Better Regulation Guidelines* of the Commission, in assessing whether or not the subsidiarity principle is respected, is must be checked

(i) whether the problem addressed has transnational aspects which cannot be adequately addressed by action by Member States (i.e. necessity), and
(ii) whether action at EU level would produce greater benefits compared to action taken solely at the level of the Member States due to its scale or effectiveness (i.e. added value).[97]

Concerning the first element, it can however be seriously doubted whether the problem *"cannot be adequately addressed by action by Member States"*. After all, the Commission identified itself a number of ways in which the Member States can resolve the matter themselves. Hence, the need for EU action seems to simply derive from the fact that Member States have not enacted appropriate measures (yet) to resolve the matter within their own national borders in the last two years only[98], but the possibility does exist, which, according to the *Better Regulation Toolbox*, seems to be sufficient.[99] Moreover, the Commission does

95 Commission Staff Working Document, Impact assessment UTP Proposal, 28.
96 *Ibid*, 28–32.
97 EUROPEAN COMMISSION, *Better regulation guidelines – Chapter III: Impact assessment*, 19, https://ec.europa.eu/info/sites/info/files/better-regulation-guidelines-impact-assessment.pdf.
98 According to the Feedback from AIM to the Initiative to improve the food supply chain, Member States should be given more time to strengthen their legislation.
99 EUROPEAN COMMISSION, *Better Regulation Toolbox – Tool 5: Legal basis, subsidiarity and proportionality*, 28, https://ec.europa.eu/info/sites/info/files/file_import/better-regulation-

not provide any reason as to whether the issue has transnational aspects that need to be regulated at the EU level.[100] It only refers to the shortcomings of the regulatory frameworks of Member States to effectively tackle UTPs, but the sole fact that the specific *content* or *enforcement* of national legislation is inadequate does not mean that the *regulation at national level as such* is inadequate. It has even been argued that, since farmers and other operators often negotiate at local or national, and various national habits and traditions in regards to negotiating in the food supply chain exist, the matter can even better be resolved at the national level.[101]

36. Concerning the second element, the Commission remains silent on which specific benefits EU regulation would, and EU regulation only could, bring forward. It remains silent on why Member States cannot resolve the matter themselves, why a homogeneous policy is needed, whether there are economies of scale etc.[102] Hence, it can seriously be doubted whether the argumentation provided is sufficient to justify EU action.

3.4. EXCLUSION OF POSSIBLE EXPANSIONS OF SCOPE – OTHER LEGAL BASIS POSSIBLE?

37. Next to possible arguments calling into question the legality of the chosen legal basis and the exercise of powers, one can also question the desirability of using Article 43(2) TFEU for this Directive. This choice namely excludes the possibility of expanding the scope of prohibited UTPs in B2B relations to other parties or sectors in the same legislative instrument, as it may only benefit the agricultural community.[103]

As set out above, however, the position that freedom of contract in B2B relations should remain untouched even outside the food sector seems to be largely abandoned at the EU level. Although the scope of the UTPD is limited to obligations for buyers in the food sector, various EU institutions have explicitly acknowledged the existence of UTPs caused by other actors and in other sectors. Not long after the Proposal for the UTPD, the Commission proposed an EU

toolbox-5_en_0.pdf: one of the questions that must be posed when assessing the 'necessity test', is *"to what extent do Member States have the ability or possibility to enact appropriate measures?"*.

100 In the same sense, see Feedback from Anonymous (France) and feedback from Handelsverband Deutschland to the Initiative to improve the food supply chain.

101 Feedback from AIM (p. 5) and Anonymous (France) to the Initiative to improve the food supply chain.

102 EUROPEAN COMMISSION, *Better Regulation Toolbox, supra* fn. 98, 28–29.

103 This stance received much criticism in the party contributions to the Initiative to improve the food supply chain: see e.g. Feedback UEAPME 22 August 2017, 1; Feedback FoodDrinkEurope, 22 August 2017, 2.

Regulation to counteract unfair contracts and trading practices in platform-to-business relations, which eventually has led to *Regulation (EU) 2019/1150 on promoting fairness and transparency for business users of online intermediation services* (which is based on Article 114 TFEU).[104] Hence, an increase in EU B2B legislation on unfair practices does not seem unthinkable.

However, such rules in other sectors – or even in relation to UTPs imposed by suppliers in the same sector (see *infra*) – will have to be taken on a different legal basis and with another legislative instrument. This will first of all create a patchwork of B2B rules at the EU level[105], which in turn may lead to serious fragmentation in the *acquis* and consequentially in Member States' private law if the EU decides to introduce more UTP legislation in B2B relations. Such additional layers of sector-specific legislation will become increasingly hard to fit in the pre-existing structures of the national legal systems and threaten their coherence ('dark side of harmonisation').[106]

38. An alternative (or additional), more product neutral, legal basis could potentially be Article 114 TFEU. Article 114 TFEU is used as a legal basis to take measures to harmonize national rules regarding the establishment and functioning of the internal market. According to the CJEU in the *Tobacco Advertising* case[107], Article 114 TFEU may form the legal basis to enact legislation only when the adopted measures will contribute to removing existing barriers in the internal market.[108] Therefore, the mere existence of different national rules on a particular topic is not enough for its application. The fact that there are different national rules must be shown to have an adverse effect upon the internal market by obstructing the fundamental freedoms or by causing significant distortions of competition.

This reasoning has been used to have Article 114 TFEU serve as legal basis for the various rules installed for protecting consumers in B2C relations. Many disparities were said to exist between the laws of the Member States in relation to unfair commercial practices (UCPD) and contract terms (UCTD), which are argued to generate distortions of competition and consequentially

104 Regulation (EU) 2019/1150 of the European Parliament and of the Council of 20 June 2019 on promoting fairness and transparency for business users of online intermediation services, *OJ* L 186, 11.7.2019, 57–79. See also V.I. DASKALOVA, "Oneerlijke *platform-to-business*-handelspraktijken: oude kwesties, nieuwe regelgeving", *SEW* 2018, 187–198; B. DEVOLDER (ed.), *The Platform Economy*, Antwerpen, Intersentia, 2019.

105 INDEPENDENT RETAIL EUROPE, see *supra*, p. 5.

106 *Ibid;* A. HARTKAMP, C. SIEBURGH and W. DEVROE, *Cases, Materials and Text on European Law and Private Law*, Bloomsbury Publishing, 2017, 404.

107 CJEU 5 October 2000, C-376/98 (*Germany v. European Parliament and Council of the European Union*), EU:C:2000:544, para. 77–79.

108 R. MANKO, "EU competence in private law: the Treaty framework for a European private law and challenges for coherence", *EPRS*, January 2015, 6.

obstacles to the smooth functioning of the internal market.[109] The uncertainty concerning the applicable rules in other Member States may deter consumers from transactions in other Member States (consumer confidence argument). The divergence in the laws of the Member States also create costs for businesses wishing to exercise their internal market freedoms (transaction cost argument).

As mentioned, similar wordings have often been used in the discussion of UTPs. Significant divergence appeared to exist between UTP laws of Member States creating similar barriers. A EU framework was considered necessary to 'level the playing field' (see *supra*). On the basis of this reasoning, Article 114 TFEU would appear a valid legal basis.

39. However, it must be noted that Article 114 TFEU can only be used as an additional legal basis when certain conditions apply. Principally speaking, the CJEU has confirmed on multiple occasions that in the field of agriculture Article 43 TFEU is considered the *lex specialis* in relation to other legal bases such as Article 114 TFEU or Article 115 TFEU. Therefore, it is considered the *sole* appropriate legal basis whenever the measures taken contribute primarily to the achievement of one or more of the objectives listed in Article 39 TFEU, even when the legislation is directed at other objectives as well, involves harmonization of provisions of national law or applies incidentally to certain products not listed in Annex I.[110] The CJEU thus favours a rather broad view on the applicability of Article 43 TFEU and easily sets aside complementary legal bases.

The use of Article 114 TFEU as an additional legal basis is only possible if it can be demonstrated that the objective in Article 39 TFEU is not the *predominant* or *main* objective of the legal measures taken, but that *"the measure pursues several objectives which are inseparably linked without one being secondary and indirect in relation to the other"*.[111] Nonetheless, as we have seen, the rather broad focus protecting a significant number of suppliers who are not agricultural producers raises serious question marks with the claim that the UTPD *primarily* wishes to protect such agricultural producers. Moreover, the underlying ratio of protecting 'the weaker party', which more than once were considered to be non-agricultural producers as well, and the focus on levelling out the divergences in the legislation of Member States reinforce the suspicion that the UTPD in fact (also) pursues other objectives.

---

109 See e.g. recital 1–3 and 5–7 of Directive 93/13 on unfair terms in consumer contracts; recital 2–4 Directive 2005/29/EC on unfair business-to-consumer commercial practices or recital 4–7 of Directive 2011/83/EU on consumer rights.

110 CJEU 2 July 2009, C-343/07 (*Bavaria v. Bayerischer Brauerbund*), EU:C:2009:415, para. 50–51; CJEU 23 February 1988, C-68/88 (*UK and Northern Ireland v Council*), EU:C:1988:85; CJEU 5 May 1998, C-180/96 (*UK v. Commission*), EU:1998:192, para. 134–135; CJEU 23 February 1988, C-131/86 (*UK and Northern Ireland*); CJEU 16 November 1989, C-11/88 (*Commission v Council*), EU:C:1989:583.

111 CJEU 11 June 2014, C-377/12 (*Commission v Council*), EU:C:2014:1903.

40. Nonetheless, even if Article 43 TFEU could be set aside due to the principal application to non-Annex I products, using Article 114 TFEU could potentially be equally problematic.

As mentioned, a mere finding of disparities or only an abstract risk that the differences in national legislation will create distortions in competition or infringe the fundamental freedoms is not considered enough. Measures adopted on the basis of Article 114 TFEU must genuinely be to improve the conditions for the establishment and functioning of the internal market.[112] The Court in *Vodafone* expressively stated that "*the emergence of such obstacles must be likely and the measure in question must be designed to prevent them.*" However, although in relation to UTPs claims have been made that the differing national rules lead to such distortions in competition, these claims remain rather abstract as evidence underpinning these claims is (still) lacking. For this reason as well, the choice for Article 114 TFEU to install EU legislation in relation to consumer protection received criticism.[113] Concerning UTPs in B2B relations, various responses to the Inception Feedback Assessment even mentioned, as already briefly indicated above, that contracts are often negotiated and concluded at the local and national level, so that differing rules across the EU are not considered a major problem.

4. CHOICE OF INSTRUMENT AND SCOPE OF APPLICATION

4.1. GENERAL OVERVIEW

41. Concerning the scope of the UTPD, four elements will be discussed.

First, although it has been recognized in various EU documents that UTPs may occur in multiple sectors, the UTPD nevertheless only applies in the case of a sale of agricultural and food products (4.2).

Second, since imbalances in bargaining power are argued to form the 'breeding ground' of UTPs, the UTPD in principle only applies between a supplier with a weaker bargaining position in comparison to a buyer with a stronger bargaining position, for which the proxy of relative annual turnover is used (4.3.1).

---

112 CJEU 8 June 2010, C-58/08 (*Vodafone*), EU:C:2010:321, para. 32.

113 J. STUYCK, "Consumer Protection against SMEs", *Journal of European Consumer and Market Law*, 2013, 3, (117) 119; R. MANKO (European Parliamentary Research Service), *EU competence in private law: The Treaty framework for a European private law and challenges for coherence*, January 2015, doi: 10.2861/292462, 6; H. COLLINS, "Why Europe Needs a Civil Code", *ERPL* 2013, 4, (907) 910: "*Despite frequent calls for evidence of obstacles to trade caused by the diversity of national laws, the Commission has never been able to obtain reliable data providing the need for a harmonization measure.*"

Furthermore, since Article 43 TFEU would not allow otherwise, the UTPD only imposes obligations and prohibitions on the buyer (4.3.2).

Lastly, the UTPD is triggered from the moment either the buyer *or* the supplier is established within the EU. The UTPD may thus impose obligations upon buyers, or offer protection to suppliers, established outside the EU (4.3.3).

42. Member States who find the scope of the UTPD too limited and/or wish to preserve the coherence within their national legal system, may opt to introduce or maintain rules that go *above and beyond* the UTPD's scope. The UTPD only offers 'a baseline' of protection and thus only installs minimum harmonisation. This is explicitly confirmed in Article 9 UTPD and reinforced by the addition in the final text of the words 'at least' in Article 3 that sums up the prohibited unfair trading practices.

This minimum harmonisation approach allows the Member States that have already introduced UTP rules, often cross-sectoral and sometimes imposing stricter rules, to keep these rules intact and solely complement them with the UTPD.[114] Furthermore, it installs a minimum of protection of those Member States which currently lack rules protecting against UTPs, or whose rules are not effective.[115] Member States are left the freedom to integrate these rules in a manner that ensures the coherence within their national system – which may potentially require an expansion of the UTP rules.[116]

43. This minimum harmonisation approach will of course not completely 'level the playing field'. Difference in competitive conditions will continue to exist between Member States due to the various layers added (or maintained) on top of the protection offered by the UTPD. As the Commission's proposal did not define the concept "unfair trading practice" – except in recital 1, which lacks binding force – the risk existed that, in the absence of a common, formal definition of UTPs, various Member States would have different understandings of what it entails and consequently adopt legislation that significantly differs as well. To minimize this risk, various Committees recommended to take up a formal definition of "unfair trading practice" in Article 2 ('Definitions') UTPD.[117] Ultimately the final text of the UTPD has taken up a description of

---

114 Recital 39–40 UTPD; UTPD Proposal, 5–6.

115 UTP Proposal, 5.

116 *Ibid*, 6.

117 Opinion of the Committee of the Regions on unfair trading practices in the food supply chain, 130th plenary session, 4–5 July 2018, C387/48; Draft European Parliament Legislative Resolution (Committee on Agriculture and Rural Development) on the proposal for a directive of the European Parliament and of the Council on unfair trading practices in business-to-business relationships in the food supply chain, 10 October 2018, A8–0309/2018, Proposed Amendment 32; Opinion of the Committee on the internal market and consumer protection, 26 September 2018, A8–0309/2018, Proposed Amendment 20; Opinion of the Committee on Development, 26 September 2018, A8–0309/2018, Proposed Amendment 9.

UTPs in Article 1, offering Member States some sort of common understanding of the concept.[118]

4.2. SCOPE *RATIONE MATERIAE*: SALES OF AGRICULTURAL AND FOOD PRODUCTS

44. In the Commission's Proposal, the scope of the UTPD was limited to "food products" only. These were defined as *"products listed in Annex I to the Treaty* [i.e. agricultural products, see *supra*] *intended for the use as food as well as products not listed in Annex I, but processed from those products for the use as food"*. Although it did not provide a definition of the term 'food', it could be deduced from the definition of 'perishable food products' and subsequent opinions on the Commission's Proposal that the term was used in a similar sense as in other EU legislation such as the *General Food Law Regulation (EC) No 178/2002*[119], namely referring to any substances intended to be or reasonably expected to be ingested by *humans*.[120] This includes drinks such as beers, but excludes animal food (referred to as 'feed'). Therefore, agricultural products (i.e. products listed in Annex I) that were *not* intended for human consumption, such as animal feed or flowers, were excluded from the scope. Consequentially, a part of the agricultural community, namely those selling Annex I products not intended for the use as food, were not offered protection against UTPs, even though they find themselves in an equally vulnerable position as agricultural producers

118 See Article 1 UTPD: *"With a view of combating practices that grossly deviate from good commercial conduct, that are contrary to good fair hand fair dealing and that are unilaterally imposed by one trading partner on another (...)."*

119 Regulation (EC) No 178/2002 of the European Parliament and of the Council of 28 January 2002 laying down the general principles and requirements of food law, establishing the European Food Safety Authority and laying down procedures in matters of food safety, *OJ* L 31/1–24.

120 In the Commission's proposal, "perishable food products" were defined as *"food products that will become unfit for human consumption (...)"* (Article 2 (e) Commission's proposal). Moreover, one of the critiques on this proposal was the fact that it only included products intended for human consumption and thus excludes agricultural products such as animal feed, see *Draft European Parliament Resolution on the proposal for a directive on unfair trading practices in business-to-business relationships in the food supply chain*, 10 October 2018, A8-0309/2018, Proposed Amendment 30 and provided justification; Opinion of the Committee of the internal market and consumer protection on the proposal, 26 September 2018, see Short Justification); see also CJEU 2 July 2009, C-343/07 (*Bavaria v. Bayerischer Brauerbund*), EU:C:2009:415, para. 49 on the classification of 'beer': *"First, it is indisputable that beer is food, in the ordinary sense of the term 'food'. Second, (...) beer is covered by the definition of 'foodstuff' in other Community legislation, such as Article 2 of Regulation (EC) No 178/2002"*; however, in the 'common sense' of the word 'food', various dictionaries define 'food' in a different manner than understood under the UTPD, e.g. 'food' in the Oxford Dictionary means *"Any nutritious substance that people or animals eat or drink or that plants absorb in order to maintain life and growth"* or in the Cambridge dictionary *"something that people and animals eat, or plants absorb, to keep them alive"*.

of products to be used as 'food'. In light of the legal basis and objectives of the UTPD, i.e. ensuring a fair standard of living for the agricultural community, this approach of excluding a part of agricultural producers, while including certain non-agricultural suppliers, could be considered problematic.

45. The matter was luckily resolved in the final text of the UTPD, which applies in relation to sales of '*agricultural and* food products'. Article 2(1) defines them as *"products listed in Annex I to the TFEU* [i.e. agricultural products, regardless whether intended for use of food] *as well as products not listed in that Annex, but processed for use as food using products listed in that Annex."* Moreover, the UTPD now clearly states that it is applicable as well, next to 'sales' of agricultural and food products, to the services provided by the buyer to the supplier that are referred to in Article 3 (e.g. marketing, promotion, listing, …).

46. In light of the principle of attributed powers and the particular legal basis used, in addition to the principle of proportionality, the limitation of the scope to 'agricultural and food products' is understandable. However, one should be mindful for the potential negative effect this *ad hoc* intervention may have on the national legal systems of the Member States.

First, the particular scope risks to *"challenge the legal order under the fundamental right to equal treatment."*[121] If a Member States implements the UTPD without offering further protection against unfair practices in B2B relations, this may lead to a discriminatory treatment of suppliers of non-food products finding themselves in equally vulnerable position.[122] As recognized in the Commission's 2013 *Green Paper*, the majority of super- and hypermarkets sell non-food products such as cosmetics or clothing as well, for which their suppliers are imposed the same (potentially unfair) terms and conditions (see already *supra*).

Moreover, we already mentioned that this sector-specific intervention may cause fragmentation and threaten the coherence of Member States' legal systems, as it will potentially not fit in the pre-existing structures (see already *supra*). To cope with this 'dark side of harmonisation', Member States may go beyond the UTPD in offering protection to parties in other B2B-relations as well or in any other way adjust their existing national law to maintain its coherence. However, in doing so, they will have to accept the risk that they might have to repeat this exercise again in light of forthcoming EU legislation on UTPs in other sectors (e.g. *Regulation (EU) 2019/1150 on promoting fairness and transparency for business users of online intermediation services*, which imposes obligations on

---

121 J. GLÖCKNER, "Unfair trading practices in the supply chain and the co-ordination of European contract, competition and unfair competition law in their reaction to disparities in bargaining power", *Journal of Intellectual Property & Practice* 2017, 5, 426.

122 *Ibid.*

'E-tailers' such as Amazon).[123] Indeed, considering the attention attributed to fairness and 'genuine' contractual freedom in B2B relations on EU level the last 10 years, it is not unthinkable that other *ad hoc* interventions in this area will follow.

4.3. SCOPE *RATIONE PERSONAE:* PROTECTION FOR SUPPLIERS FROM BUYERS WITH A STRONGER BARGAINING POSITION

4.3.1. Imbalance in bargaining position: relative turnover scales

47. We already mentioned that UTPs occur in relations where an imbalance of bargaining power exists that is being abused by the party in the stronger position.[124] Whereas in more balanced commercial relations, parties may negotiate contractual terms to their benefit that restrain potential unfair conduct in the future, parties finding themselves in a weaker, dependent position may have to accept the terms imposed on them. In addition, even when the terms of the existing supply agreement are violated, due to their fear of retaliation, legal action to rectify the situation is hardly taken. Consequentially, since this unequal distribution of power, and more particularly the abuse thereof, is considered the problem driver of UTPs, only parties in such a relation are (theoretically) targeted by the UTPD.[125]

48. In the Commission's Proposal, the prerequisite of this imbalance was translated into the application of the UTPD to UTPs conducted by non-SME buyers to SME suppliers of food products. Hence, the difference in size of the undertakings was used as 'proxy' for their difference in bargaining power. The use of a proxy was preferred over establishing the existence of weak bargaining power on a case-by-case basis to increase predictability. 'SMEs' were defined according to the criteria set out in *Commission Recommendation 2003/361/ EC*[126] and cover enterprises with less than 250 employees and with an annual turnover not exceeding EUR 50 million and/or an annual balance sheet in total not exceeding EUR 43 million.

---

123 Regulation (EU) 2019/1150 of the European Parliament and of the Council of 20 June 2019 on promoting fairness and transparency for business users of online intermediation services, *OJ* L 186/57–79.

124 Recital 14 UTPD; Commission Staff Working Document, 20.

125 Commission Staff Working Document, Impact assessment UTP Proposal, 45–46; However, they are only targeted at the supplier side and not on the buyer side, see 4.3.2.

126 Commission Recommendation of 6 May 2003 concerning the definition of micro, small and medium-sized enterprises, *OJ* L 124/36–41.

49. Whereas the Council agreed with the Commission on this approach, Members of the European Parliament still believed the scope to be too narrow. In the Draft Legislative Resolution of the European Parliament, it was suggested to expand the scope to UTPs enacted by *all* buyers to *all* suppliers, thus regardless of their size.[127] The rapporteur of the draft legislative resolution justified the proposal to expand the scope to cover all suppliers by the argument that trade would otherwise be diverted away to larger players. Other arguments given by the Committees asked for an opinion were that "*if these practices are unfair, they must be prohibited to all operators*"[128] and that "*legal protection should be enlarged to cover the whole spectrum of unfair situations.*"[129] However, not only are such arguments inconsistent with the imposition of obligations and prohibitions on the buyer only (see also *infra*) or the legal basis which principally only attributes power to the EU to protect the agricultural community (see *supra*), it is also disconnected from the initial purpose of the Directive, i.e. to address the power imbalances between the parties.[130] According to this initial view of the European Parliament, the UTPD would limit the contractual freedom of buyers even when they deal with equally powerful suppliers. More than that, small, local shops could be held liable under the UTPD for breaches towards large manufacturers of famous brands.

50. The final text of the UTPD does not go this far and holds on to the prerequisite of imbalanced bargaining power, but nevertheless has significantly expanded the reach of the Commission's Proposal. Instead of the size of the undertaking, the proxy used for the relative bargaining power in the UTPD as finally adopted is that of the annual turnover of the undertaking. An imbalance in bargaining power is presumed to exist if the annual turnover of a supplier is in a lower turnover category than that of the buyer ('dynamic approach'), up to a threshold of EUR 350 million: if the supplier has an annual turnover exceeding this amount, he is not protected by the UTPD (Article 1(2) UTPD). Public authorities acting as buyers of agricultural and food products must always

---

127 Draft European Parliament Legislative Resolution, *supra*, Proposed Amendment 12 and 37; this stance is supported by the Committee on the internal market and consumer protection and the Committee on Development and the Committee on the Environment (see for their respective opinions *supra*) and the opinion on the Commission's proposal by the Committee of Public Health and Food Safety, 17 September 2018, A8-0309/2018.

128 Opinion of the Committee on the internal market and consumer protection, *supra*.

129 Opinion of the Committee on the Environment, *supra*.

130 It must be noted that the inequality of power between the parties is taken into account by the European Parliament in relation to the 'grey list'. The grey list concerns practices that are allowed on the condition that they are agreed upon at the conclusion of the supply agreement in clear and unambiguous terms (see *infra*, Chapter 2). In addition to these requirements, the European Parliament proposed to add the condition that the terms may not result from an abuse of economic dependence which enabled the buyer to impose those terms (Draft Legislative Resolution, *supra*, proposed amendment 88). This amendment did not make it into the final text of the UTPD.

respect the UTPD when dealing with a supplier with an annual turnover not exceeding EUR 350 million.

The UTPD uses the following turnover scales:

Supplier with annual turnover...	Buyer with annual turnover...*
≤ EUR 2 000 000	> EUR 2 000 000
> EUR 2 000 000 and ≤ EUR 10 000 000	> EUR 10 000 000
> EUR 10 000 000 and ≤ EUR 50 000 0000	> EUR 50 000 000
> EUR 50 000 000 and ≤ EUR 150 000 0000	> EUR 150 000 000
> EUR 150 000 000 and ≤ EUR 350 000 0000	> EUR 350 000 000

51. The annual turnover of undertakings is determined on the basis of the rules set out in the Annex to *Commission Recommendation 2003/361/EC*. On the basis of this Recommendation, the annual turnover of any partner[131] or linked enterprise[132] of the supplier or buyer in question must be (partially) added to the annual turnover of the latter. This prevents larger buyers from establishing smaller subsidiaries to handle transactions that may otherwise not have fallen under the turnover threshold.

52. Considering that according to the Commission's Proposal the UTPD was only meant to offer protection to undertakings with a turnover not exceeding EUR 50 million (see *supra* on the definition of SME), the threshold to fall outside its scope has significantly been raised. As already explained, this particular threshold of EUR 350 million has been chosen to absorb the 'cascading effect' and to avoid trade being diverted to larger suppliers (see also *supra*).[133] This cascading effect is argued to be particularly significant for enterprises with an annual turnover of EUR 350 million.[134] Moreover, suppliers with an annual turnover succeeding this amount are not considered vulnerable, or at least significantly less vulnerable than smaller operators.[135]

---

131 See Article 3(2) Annex: enterprises are in principle classified as 'partner enterprises' if the upstream enterprise holds, either solely or jointly with one or more linked enterprises, 25% or more of the capital or voting rights of the downstream enterprise.

132 See Article 3(3): enterprises are in principle classified as 'linked enterprises' if the upstream enterprise either (i) holds the majority of shareholders' or members' voting rights in the downstream enterprise, (ii) has the right to appoint or remove the majority of the administrative, management or supervisory body of the downstream enterprise, (iii) has the right to exercise a dominant influence in the downstream enterprise, or (iv) as a shareholder or member of the downstream enterprise controls alone, pursuant to an agreement with other shareholders or members in that enterprise, a majority of the shareholders' or members' voting rights in that enterprise.

133 Recital 9 UTPD.

134 Recital 9 UTPD.

135 Recital 14 UTPD.

53. By installing an upper limit and thus not extending the scope to protect all suppliers, the UTPD aims to hold on to the focus on unequal bargaining power and aiding the most vulnerable undertakings against abuse thereof.[136] However, it is questionable to what extent this will hold true in practice.

First, the UTPD applies as soon as the buyer is in a higher turnover category than the supplier, regardless whether the difference between these numbers is significant or insignificant. Concretely, this means that a commercial relationship between a buyer with EUR 2,1 million and a supplier with EUR 1,9 million in turnover is considered imbalanced, triggering the protection of the UTPD. It is doubtful whether a restriction of the parties' contractual freedom is necessary in this instance.

Second, a difference in turnover – perhaps even a significant one – may not necessarily coincide with different levels of bargaining power or dependence. The latter[137] can be influenced by other elements such as the strong reputation of the counterparty, the absence of sufficient alternative trading partners or sales outlets or the percentage one party accounts for in the turnover of the other party.[138] Although for reasons of predictability it is understandable that a proxy is used to determine the imbalance, the proxy of (sometimes even an insignificant) difference in turnover may not be the most optimal.

4.3.2. One-way street: obligations for the buyer only

54. Another important element of the UTPD's scope is that it only offers protection to one side of the bilateral relations in the food supply chain, namely to the suppliers. The reasoning used to support this one-way application is that buyers generally speaking find themselves in a strong bargaining position towards suppliers, due to the concentration and vertical integration on the

136 To this extent, the explanatory memorandum of the Commission's proposal draws comparisons with B2C laws, see Explanatory memorandum UTP Proposal, 3; Recital 4 UTPD.

137 In the text of the UTPD an imbalance in bargaining power is equated with economic dependence, see recital 9 UTPD.

138 Opinion of the European Economic and Social Committee on the Commission's proposal, 19 September 2019, C 440/28: "*The proposal also fails to address the issue of unequal bargaining power and economic dependence, which does not necessarily coincide with the economic dimension of operators.*"; As mentioned, various committees of the European Parliament suggested to add the criterion of (abuse of) economic dependence to determine the lawfulness of the practices on the 'grey list'. The mentioned elements were used to define a situation of 'economic dependence' (see Opinion of Committee IMCO (*supra*): presumption of economic dependence "*when the buyer accounts for at least 40% of the supplier's turnover*"; Opinion of Committee ENVI (*supra*): presumption of economic dependence when "*the buyer accounts for at least 30% of the supplier's turnover*"; Draft Legislative Resolution (*supra*): economic dependence of the supplier on the buyer because of "*the buyer's reputation, its market share, the absence of sufficient alternative sales, possibilities or because the total sum for which the supplier invoiced the buyer accounts for a significant amount of the supplier's turnover*").

downstream side of the market, whereas farmers (and other suppliers) remain largely fragmented and become dependent on the scarce number of buyers. The increasing market-orientation of the CAP increases their vulnerable position. As a result, UTPs mostly affect farmers and SME suppliers (see already *supra*).

55. However, caution should be taken in dividing the food supply chain too strictly in a fragmented upstream market and a concentrated downstream market, as levels of concentrations vary considerable per sector.

For instance, the AMFT report itself described the dairy, meat, cereal and sugar sector (primary processing stage) to consist of mostly larger enterprises and the secondary processing stage generally to be highly concentrated and dominated by one or two large processing companies, although it also comprises SMEs for specialized and/or perishable products.[139] Thus, in some occasions there may exist an imbalance of power to the benefit of the supplier as well.[140] This is for instance the case when a small, local supermarket wishes to sell certain popular products from an international consumer brand manufacturer such as Coca-Cola or Lays.[141]

Moreover, even multinational retailers may be put under pressure by such manufacturers, as brand loyalty may be higher than store loyalty when it comes to such popular brands and customers may switch stores instead of brands if these products are not available on its shelves.[142]

Bottom line, although it may be true that the imbalance in contractual relations most often exists in favour of the buyer, that observation does not detract from the fact that it is still the (abuse of that) imbalance that constitutes the problem driver and not the buyer per se. From that perspective, the exclusion of suppliers as 'offenders' of UTPs – when they are in fact in a stronger bargaining position and abuse it – is highly questionable.

56. The argumentation used to support the one-way application may in fact also partially be a form of window dressing of the choice for Article 43 TFEU as legal basis. Since the legal basis may only be used to (principally) protect the agricultural community, it does not allow for measures taken to protect

---

139 AMTF report, *supra*, 29.

140 This has even been explicitly recognized by the Commission's (then still DG INT) Green Paper of 2013: *"It is important to note that the situation of imbalance can exist from any side of the B2B relationship: retailers as well as suppliers can be the victims of UTPs and they can occur at any stage of the B2B retail supply chain."*, see European Commission, *Green Paper*, 2013, 6.

141 Commission Staff Working Document, *Retail services in the Internal Market*, Accompanying document to Report on Retail Market Monitoring: "Towards more efficient and fairer retail services in the Internal Market", 5 July 2011, SEC(2010) 807, 41.

142 J. VAN DER MAELEN, E. BREUGELMANS and C. CLEEREN, "The clash of the Titans: On Retailer and Manufacturer Vulnerability in Conflict Delistings", *Journal of Marketing* 2017, 1, 118–135; L. SLOOT and P. VERHOEF, "The impact of Brand Delisting on Storeswitching and Brand Switching Intentions", *Journal of Retailing* 2008, 3, 281–296.

the buyer-side of the supply chain as well. Whereas the protection for non-agricultural suppliers with an annual turnover of maximum EUR 350 million can (arguably) still be justified with the cascading effect and trade diversion argument, the same is not possible for buyers. It seems that at some occasions, certain EU bodies seem to forget themselves the need for this window dressing, when stating that the scope of the Directive must be broadened "*by prohibiting UTPs to the benefit of all producers and purchasers*"[143] or that "*This Directive must apply to the business conduct of larger operators towards operators who have less bargaining power*".[144]

4.4. APPLICATION TO BUYER OR SUPPLIER OUTSIDE THE UNION

57. Finally, the UTPD does not only apply to buyers and suppliers within the EU, but already when *either* the buyer *or* the supplier is established in the Union.

This implies, first, that buyers established in the EU must comply with the UTPD when they are dealing with third country suppliers as well. One argument used to justify this expansion to non-EU suppliers, is (again) that trade would otherwise be diverted away towards non-protected suppliers such as non-EU suppliers, which in turn could undermine the protection of suppliers in the Union.[145] Furthermore, it is argued that "*such suppliers [are] equally vulnerable to unfair trading practices*"[146] and that the diminishing share of revenues reaching small scale food producers and workers in developing countries and their working conditions as a consequence of UTPs could undermine the Union's development policy and its objectives under the 2030 Agenda for Sustainable Development.[147]

Second, in comparison with the Commission's Proposal, the scope has also been expanded to cover buyers who are not established in the Union when they deal with EU suppliers. In this case, non-EU buyers are thus nevertheless bound by EU rules "*to avoid possible unintended consequences, such as choosing the place of establishment on the basis of the applicable rules.*"[148] However, it must be noted that the much used 'trade diversion' argument from above can be applied here as well: the application of the UTPD to non-EU buyers in relation to supply agreements with EU suppliers may result in diminished export, as non-EU buyers will prefer to buy from non-EU suppliers that do not enjoy such protection against UTPs.

[143] Opinion IMCO (Short Justification), *supra*.
[144] Recital 14 UTPD.
[145] Recital 12 UTPD; See also Feedback European Environmental Bureau, 2.
[146] *Ibid.*
[147] Opinion of the Committee on Development, *supra*, Proposed Amendment 4.
[148] Recital 12 UTPD.

5. CONCLUSION

58. In this chapter, we have first examined the run-up to and the political background of the UTPD which may well be a first step in slowly breaking down the wall between the regulatory approach towards B2C and B2B (contractual) relations.

59. Next, we have argued that the choice for Article 43(2) TFEU as legal basis is contentious to say the least. First, the scope of the UTPD reaches well beyond the agricultural products and producers thereof for which measures under the CAP may principally be taken and it is doubtful whether the reasons brought forward to justify this expansion hold true. Second, questions arise on whether the principle of proportionality and subsidiarity have been respected. Third and finally, the choice for a sector-specific basis excludes the possibility of any future expansion of the UTP rules to other parties and sectors in the same Directive.

60. Finally, we have critically discussed four elements as regards the scope of the UTPD. First, although it has been recognized in various EU documents that UTPs may occur in multiple sectors, the UTPD nevertheless only applies in the case of a sale of agricultural and food products. Second, since imbalances in bargaining power are argued to form the 'breeding ground' of UTPs, the UTPD in principle only applies between a supplier with a weaker bargaining position in comparison to a buyer with a stronger bargaining position, for which the proxy of relative annual turnover is used. Furthermore, since Article 43 TFEU would not allow otherwise, the UTPD only imposes obligations and prohibitions on the buyer. Lastly, the UTPD is triggered from the moment either the buyer or the supplier is established within the EU. The UTPD may thus impose obligations upon buyers, or offer protection to suppliers, established outside the EU.

CHAPTER 2

PROHIBITED AND CONDITIONALLY PERMITTED UNFAIR TRADING PRACTICES

Sofie De Pourcq*

PhD of KU Leuven; Lawyer at IP Porta

Evelyne Terryn

Full professor KU Leuven, guest professor UHasselt, co-director Consumer Competition Market, lawyer at Roots advocaten

1. INTRODUCTION

Article 3 is at the heart of Directive 2019/633/EU. This Article sets out the unfair trading practices which are prohibited. Instead of creating a general prohibition on unfair trading practices in the contractual B2B relationship, the European legislator chooses to define a list of concrete prohibited unfair trading practices. In this chapter, we provide a critical analysis of these specifically prohibited unfair trading practices.

First, we will give a short overview of the existing EU legislative framework on unfair trading practices in the contractual B2B relationship. Afterwards, we will discuss the prohibited practices mentioned in article 3 Directive 2019/633/EU. Whereas the first paragraph of that key Article lists practices which are prohibited per se, the second paragraph relates to practices which are permitted if they are agreed upon. By comparing the approach of the European legislator to the approach in France, Germany, Belgium and the UK, we conclude that there is still room for improvement of European rules on unfair trading practices in the contractual B2B relationship.

---

* See for a more extensive analysis of the issue of unfair commercial practices between businesses: S. De Pourcq, *Oneerlijke handelspraktijken en bedingen in contracten tussen ondernemingen*, Antwerpen, Intersentia, 2018, 777 p.

2. EXISTING EU LEGISLATIVE FRAMEWORK

Before the adoption of Directive 2019/633/EU, the EU legislative framework on the issue of unfair trading practices in the contractual B2B relationship was limited. That framework only consisted of Directive 2011/7/EU of the European Parliament and of the Council of 16 February 2011 on combating late payment in commercial transactions[1] (hereafter: "Late payment directive") (2.1) on the one hand and the so-called Supply Chain Initiative on the other hand (2.2).

2.1. LATE PAYMENT DIRECTIVE

In contrast to the Directive 2019/633/EU, the Late payment directive applies to every B2B relationship.[2] Quite logically, the directive only aims to regulate late payment. As Article 3, 1, (a) of Directive 2019/633/EU confirms, such a practice can also be considered an unfair trading practice.

The Late payment directive determines, amongst other things, a default payment term of 30 days[3] and a maximum payment term of 60 days, unless otherwise expressly agreed.[4] As mentioned below, the Directive 2019/633/EU now also prescribes a maximum payment term.

With regard to the issue of unfair trading practices, however, Article 7 of the Late payment directive is of more importance. That Article obliges Member States to "*provide that a contractual term or a practice relating to the date or period for payment, the rate of interest for late payment or the compensation for recovery costs is either unenforceable or gives rise to a claim for damages if it is grossly unfair to the creditor.*"[5] Consequently, this directive creates a general prohibition on grossly unfair terms and practices with regard to the payment of the contract. By doing so, the European legislator recognises that unfair commercial practices and terms do occur in the contractual B2B relationship as well. However, the protection offered by this directive is limited to terms or practices which are unfair from the point of view of the creditor. Moreover, application in case law of this prohibition seems to be absent.

---

1 This directive was transposed in Belgian law in the "*Wet betreffende de bestrijding van de betalingsachterstand bij handelstransacties", Parl.St. Kamer 2012–2013, nr. 53K2927/003, 5*" (hereafter: law on combating late payment in commercial transactions).

2 "Undertaking" being defined as "*any organisation, other than a public authority, acting in the course of its independent economic or professional activity, even where that activity is carried out by a single person": Art. 2, 3) Late payment directive.*"

3 Art. 3, 3, (b) Late payment directive.

4 Art. 3, 5 Late payment directive.

5 Our underlining.

Besides this general prohibition, the Late payment directive describes one contractual term or practice that is definitely grossly unfair[6] and one term or practice that is presumed to be grossly unfair.[7]

With regard to unfair terms, the Late payment directive specifies how to determine whether a contractual term is grossly unfair. All the circumstances of the case need to be taken into account, including[8]:

> "(a) *any gross deviation from good commercial practice, contrary to good faith and fair dealing;*
> (b) *the nature of the product or the service; and*
> (c) *whether the debtor has any objective reason to deviate from the statutory rate of interest for late payment, from the payment period as referred to in Article 3(5), point (a) of Article 4(3), Article 4(4) and Article 4(6) or from the fixed sum as referred to in Article 6(1).*"

Quite remarkably, the Belgian equivalent of the general prohibition on unfair terms and practices with regard to contractual payments, seems to be restricted to unfair *terms*.[9] However, given the broader scope of that prohibition as mentioned in the directive, the Belgian prohibition must be thus interpreted that it also prohibits grossly unfair *practices*.

As regards the criteria for assessing the unfair character, the Belgian law on combating late payment in commercial transactions differs somewhat from the Late payment directive. According to the Belgian legislator, it is also necessary to verify whether there is a significant imbalance between the rights and obligations of the parties, to the disadvantage of the creditor.[10]

2.2. SUPPLY CHAIN INITIATIVE

The so-called Supply Chain Initiative (hereafter: "SCI") tackles the problem of unfair commercial practices in the contractual B2B relationship too. This initiative, which only concentrates on the food supply chain, was created by the High Level Forum for a better functioning food supply chain. In 2010, that High Level Forum was set up by the European Commission.[11]

---

6 Art. 7, 2 Late payment directive: "*a contractual term or a practice which excludes interest for late payment shall be considered as grossly unfair*".

7 Art. 7, 3 Late payment directive: "*a contractual term or a practice which excludes compensation for recovery costs as referred to in Article 6 shall be presumed to be grossly unfair*".

8 Art. 7, 1, second paragraph Late payment directive.

9 Art. 7, first paragraph law on combating late payment in commercial transactions.

10 Art. 7, second paragraph law on combating late payment in commercial transactions.

11 Commission Decision of 30 July 2010 establishing the High Level Forum for a Better Functioning Food Supply Chain, *OJ C* 3 August 2010, 210, 4.

The SCI is structured around a set of Principles of Good Practice in vertical relationships in the Food Supply Chain (hereafter: "Principles of Good Practice").[12] Since those principles are a result of a dialogue between several European organizations involved in the food supply chain[13], they form a self-regulatory document. In 2014, the Belgian "Code of conduct for fair relationships between suppliers and buyers in the agri-food chain" (hereafter: "Code of conduct for fair relationships") has been recognized as an equivalent of the European Principles of Good Practice.

The Principles of Good Practice formulate three general principles on the one hand and seven specific principles on the other. In the context of this chapter, the second as well as the sixth specific principle, relating to the issue of unilateral changes to the contract and responsibility for risk respectively, are particularly relevant. The second principle states that: "*Unilateral change to contract terms shall not take place unless this possibility and its circumstances and conditions have been agreed in advance. The agreements should outline the process for each party to discuss with the other any changes necessary for the implementation of the agreement or due to unforeseeable circumstances, as provided in the agreement.*"[14] According to the sixth principle, concerning responsibility for risk, "*all contracting parties in the supply chain should bear their own appropriate entrepreneurial risks*".[15] Of course, it can be discussed what should be considered an "appropriate" entrepreneurial risk.

3. DIRECTIVE 2019/633/EU: PROHIBITED UNFAIR PRACTICES

3.1. INTRODUCTION

The adoption of Directive 2019/633/EU extends the current European protection against unfair commercial practices in the contractual B2B relationship. However, the European legislator did not opt for a general prohibition, but only

---

12 See www.supplychaininitiative.eu/about-initiative/principles-good-practice-vertical-relationships-food-supply-chain.

13 AIM (European Brands Association), CEJA (Conseil Européen des Jeunes Agriculteurs), CELCAA (European Liaison Committee for Agricultural and Agri-Food Trade), CLITRAVI (Liaison Center for the Meat Processing Industry in the EU), COPA-COGECA (Committee of Professional Agricultural Organisations – General Confederation of Agricultural Cooperatives), ERRT (European Retail Round Table), EUROCOMMERCE, EuroCoop (European Community of Consumer Cooperatives), FoodDrinkEurope, UEAPME (European Association of Craft, Small and Medium-sized Enterprises) and UGAL (currently: Independent Retail Europe).

14 Principles of Good Practice, principle 2 (our underlining).

15 Principles of Good Practice, principle 6.

indicates eight unfair trading practices in Article 3. Consequently, the impact of this European initiative should not be overestimated.

The European legislator nevertheless emphasizes the importance of this Article 3, by requiring the Member States to include the content of its two first paragraphs in mandatory provisions "*which are applicable to any situation falling within the scope of those prohibitions, irrespective of the law that would otherwise be applicable to the supply agreement between the parties*".[16]

A clear distinction is made between the practices mentioned in the first paragraph of Article 3, which are prohibited, on the one hand, and those mentioned in the second paragraph. The latter are only prohibited if they have not been "*previously agreed in clear and unambiguous terms in the supply agreement or in a subsequent agreement between the supplier and the buyer*".[17] Consequently, those practices are left to the contractual freedom of the parties. In this way, this second paragraph actually also refers to the issue of unfair *terms*.

As the directive is a minimum harmonisation directive, Member States remain free to adopt stricter rules.[18] They can still choose to introduce a general norm or to maintain a pre-existing national general norm. Member States may also choose to introduce or maintain stricter or different per se prohibitions to combat unfair trading practices.

3.2. PRACTICES INCLUDE TERMS – THE ABSENCE OF CONTRACTUAL REMEDIES

This Directive 2019/633/EU clearly uses the term '*practices*' in a broad sense that also encompasses the use of unfair terms. This is of course not completely new for EU law, as it was already accepted in a B2C context that the use of a term may be considered as an unfair commercial practice. Indeed, the ECJ decided in *Perenicova v Perenic* that the use of a term may be an unfair commercial practice.[19] The case concerned a credit contract indicating an incorrect annual percentage rate of charge.

What is however problematic is that this Directive fails to set out the consequences of the use of an unfair trading practice for the validity of the contract that may be concerned. This is all the more problematic as this Directive focuses on the food supply chain and thus on vertical relationships between non-competitors which will mostly be *contractual* relationships. The silence of this Directive on the consequences of the use of an unfair trading practice on the validity of those contracts creates legal uncertainty and questions on the impact on the validity of the contract will pop up inevitably.

16 Art. 3, 4 Directive 2019/633/EU.
17 Art. 3, 2 Directive 2019/633/EU.
18 Art. 9 Directive 2019/633/EU.
19 In Case C-453/10, Jana Pereničová v Vladislav Perenič, ECLI:EU:C:2012:144.

In a B2C context, the Unfair Contract Terms Directive 93/13/EEC also prohibits unfair terms. It provides however for a clear sanction: an unfair term does not bind the consumer; the contract nevertheless continues to be binding if it is capable of continuing in existence without the unfair term.[20] In a B2C context, unfair *practices* are dealt with in a separate instrument: the Unfair Commercial Practices Directive 2005/29/EC. That directive currently also fails to set out its relation with contract law and even provides that it is '*without prejudice to contract law, and in particular, to the rules on the validity, formation or effect of a contract*'.[21] This failure was precisely identified as one of the shortcomings of this directive[22] and the New Deal for consumers is now trying to remedy this lacuna by requiring Member States to provide for contractual (and non-contractual) remedies for breaches of the directive.[23]

The same problem now arises in Directive 2019/633/EU as the contractual consequences of the use of an unfair trading practice in the B2B sector are not spelled out. Given the minimum harmonisation character of this directive, there is no doubt that Member States remain free to provide such contractual remedies. Nevertheless, the fact that this is not regulated at EU level is regrettable and may hinder the effectiveness of this Directive.

3.3. PROHIBITED PRACTICES

3.3.1. Payment term exceeding 30 or 60 days

In Article 3, 1, a) Directive 2019/633/EU, late payment practices are tackled. This Article defines maximum payment terms for perishable as well as non-perishable agricultural and food products. With regard to the former, the maximum payment term is 30 days. For non-perishable agricultural and food products, the maximum payment term is 60 days.

The starting point of the payment term depends on whether the products are delivered on a regular basis or not. If they are delivered on a regular basis, the term starts as from "*the end of the agreed delivery period in which deliveries have*

---

20 Art. 6, 2 Directive 93/13/EEC.

21 Art. 3, 2 Directive 2005/29/EC.

22 Civic consulting in cooperation with KU Leuven CCM, Study for the Fitness Check of European consumer and marketing law, https://publications.europa.eu/en/publication-detail/-/publication/f7b3958b-772b-11e7-b2f2-01aa75ed71a1/language-en, p. 269.

23 See Art. 3 Directive (EU) 2019/2161 of the European Parliament and of the Council of 27 November 2019 amending Council Directive 93/13/EEC of 5 April 1993, Directive 98/6/EC of the European Parliament and of the Council, Directive 2005/29/EC of the European Parliament and of the Council and Directive 2011/83/EU of the European Parliament and of the Council as regards better enforcement and modernisation of EU consumer protection rules, *OJ L* 328, 18.12.2019 (inserting a new art. 11a 'Redress' in Directive 2005/29/EC').

been made or [as from] the date on which the amount payable for that delivery period is set, whichever of those two dates is the later".[24] In order to increase the level of protection, it is specified that the agreed delivery period "*shall in any event be considered not to exceed one month*".[25] Moreover, the Directive defines the starting point if the amount payable is set by the buyer. In that event, the payment term starts to run from the end of the agreed delivery period in which the deliveries have been made, if the products are delivered on a regularly basis.[26] If they are not delivered on a regularly basis, the term starts to run from the date of delivery.[27]

As a result, with regard to perishable agricultural and food products, the current maximum payment term of 60 days established in the Late payment directive[28] is halved. The maximum payment term thus prescribed in Directive 2019/633/EU corresponds with the default payment term[29] mentioned in the Late payment directive.[30]

The concept of "perishable agricultural and food products", which limits the scope of this specific prohibition, is defined in art. 2, 5) Directive 2019/633/EU. These are "*agricultural and food products that by their nature or at their stage of processing are liable to become unfit for sale within 30 days after harvest, production or processing*".[31] By contrast, the French Code de commerce provides a more detailed definition, by referring to frozen meat, frozen fish, ready-made meals and canned perishable food.[32] Since the European definition leaves more leeway for interpretation, we believe it would be useful to make a non-exhaustive list of products which should be considered perishable agricultural and food products on the one hand, and a non-exhaustive list of agricultural and food products which fall outside the scope of the definition on the other hand.

With regard to non-perishable food, the maximum payment term coincides with the current maximum payment term of 60 days established in the Late payment directive. However, whereas the latter directive still allows to agree otherwise if this is done expressly and if it is not grossly unfair to the creditor[33], Directive 2019/633/EU that takes precedence over the Late payment directive does not foresee such an exception.

---

24 Art. 3, 1 Directive 2019/633/EU.
25 *Ibid.*
26 *Ibid.*
27 *Ibid.*
28 Art. 3, 5 Late payment directive.
29 Art. 3, 3, (b) Late payment directive.
30 For public authorities the Late payment directive however also provides for a maximum payment term of 30 calendar days, with a limited number of exceptions. Art. 4, 3 and 4, 4 Late payment directive.
31 Art. 2, 5 Directive 2019/633/EU.
32 Art. L441–11 C. com. Before 26 April 2019, this was specified in art. L-443–1 C. Com.
33 Recital 13 and Art. 3, 5 Late payment directive.

3.3.1.1. Consequences of late payments and remedies

One of the flaws of Directive 2019/633/EU is that it fails to provide concrete remedies if unfair terms or practices are used (see above). For late payments, this is solved by referring to the '*consequences and remedies*' the Late Payment Directive provides. These consequences and remedies shall apply '*on the basis of the payment periods set out in this Directive [2019/633/EU]*', '*by derogation from the payment periods set out in the [Late Payment Directive]*'.[34]

This seems to imply that the supplier will be entitled to the interest for late payment provided by the Late payment directive, without the necessity of a reminder if he does not receive payment on time (Article 3 Late payment directive *juncto* art. 3, 1, *in fine* Directive 2019/633/EU); provided of course that the supplier has fulfilled its contractual and legal obligations and unless the buyer is not responsible for the delay (Article 3, 1 Late payment directive).

It also seems to imply that the supplier must be able to obtain compensation for recovery costs where interest for late payment becomes due (Article 4 Late payment directive *juncto* art. 3, 1, *in fine* Directive 2019/633/EU).

And lastly, it is not entirely clear how the '*consequences and remedies*' of Article 7 Late payment directive should be applied to the payment terms provisions of Directive 2019/633/EU. Article 7 Late payment directive requires Member States to provide that contractual terms or practices relating i.a. to the period for payment that are '*grossly unfair*' are either unenforceable or give rise to a claim for damages. This is logical in a system that still allows to deviate from the payment terms provided for. Directive 2019/633/EU does not give such leeway and simply prohibits longer terms. It would then seem logical to require that terms providing for longer payment periods are automatically unenforceable or void without any need to further assess their unfair character. Unfortunately Directive 2019/633 is not clear in this regard. Member States of course have the possibility to provide so in their national laws.

Although it is laudable that the EU legislator tries to achieve some consistency between both directives, the formulation of this reference to the '*consequences and remedies*' of the Late payment directive poses interpretation problems.

3.3.1.2. Value sharing clause

The Directive furthermore provides that its late payment provisions are without prejudice '*to the option of a buyer and a supplier to agree on a value sharing clause within the meaning of Article 172a of Regulation (EU) No 1308/2013*'.[35, 36]

---

34 Art. 3, 1, *in fine* Directive 2019/633/EU.

35 Regulation (EU) No 1308/2013 of the European Parliament and of the Council of 17 December 2013 establishing a common organisation of the markets in agricultural products and repealing Council Regulations (EEC) No 922/72, (EEC) No 234/79, (EC) No 1037/2001 and (EC) No 1234/2007.

36 See Recital 18 Directive and art. 3, 1, *in fine* Directive 2019/633/EU.

This provision allows farmers (including farmers' associations) and their first purchaser to agree on value sharing clauses, whereby they determine how any evolution of relevant market prices is to be allocated between them.[37] Such clauses were formerly only allowed in the sugar sector[38], but this was extended to all agricultural sectors[39] and these clauses are widely used.[40]

3.3.1.3. Exemptions from the payment provisions of Directive 2019/633/EU

The late payment provisions furthermore do not apply to payments made by a buyer in the framework of a school scheme, as set out in Regulation (EU) No 1308/2013. That regulation provides for an aid system for the supply of fruit and vegetables and milk (products) in schools and other educational establishments.[41] The aid applicant will not be submitted to the clauses on late payment in order not to undermine the functioning of this system.[42]

A further exception is made for public entities providing healthcare.[43] These entities still need to comply with the provisions of the Late payment directive, that however also provides for an exceptional regime in that Member States may extend the maximum payment term for these public entities to a maximum of 60 calendar days.

A final exception concerns supply agreements between *'suppliers of grapes or must for wine production and their direct buyers'* provided a number of conditions have been met that should ensure the balanced character of such supply agreements.[44] As grapes are harvested only during a very short period but used to produce wine that may be sold several years later, the sector has developed standard contracts with specific payment arrangements with installments.[45] This exception takes these specific characteristics into account.

---

37 Art. 172a Regulation (EU) No 1308/2013.

38 See Commission Delegated Regulation (EU) 2016/1166.

39 *Article 172a of Regulation (EU) No 1308/2013.*

40 See, for the sugar sector, Commission Report on The application of the Union competition rules to the agricultural sector, COM(2018) 706 final, nr. 30.

41 See art. 22 et seq. of Regulation EU) No 1308/2013.

42 Recital 18 Directive 2019/633/EU.

43 In the meaning of point (b) of Article 4, 4 of the Late payment directive 2011/7/EU; i.e.: "*public entities providing healthcare which are duly recognised for that purpose*".

44 These conditions entail: '*(i) that the specific terms of payment for the sales transactions are included in standard contracts which have been made binding by the Member State pursuant to Article 164 of Regulation (EU) No 1308/2013 before 1 January 2019, and that this extension of the standard contracts is renewed by the Member States from that date without any significant changes to the terms of payment to the disadvantage of suppliers of grapes or must; and (ii) that the supply agreements between suppliers of grapes or must for wine production and their direct buyers are multiannual or become multiannual*' (art. 3, 1, *in fine* Directive 2019/633/EU).

45 Recital 19 Directive 2019/633/EU.

3.3.2. Short notice order cancellation

The second practice which is prohibited by Article 3, 1) of Directive 2019/633/EU, relates to "short notice order cancellations". This occurs when "*a buyer cancels orders of perishable agricultural and food products <u>at such short notice</u> that a supplier <u>cannot reasonably be expected to find an alternative means</u> of commercialising or using those products*".[46] According to the directive, notice of less than 30 days shall always be considered as short notice. Probably, this criterion should be understood as less than 30 days *before the agreed delivery date of the products.* Member States remain free to set periods shorter than 30 days for specific sectors in duly justified cases.[47]

This prohibition only aims at protecting suppliers of *perishable* agricultural and food products. This restriction seems to be justified. One can presume that short notice order cancellations of perishable agricultural and food products will indeed have a greater impact than the cancellation of other agricultural and food products. As regards the definition of the concept "perishable food product", we refer to the aforementioned remark.

The European legislator tries to facilitate the use of this prohibition by creating a non-refutable presumption with regard to cancellations which take place with a notice of less than 30 days. However, one can question whether this prohibition will create sufficient certainty if the cancellation takes place with a longer notice period. In that case, the prohibition will only be infringed if the supplier cannot *reasonably* be expected to find an alternative after cancellation. The degree of reasonableness will highly depend on the specific supply agreement and the products concerned.[48] To determine whether the supplier can reasonably be expected to find an alternative, account should be taken, in particular, to the extent to which a perishable food product can be processed. The range of alternatives will be wider for products that can easily be processed. Besides, the volume of the cancelled order will be relevant as well. Hence, a concrete assessment will be necessary in order to decide whether a cancellation of an order accounts for an unfair practice. The experience with the UCPD demonstrates that the use of vague terms necessitating a concrete assessment in

---

46 Art. 3, 1, b) Directive 2019/633/EU; our underlining.

47 Art. 3, 1, b) Directive 2019/633/EU.

48 Compare with the French case law applying art. L-442–6, I, 5° C. com. (since 26 April 2019: art. L-442–1, II, first paragraph C. com.). That Article prohibits the sudden termination of a commercial relationship. The French courts takes i.a. the following criteria into account: the scope of the commercial relationship, the investments made, the specific characteristics of the goods concerned, see CA Paris 21 March 2018, nr. 16/07984, www.dalloz.fr; CA Paris 14 March 2018, nr. 16/09127, www.dalloz.fr; CA Paris 9 May 2018, nr. 16/02810, www.lexisnexis.com; CA Paris 22 November 2017, nr. 15/01067, www.dalloz.fr.

a blacklist make such a list difficult to apply in practice.[49] The same problems may occur in the application of Directive 2019/633/EU.

3.3.3. *Unilateral and retroactive change of the supply agreement*

Thirdly, the European legislator prohibits "*unilateral changes of the terms of the supply agreement concerning the frequency, method, place, timing or volume of the supply or the delivery of the agricultural and food products, the quality standards, the terms of payment or the prices, or as regards the provision of services insofar as these are explicitly referred to in paragraph 2*".[50]

In contrast with the proposal, the scope of this prohibition is no longer limited to unilateral changes with retroactive effect.

Since the practices mentioned in the first paragraph of Article 3 are not left to contractual freedom[51], it seems to follow from the structure and the wording of the directive that contractual terms allowing one or both parties to unilaterally change the contract, are forbidden as well. This differs from the Principles of Good Practice. Those principles allow non-retroactive, unilateral changes to the contract if that possibility and the circumstances and conditions of such a unilateral change have been agreed in advance.[52] This provision also goes further than the recently introduced Belgian provisions on unfair contract terms between businesses. The newly introduced Article VI.91/5, 1° Code of economic law merely creates a *presumption* that a clause that allows an undertaking to unilaterally and without a valid reason change the price, characteristics or conditions of the agreement is unfair and therefore invalid. The Belgian provision will need to be adapted to implement the Directive correctly. It also differs from French law. Under French law there is no *per se* prohibition of a contractual terms that allows unilateral changes. Such clauses can however be considered unfair in particular circumstances under the open norm of Article L. 442-1, I, 2° C. com.[53] if they create a significant imbalance.[54] For clauses allowing a *retroactive* change, Article L. 442-3, a) C. Com.[55] of the black list could be invoked.[56] German law also accepts clauses that allow undertakings to unilaterally change certain elements under certain conditions, including that the company should have a legitimate interest in the adaptation, the circumstances

49 See e.g. the Study for the Fitness Check of consumer and marketing law, May 2017, http://ec.europa.eu/newsroom/document.cfm?doc_id=44840, p. 35.

50 Art. 3, 1, (c) Directive 2019/633/EU; our underlining.

51 Cf. proposal for a directive on unfair trading practices, COM (2018) 173 final, p. 13.

52 Principles of Good Practice, principle 2.

53 Former art. L442-6, I, 2° C. com.

54 E. KERGUELEN, JurisClasseur Commercial, Fasc. 280: le déséquilibre significatif entre les droits et obligations des parties (pratiques commerciales restrictives), 15 December 2015, nr. 43-45.

55 Former art. L442-6, II, a) C. com.

56 That clause prohibits retroactive rebates and price reductions in all circumstances.

and conditions of such unilateral change should be set out and the interests of the other contractual party should be taken into account.[57] This finally also differs from the Unfair Contract Terms Directive 93/13/EC, that is less strict on clauses allowing unilateral changes as it only considers such clauses '*potentially*' unfair if they '*enable the seller or supplier to alter the terms of the contract unilaterally without a valid reason which is specified in the contract*'.[58] One may therefore wonder whether the European legislator really intended to be stricter in a B2B than in a B2C context. It would have contributed to legal certainty to set out explicitly whether contractual clauses allowing unilateral changes are indeed covered by Article 3, 1, c).

The scope of this far reaching provision is in any event somewhat attenuated as a difference is made (in the recitals) between unilateral changes and unilateral specifications. Whereas the former are per se prohibited, recital 21 explains that clauses allowing a buyer to *specify* an element at a later stage for future orders are still allowed.

3.3.4. *Payments not related to the contract*

According to Article 3, 1, d) buyers may not require payments from the supplier which are "*not related to the sale of the agricultural and food products of the supplier*".

One can presume that such payments will often arise from a contractual term. Hence, this fourth prohibition of unfair trading *practices* also refers to prohibited unfair *terms*. By considering such term as an unfair trading practice, the European legislator abandons the distinction between unfair *practices* and unfair *terms*, made in the legislation regulating the B2C-relationship. We support this approach as this distinction is in practice sometimes difficult to make. Unfortunately, Directive 2019/633/EU does not explicitly provide that such an unfair term should be declared void. The absence of such sanction was discussed in more detail above.

This broadly formulated prohibition is open to interpretation. The second paragraph of Article 3 can somewhat help to interpret Article 3, 1, d). In that second paragraph, several payments are specified which may be required by the buyer if they are agreed in clear and unambiguous terms in the supply agreement or in a subsequent agreement between the supplier and the buyer. Hence, those payments can be considered as payments *related* to the sale of the agricultural or food products.

This prohibition is in any event broad enough to also tackle '*the payment for fictitious and unsolicited services*', as suggested in the opinion of the EESC of

57 See S. De Pourcq, *Oneerlijke handelspraktijken en bedingen tussen ondernemingen*, Antwerpen, Intersentia, 2019, 247–249.

58 Point j) Annex to Directive 93/13/EEC.

2013.[59] It indeed appears from the recitals that these are the practices envisaged: according to recital 22, it is allowed to negotiate and charge payment for services provided by the seller, such as listing, marketing and promotion. '*However, where a buyer charges a supplier payments which are not related to a specific sales transaction, this should be considered unfair and should be prohibited under the directive*'.

Such practices would indeed be widespread. According to the Confederation of the Food and Drink Industries of the EU (FoodDrinkEurope) and the European Brands Association (AIM), 60% of European suppliers to the large retail sector would have been forced to make payments for which there was nothing in return.[60] Examples of such practices include invoices mentioning 'payment for stable cooperation', 'payment for issuing invoice', 'payment for settling invoice', or 'contribution to the costs of the company party', for fictitious services.[61]

A similar prohibition exists in France, where art. L442-1-I, 1° C. Com. provides that it is '*prohibited to obtain or try to obtain an advantage of any kind that is not related to a commercial service that has effectively been provided or that is manifestly disproportionate*'. In the former provision, the French legislator in addition included several examples of such practices, including the financial participation in a commercial promotion campaign or new sales strategy, not justified by a common interest and without proportionate consideration; in the investment, in particular in the context of the renovation of stores; in the merger of brands; in the payment for services provided by an international center grouping distributors.[62]

Unlike the similar French provision, art. 3, 1, d) of the Directive does permit payments that are '*manifestly disproportionate*', as long as they are 'related to the sale'.

---

59 European Economic and Social Committee, Opinion of 11.7.2013 on the Green Paper on unfair trading practices in the business to business food and non-food supply chain in Europe, COM(2013) 37 final, at point 6.4.

60 In 2009, cited in Opinion of the European Economic and Social Committee on 'The current state of commercial relations between food suppliers and the large retail sector' (own-initiative opinion) 2013/C 133/03, point 2.3.3.2.

61 Opinion of the European Economic and Social Committee on 'The current state of commercial relations between food suppliers and the large retail sector' (own-initiative opinion) 2013/C 133/03, point 2.3.3.

62 See Art. L 442-6, I, 1° C. Com. (text in force until 26 april 2019): '*Un tel avantage peut notamment consister en la participation, non justifiée par un intérêt commun et sans contrepartie proportionnée, au financement d'une opération d'animation ou de promotion commerciale, d'une acquisition ou d'un investissement, en particulier dans le cadre de la rénovation de magasins, du rapprochement d'enseignes ou de centrales de référencement ou d'achat ou de la rémunération de services rendus par une centrale internationale regroupant des distributeurs. Un tel avantage peut également consister en une globalisation artificielle des chiffres d'affaires, en une demande d'alignement sur les conditions commerciales obtenues par d'autres clients ou en une demande supplémentaire, en cours d'exécution du contrat, visant à maintenir ou accroître abusivement ses marges ou sa rentabilité.*'

Once more, it is regrettable that the prohibition of the Directive is not formulated more precisely as the broad wording is likely to give rise to interpretation problems.

3.3.5. *Payment for deterioration or loss*

Article 3, 1, e) prohibits the fact that the supplier is required to pay for the deterioration or loss of agricultural and food products if that deterioration or loss "*occurs on the buyer's premises or after ownership has been transferred to the buyer*" and "*is not caused by negligence or fault of the supplier*".[63]

This prohibited type of payment will also often be incorporated into a contractual term.[64] The application in practice of the prohibition as formulated by Directive 2019/633/EU will probably cause problems. It will be difficult to determine whether or not the deterioration or loss was caused by negligence or fault of the supplier. The English supply code which applies to the groceries supply chain, known as the GSCOP[65], requires the parties to anticipate to such a discussion. More precisely, the GSCOP accepts payment for wastage if the wastage "*is due to the negligence or default of that Supplier, and the relevant Supply Agreement sets out expressly and unambiguously what will constitute negligence or default on the part of the Supplier*".[66] Interpretation and application problems could thus have been avoided by only allowing a contractual shift of the risk for deterioration or loss if it is set out expressly and precisely what constitutes negligence or fault of the supplier. Although the Directive does not impose this requirement, the minimum harmonization character allows Member States to add such requirement when implementing the Directive.

The way the Principles of Good Practice deal with this issue, by contrast, is not a source of inspiration to solve this application problem. The sixth principle only vaguely stipulates that "*all contracting parties in the supply chain should bear their own appropriate entrepreneurial risks*".[67] The same principle is recorded in the Belgian Code of conduct for fair relationships.[68] The recently adopted

---

63 Our underlining.

64 See for an example of a clause regulating deterioration and more generally the risk allocation between parties in contracts in France, Court of Appeal Paris 25 November 2015, nr. 12/14513, Jurisdata nr. 2015–026641.

65 Groceries Supply Code of Practice, www.gov.uk/government/publications/groceries-supply-code-of-practice/groceries-supply-code-of-practice. The GSCOP only applies in the relationship between retailers and their direct suppliers: see Groceries Market Investigation Order 2009: https://assets.publishing.service.gov.uk/government/uploads/system/uploads/attachment_data/file/461114/GSCOP-Order_v2.pdf.

66 Art. 8 GSCOP. Besides, regardless of who is responsible for the wastage, the GSCOP allows payments for wastage if "*the basis of such Payment is set out in the Supply Agreement*": *ibid.*

67 Principles of Good Practice, principle 6.

68 Code of conduct for fair relationships, http://supplychaininitiative.be/_library/_files/Code_140610_NL.pdf.

Belgian Act on 'abuse of economic dependence, unfair contract terms and unfair trade practices'[69], still takes a different approach and creates a rebuttable presumption that clauses that entail a transfer of risk without consideration are considered unfair (and void).[70]

3.3.6. *Refusal of confirmation in writing*

According to Article 3, 1, f) an unfair trading practice occurs when the buyer refuses to confirm in writing the terms of a supply agreement, although the supplier has asked for written confirmation. Hence, the European legislator does not require *each* supply agreement to be specified in writing. This is only required if the supplier asks for a written confirmation.[71]

A lot of discussion and possible abuses can indeed be avoided through the use of written agreements. Having the terms of an agreement in writing will often also be a necessary condition for the supplier to be able to prove an unfair trade practice, such as e.g. the later unilateral change of a term.

This obligation to confirm the terms in writing, does not apply "*where the supply agreement concerns products to be delivered by a member of a producer organisation, including a cooperative, to the producer organisation of which the supplier is a member, if the statutes of that producer organisation or the rules and decisions provided for in, or derived from, those statutes contain provisions having similar effects to the terms of the supply agreement*".[72]

The enforcement of this prohibition seems to be quite straightforward. It will suffice for the supplier to provide evidence of his request for a confirmation in writing on the one hand, and the buyer's refusal on the other. Consequently, one can expect this prohibition to be quite relevant in practice, provided appropriate sanctions are foreseen in case of non-compliance with this prohibition. As the Directive leaves this to the Member States (see below), much will depend on the implementation.

3.3.7. *Unlawful acquirement, use or disclosure of trade secrets*

Art. 3, 1, g) Directive 2019/633/EU concerns the fact that the buyer "*unlawfully acquires, uses or discloses the trade secrets of the supplier within the meaning of Directive (EU) 2016/943 of the European Parliament and of the Council*".

---

69 Act of 4 April 2019 amending the Code of Economic law concerning the abuse of economic dependence, unfair contract terms and unfair trade practices, *Belgian Offical Gazette* 24 May 2019.

70 Art. VI.91/5, 3° Code of Economic Law.

71 See also Recital 23 Directive 2019/633/EU.

72 Art. 3, 1, f) Directive 2019/633/EU.

Directive 2016/943/EU on the protection of trade secrets[73] already requires Member States to ensure that remedies are available to both prevent and obtain redress from the unlawful acquisition, use and disclosure of trade secrets.[74] By qualifying such a practice as an unfair trading practice, an additional set of enforcement tools seems to be made available to ensure compliance with Directive 2016/943/EU in the agricultural and food supply sector.

Unfortunately, it is not made clear what provisions are to take precedence in case of a conflict.[75] Whereas Directive 2016/943/EU e.g. provides detailed safeguards for protecting the interests of both parties, no similar measures are foreseen in the enforcement provisions of Directive 2019/633/EU. It would seem logical that the safeguards provided for under the trade secrets directive also find application when the enforcement tools of Directive 2019/633/EU are applied.[76]

3.3.8. *Hampering the exercise of contractual or legal rights*

It is forbidden for the buyer to threaten to carry out, or to carry out, "*acts of commercial retaliation against the supplier if the supplier exercises its contractual or legal rights, including by filing a complaint with enforcement authorities or by cooperating with enforcement authorities during an investigation.*"[77]

The European legislator sees i.a. the following actions (or threat thereof) as acts of commercial retaliation: delisting products, reducing the quantities of products ordered or stopping certain services which the buyer provides to the supplier such as marketing or promotions on the suppliers' products.[78]

Once more, the effectiveness of such prohibition that tries to tackle the 'fear factor' will depend on the available enforcement tools. The possibility of '*fines or other equally effective penalties*' being imposed, as required by Article 6, 1), e) Directive 2019/633, should be an incentive to refrain from the mentioned practice.

---

73 Directive (EU) 2016/943 of the European Parliament and of the Council of 8 June 2016 on the protection of undisclosed know-how and business information (trade secrets) against their unlawful acquisition, use and disclosure.

74 Art. 4 Directive 2016/943/EU.

75 As is for example done in recital 39 of the trade secrets directive for a potential overlap between the trade secrets directive and Directive 2004/48/EC on the enforcement of intellectual property rights.

76 Recital 10 trade secrets directive seems to confirm this reasoning as it sets out that Member States may provide more far-reaching protection against the unlawful acquisition use or disclosure of trade secrets than provided for in the Trade secrets directive as long as the safeguards provided for in that directive are respected. This should also be the case when Member States implement Directive 2019/633/EU.

77 Art. 3, 1, h) Directive 2019/633/EU.

78 Recital 25 Directive 2019/633/EU.

3.3.9. *Payment for the examining of customer complaints*

Article 3, 1, i) Directive 2019/633/EU forbids the buyer to require "*compensation from the supplier for the cost of examining customer complaints relating to the sale of the supplier's products despite the absence of negligence or fault on the part of the supplier*".

This type of payment is also regulated in the aforementioned GSCOP, the English supply code which applies to the groceries supply chain.[79] The relevant provisions can be a source of inspiration for the Member States when implementing the Directive, as it distinguishes between various types of complaints and it sets out what evidence must be provided by the buyer to be able to request such payment.[80]

3.4. CONDITIONALLY PERMITTED PRACTICES

The second paragraph of Article 3 of Directive 2019/633/EU contains six practices which are, according to the proposal of the directive, believed to "*yield efficiencies in favour of both contract partners and thus lead to win-win situations*".[81] For that reason, they are permitted, provided that they are "*agreed in clear and unambiguous terms in the supply agreement or in a subsequent agreement between the supplier and the buyer*".[82] Except for the first practice, all practices mentioned in this second paragraph concern payments made by the supplier to the buyer. By taking this approach, the European Commission at the same time implicitly accepts that it is *fair* to stipulate these terms. It is merely sufficient that the practice is agreed in clear and unambiguous terms in the supply agreement or in a subsequent agreement between the supplier and the buyer.

The choice of the European legislator not to pay any attention to the concrete *content* of the terms in question significantly limits the importance of the Directive 2019/633/EU and can be regretted. It prevents Directive 2019/633/EU from giving an adequate answer to the imbalance of contractual bargaining power which often exists between suppliers and sellers. The current approach assumes that contractual negotiations about these payments will in any event lead to fair contract terms.

---

79 Art. 15 GSCOP.

80 Www.gov.uk/government/publications/groceries-supply-code-of-practice/groceries-supply-code-of-practice#no-unjustified-payment-for-consumer-complaints.

81 Proposal for a Directive of the European Parliament and of the Council on unfair trading practices in business-to-business relationships in the food supply chain, 2018/0082 (COD), Explanatory memorandum, 14.

82 Art. 3, 2 Directive 2019/633/EU.

Moreover Directive 2019/633/EU also fails to set out what the (contractual) sanction is if a term is not formulated in a clear and unambiguous way. This is once more regrettable.

In a B2C context, there is a similar but more general obligation to draft (B2C) contract terms in '*plain, intelligible language*'[83] and extensive ECJ case law clarifying the exact meaning of this transparency requirement.[84] Especially the clarification of the Court that this requirement entails not only that a term must be '*formally and grammatically intelligible*', but that it is also required that the consumer must be able to ascertain the economic consequences that result from a term has been particularly useful.[85] By analogy, as the supplier is considered to be the weaker party in Directive 2019/633/EU, the same interpretation could be applied here: in order to be clear and unambiguous, the clauses listed in Article 3, 2 Directive 2019/633/EU should not only be formally and grammatically intelligible, the supplier must also be able to ascertain the economic consequences that result from it.

Directive 93/13/EEC furthermore provides for concrete sanctions in case clauses are not drafted in '*plain and intelligible language*'. First, the directive has an interpretation rule: '*Where there is doubt about the meaning of a term, the interpretation most favourable to the consumer shall prevail*'.[86] It would have been possible to provide a similar rule in Directive 2019/633/EU stating that the interpretation most favourable to the supplier prevails, given that the scope of application of the Directive is thus determined that the supplier would normally be the weaker party. Once more, Member States remain free to adopt such a rule when implementing the directive. However, in Member States that allow for a control of unfair terms and practices between undertakings in general, such a rule of interpretation is more difficult to implement as it may not be possible to determine in advance who is the weaker party of the undertakings involved.[87]

Second, although not made explicit in Directive 93/13/EEC, the ECJ has made clear that the lack of transparency is an element to be taken into account when declaring a clause unfair (and thus non-binding) under the general clause of the directive.[88] This seems to be a balanced sanction, whereby the courts can

---

83 Art. 5 Directive 93/13/EEC.

84 See i.a. M. Loos, "Transparency of standard terms under the Unfair Contract Terms Directive and the Proposal for a Common European Sales Law", *ERPL* 2015; E. Terryn, "Transparantie en Algemene Voorwaarden: Nood aan Hervorming?", *TPR* 2017, 15–70.

85 Case C-26/13 *Kasler* [2014] ECLI:EU:C:2014:282, para 73.

86 Art. 5 Directive 93/13/EEC. This rule does however not apply in the context of the procedures laid down in Art. 7 (2) Directive 93/13/EEC – i.e. in actions to prevent the continued use of such terms.

87 Thus e.g. in Belgium, where a general provision allowing for a control of unfair terms between all undertakings was recently introduced, no interpretation rule was adopted (see Articles VI.91/2 and VI.91/3 Code of Economic Law).

88 Case C-96/14 Van Hove [2015] ECLI:EU:C:2015:262, para 27; Case C-191/15 Amazon EU [2016] ECLI:EU:C:2016:612, paras 65 and 68.

take into account all the relevant circumstances. In the absence of a general norm under Directive 2019/633/EU, this sanction of Directive 93/13/EEC can in any event not be applied by analogy.

In the system of Directive 2019/633/EU, the consequence of an unclear or ambiguous term is that the term is 'prohibited'[89] and Member States will at least have to ensure that the use of such terms can be stopped.[90] Whether the ambiguity also has implications on the validity of the clause is not spelled out nor explicitly required by the Directive. It remains however possible for the Member States to provide that the ambiguity can be an element for their courts to take into account to declare such a term void. Such sanction has for example been adopted in the new Belgian legislation on unfair B2B practices and terms.[91]

Providing a clear sanction for non-compliance with the transparency requirement will in any event be a point of attention for the Member States when implementing the directive.

3.4.1. *Payment for unsold products*

Article 3, 2, a) of Directive 2019/633/EU relates to clauses allowing the buyer to return unsold agricultural and food products without paying for those unsold products or without paying for the disposal of those products, or both. Such a right is often included in contracts between suppliers and sellers in the food supply chain. According to Directive 2019/633/EU, it is permitted to agree on such an obligation, provided it is agreed upon in clear and unambiguous terms.

It is interesting to compare this view to the approach in the French case law. In 2017, the court of appeal of Paris was asked to assess whether or not the contractual obligation for a supplier to take back 7% of the unsold goods was fair.[92] The court of appeal concluded that such contractual terms do not infringe the French prohibition on unfair commercial practices, stated in art. L442-1, I, 2° C. com. The court took the limited extent to which the products were returned, into account. This balanced approach can be supported.

3.4.2. *Payment for stocking, displaying, listing or making available on the market*

Secondly, it is permitted, if it is agreed upon in clear and unambiguous terms, to charge a supplier a payment as a condition for the stocking, displaying, listing of his agricultural and food products or as a condition for making such products available on the market.[93]

---

89 Art. 3, 2) Directive 2019/633/EU.
90 Art. 5, 7) and art. 6, 1, d) Directive 2019/633/EU.
91 See Article VI.91/3, §2 Code of Economic Law. The Belgian legislation also has a general norm in addition to black and grey clauses.
92 CA Paris 8 February 2017, No. 15/02170, JurisData No. 2017-002438.
93 Art. 3, 2, b) Directive 2019/633/EU.

This type of payments is rather contested. In Germany, no unified vision can be identified. In 1976, the Bundesgerichtshof judged that "*Eintrittsgeld*" was unfair.[94] However, some legal scholars believe that "*Eintrittsgeld*" and "*Listungsentgelte*" should be allowed if they are aligned with the costs and the potential risks connected to contracting with a new supplier or to selling new products.[95]

Article 3, 3 Directive 2019/633/EU adds that the supplier can request an "*estimate of the payments per unit or overall, whichever is appropriate*" and "*an estimate of the costs and the basis for such estimate*". The European legislator aims to create additional transparency for the supplier. This obligation should also help to avoid that buyers impose merely arbitrary payments on their suppliers. Once more, a sanction is missing in case such an estimate is not provided. Several options are possible (for the Member States); such charges could e.g. be prohibited if the requested estimates were not provided; or there could be a (rebuttable) presumption that the charges are unfair (and prohibited) if the requested estimates were not provided.

3.4.3. *Payment for discounts*

The third type of payment which is implicitly accepted by Directive 2019/633/EU, relates to discounts on the agricultural and food products sold by the buyer as part of a promotion.[96] Clauses requiring the supplier to bear all or part of the costs are once more allowed, provided they were previously agreed upon in clear and unambiguous terms. With regard to these payments, Directive 2019/633/EU however imposes an information obligation on the buyer if the promotion is initiated by him. This information includes a specification of the period of the promotion and the expected quantity of the agricultural and food products to be ordered. In addition, the supplier is also offered the possibility to request an estimate of the payment.

The GSCOP also deals with payments for promotions. First, it determines the extent to which a supplier can be asked to make payments for promotions, by stipulating that a retailer should not "*directly or indirectly, require a supplier predominantly to fund the costs of a promotion*".[97] The Directive does not exclude such practice if it is clearly agreed upon. Besides, according to the GSCOP the retailer can only hold a promotion "*after reasonable notice has been given to that*

---

94 BGH 17.12.1976, I ZR 77/75, *GRUR* 1977, 619.

95 J. Nothdurft, "§19 GWB Verbotenes Verhalten von marktbeherrschenden Unternehmen" in H.J. Bunte (ed.), *Langen/Bunte, Kartellrecht – Kommentar*, I, Keulen, Luchterhand Verlag, 2014, (422) 488, No. 170; cf. J. Säcker and J. Mohr, "Forderung und Durchsetzung ungerechtfertigter Vorteile – Eine Analyse des §20 Abs. 3 GWB", *WRP* 2010, (1) 11.

96 Art. 3, 2, c) Directive 2019/633/EU.

97 Art. 13 (1) GSCOP.

supplier in writing".[98] Thirdly, the GSCOP explicitly states that it is not allowed to pay for promotions "*where this would entail a retrospective variation to the supply agreement*".[99] The latter two practices also seem to be covered by the Directive, as an explicit agreement in writing is necessary and as it is specified that the details of the planned promotion need to be set out prior to the promotion.[100]

3.4.4. Payment for advertising & payment for marketing

As a fourth type of payment, the Directive allows suppliers and buyers to agree on (clear and unambiguous) clauses requiring the suppliers to pay for *advertising* by the buyer of agricultural and food products.[101] The fifth type of payment mentioned in Article 3, 2 Directive 2019/633/EU, is payment for *marketing* of agricultural and food products by the buyer.[102]

Unfortunately, Directive 2019/633/EU does not describe how advertising or marketing costs should be understood. The provisions furthermore broadly describe the payments that may be allowed, as they do refer in general to advertising and marketing 'by the buyer of agricultural and food products'. They do not explicitly refer to advertising of *the* agricultural and food products of the supplier. The exact scope of these provisions is therefore unclear.

It is regrettable that the Directive does not define advertising and marketing costs. Here again, it is interesting to make a comparison with the GSCOP. Similar to Directive 2019/633/EU, the GSCOP requires that payments for marketing costs are agreed in the supply agreement. However, since "marketing" is a broad concept in the GSCOP, which is not restricted to the products of that specific supplier, buyers are able to pass on a wide range of costs to their suppliers. More precisely, marketing costs in the meaning of the GSCOP refer to retailer's costs of "*buyer visits to new or prospective suppliers, artwork or packaging design, consumer or market research, the opening or refurbishing of a store or hospitality for that retailer's staff*".[103]

One may wonder whether the European legislator intended to apply a similarly broad definition. The idea to require payment from suppliers for the opening or refurbishing of a store, for instance, would clearly deviate from the approach in Germany and France. The French Code de commerce forbids such payments in art. L442-1, I, 1° C. com., and such payments were considered unfair by the German Bundesgerichtshof in January 2018.[104] Such a broad approach also seems to conflict with art. 3, 1), d) of the Directive that prohibits

98 Art. 13, 2 GSCOP.
99 *Ibid.*
100 Art. 3, 2, *in fine* Directive 2019/633/EU.
101 Art. 3, 2, d) Directive 2019/633/EU.
102 Art. 3, 2, e) Directive 2019/633/EU.
103 Art. 6 GSCOP.
104 BGH 23.01.2018, KVR 3/17, No. 19, www.bundesgerichtshof.de.

payments *'that are not related to the sale of the agricultural and food products of the supplier'*.

Clarification of the exact scope of the payments for advertising and marketing that may be allowed will be necessary when implementing the Directive. The apparently broad wording of art. 3, 2, d) and e) of the Directive does not prevent Member States to require a link between the advertising or marketing costs and the products of the supplier or at least to require a mutual interest in the advertising or marketing the supplier is required to pay for.

3.4.5. Payment for staff for fitting-out premises used for the sale of the supplier's products

The Directive lastly allows the buyer, if agreed upon in clear and unambiguous terms, to charge the supplier for the costs of staff for *'fitting-out premises used for the sale of the supplier's products'*.[105] Such payment seems less problematic than the payment for advertising and marketing, as at least a clear link with the supplier's products and thus some mutual interest is required by the Directive.

4. CONCLUSION

The current European legal framework on unfair trading practices in the contractual B2B relationship only consists of the Late payment directive and the Supply Chain Initiative. The adoption of Directive 2019/633/EU will definitely extend the protection provided to suppliers in the food supply chain.

However, the protection provided by the Directive is rather limited.

Firstly, Directive 2019/633/EU does not create a general prohibition on unfair trading practices, but merely defines a list of concrete prohibited unfair trading practices in Article 3. Secondly, only the first paragraph of Article 3 genuinely prohibits certain unfair trading practices, since the second paragraph mentions practices which are permitted if they are agreed upon in clear and unambiguous terms.

Thirdly, the effectiveness of the Directive may be further reduced as many of its provisions are open to interpretation and as in particular some of the provisions allowing certain contractual clauses (provided they are clear and unambiguous) can be given a broad interpretation, thereby seemingly allowing certain practices/contractual clauses that are now considered unfair in several Member States.

Fourth, clear sanctions are missing as it is left to the Member States to ensure that the penalties shall be *'effective, proportionate and dissuasive'*.[106] The Directive

105 Art. 3, 2, f) Directive 2019/633/EU.

106 Art. 6 Directive 2019/633/EU.

in particular fails to set out the (contractual) consequences of an unfair trading practice.

The effectiveness of the legislation will therefore to a large extent depend on the willingness of the Member States to maintain or introduce stricter rules when implementing this directive and to provide for effective sanctions. The minimum harmonisation character of this instrument is in any event to be welcomed as it still gives the Member States the possibility to adopt effective legislation on unfair B2B trading practices. A copy paste implementation of this Directive will in any event not be sufficient to reach that aim.

CHAPTER 3

ENFORCEMENT IN THE DIRECTIVE (ARTICLES 4 TO 11)

Muriel CHAGNY[*, **]

Academic Director of the LLM in Competition and Contract Law (University of Versailles – Paris Saclay); President of the French Association for the Study of Competition (AFEC); Vice-President of the International League of Competition Law (LIDC)

Enforcement is undoubtedly "the key element"[1] of any system addressing unfair trading practices and, as already stated, "the core"[2] of the Directive on unfair trading practices in business-to-business relationships in the agricultural and food supply chain (hereafter "the Directive").[3]

Published approximately one year after the Proposal for a Directive submitted by the European Commission[4] (hereafter "the Proposal"), the Directive is, as usual, the result of a compromise reached after political negotiations.

It is worth noting that the comparison between the Proposal and the Directive reveals some differences, in particular as regards the institutional enforcement mechanism.

The Explanatory Memorandum added to the proposed Directive explains that the Proposal, as regards enforcement, is "inspired by best practices in Members States's existing regimes".

---

* The views expressed are personal ones and should not be regarded as an official position of the CEPC (Commercial Practices Review Commission).

** Special thanks to the organizers of the conference and editors, Evelyne Terryn and Bert Keirsbilck, for inviting me to deal with this hot topic.1 European Parliament, Briefing Unfair Trading Practices in the Business-to-Business Food Supply Chain, PE 563.430, p. 1.

1 European Parliament, Briefing Unfair Trading Practices in the Business-to-Business Food Supply Chain, PE 563.430, p. 1.

2 F. Cafaggi &P. Iamiceli, Unfair Trading Practices in Food Supply Chain. Regulatory Responses and Institutional Alternatives in the Light of the New EU Directive European Review of Private Law 5–2019, 1075–1114, n° 45.

3 Directive 2019/633 of the European Parliament and of the Council of 17 April 2019, OJEU 25 April 2019, L. 111/59.

4 Proposal for a Directive on unfair trading practices in business-to-business relationships in the food supply chain, 12 April 2018, COM (2018) 173 final.

Indeed, French law has undeniably a lot of experience with regard to tackling UTPs in B-to-B relationships through specific UTP legislation. Numerous entities are involved in the enforcement of this specific legislation: judicial courts, the minister of Economic affairs, the DGCCRF, the mediator for agricultural trade relations, but also administrative courts as well as the Commission for the Examination of Commercial Practices (CEPC). Various measures can be adopted: from criminal sanctions, over fines and administrative injunctions, civil sanctions including fines, to opinions and recommendations. In brief, nothing beats a French lawyer to deal with UTPs. This is especially true given that many (too many?) reforms have been carried out in this field in France, so that the famous French critical thinking which could work wonders when assessing the new EU Directive.

As stated in the Proposal, the EU legislation aims at "laying down effective enforcement powers that have proven effective in tackling the fear factor, as well as enhancing the deterrent effect and improving redress possibilities in Member States". The European Parliament also emphasizes the need for an effective enforcement mechanism".[5] Consequently, it should be assessed to what extent Articles 4 to 11 of the Directive allow an effective implementation, and more precisely how they ensure firstly effectiveness in tackling UTPs (I) and secondly whether the result is satisfactory in terms of efficiency of the measures (II). These two perspectives will be successively considered bearing in mind that the Directive only provides minimum harmonization, so that MSs are free to adopt stricter enforcement provisions.

1. EFFECTIVENESS IN TACKLING UNFAIR TRADE PRACTICES

The Directive underlines the major hurdle as being the "fear factor", namely unwillingness of direct victims of UTPs to report them due to fear of commercial retaliation.[6] It is thus not surprising that the Directive includes provisions aiming at overcoming the fear factor (A). This explains also a strong preference in favour of public enforcement through the institutional framework based on designated enforcement authorities in each Member State that are intended to play a crucial part in tackling UTPs (B).

---

5 European Parliament, Briefing Unfair Trading Practices in the Business-to-Business Food Supply Chain, PE 563.430, p. 5.

6 See also European Parliament, Briefing Unfair Trading Practices in the Business-to-Business Food Supply Chain, PE 563.430, p. 5: "The greatest challenge for achieving the effectiveness of a system aimed at combatting unfair trade practices is overcoming the problems that stem from the fear factor".

1.1. THE DEVICE DESIGNED TO OVERCOME THE FEAR FACTOR

Two sets of measures are intended to address the fear of retaliation: on one side, the Directive expands the categories of people authorized to start UTP proceedings by going beyond the direct victim (1); on the other side, it seeks to encourage the direct victim to effectively file a complaint while ensuring confidentiality (2).

1.1.1. Expanding the categories of right of action holders beyond the direct victim

Firstly, the enforcement authority should be able to act, not only by way of complaints, but also on its own initiative.[7]

An infringement can also be brought to the attention of the authority by a complaint, being specified that the authority is allowed to not pursue if it considers that the grounds for acting are not sufficient. In that case, it must however inform the complainant of the reasons for such a decision. It should be noticed that, contrary to the Proposal, the Directive provides that this information must be given "within a reasonable period of time after the receipt of the complaint".[8]

As regards complaints, Article 5.2 allows "*producer organisations, other organisations of suppliers and associations of such organisations,* [...]"" to file a complaint, "*at the request of one or more of their members or, where appropriate, at the request of one or more members of their member organisations, where those members consider that they have been affected by a prohibited trading practice*". In addition to the Proposal's content, the final Directive grants "*other organisations that have a legitimate interest in representing suppliers*" the right to "*submit complaints, at the request of a supplier, and in the interest of that supplier, provided that such organisations are independent non-profit-making legal persons*". As stated in Recital 31, the objective is clearly "*to protect the identities of individual members of the organisation who consider that they are affected by unfair trading practices.*" As an example, it is possible to refer to Article L. 440–1 of the French Commercial Code which provides that professional organisations or trade unions, consular chambers or agricultural chambers as well as recognized consumer associations are entitled to bring a case to the CEPC.

Of course, the supplier, which is injured by UTPs, has also the right to submit a complaint, unless he refrained from the right to do so. This is the reason why

7 Article 6.1 (a) of the Directive.

8 Comp. Article 5.5 of the Directive and Article 5.4 of the Proposal: "*Where the enforcement authority considers that there are insufficient grounds for acting on a complaint, it shall inform the complainant about the reasons.*"

the Directive provides measures intended to encourage the direct victim to effectively file a complaint.

1.1.2. Encouraging enforcement through confidentiality of the complaints

In order to overcome the fear of retaliation, the Directive grants the possibility of anonymous complaints.

Pursuant to Article 5 (3), on request of the complainant, "*the enforcement authority shall take the necessary measures for the appropriate protection of the identity of the complainant or the members or suppliers referred to in paragraph 2 and for the appropriate protection of any other information in respect of which the complainant considers that the disclosure of such information would be harmful to the interests of the complainant or of those members or suppliers*", the complainant being responsible for identifying "*any information for which it requests confidentiality*".

It is also provided in Article 6.1(d) that "*the authority may abstain from taking any such decision, if that decision would risk revealing the identity of a complainant or would risk disclosing any other information in respect of which the complainant considers that such disclosure would be harmful to its interests, and provided that the complainant has identified that information in accordance with Article 5(3)*".

As regards the French CEPC, anonymity of the complainants, but also of the offenders concerned, is the rule[9]: only members of the Board and the "Rapporteurs" have access to this information and are compelled by professional secrecy. However, it should be noted that the CEPC (to this day) lacks coercive powers and has only a consultative role.

Confidentiality is apt to address the root causes for the victims not to seek redress. But it has to be considered with caution due to the effect on due process. It shall be balanced with the right of defense of potential infringers. As explained in the Explanatory Memorandum to the Commission's Proposal, "for the confidential treatment of complaints, a balance must struck in relation to the rights of defence". Contrary to the Proposal, the Directive as finally adopted fortunately underlines in Article 6.2 the need for "appropriate safeguard in respect of rights of defense", with an explicit reference to "cases where the complainant requests confidential treatment of information".

Moreover, there could be practical difficulties. Confidentiality may be difficult to ensure in all those cases in which practices are imposed on a single

---

[9] "The Commission ensures, under the supervision of its President, anonymity of the complaint and the documents provided, including for its members". A Decree determines the organization, the means and the modalities of the functioning of the Commission as well as the conditions necessary to ensure anonymity of economic players mentioned in the advice and recommendations of the Commission.

counter-party or a limited number thereof. It might be hindered by the need to provide detailed information, whose origin may be traced back to the victim.

In addition to the fear factor, other obstacles, such as the cost of proceedings and evidentiary difficulties, might discourage undertakings or professional organizations to act. These issues are not directly addressed by the Directive. In particular, Recital 24 underlines that it "does not harmonize the rules on the burden of proof to be applied before the national enforcement authorities". It is worth noting that Article 7 of the Directive newly requires that Member States "promote the voluntary use of effective and independent alternative dispute resolution mechanism, such as mediation". As explained in Recital 41, this new provision aims at explicitly encouraging "the use of voluntary alternative dispute resolution", with the view to reach a settlement. However, the use of ADR may fail. Moreover, despite the current promotion of negotiated solutions, some people are reluctant to make use of this possibility. In addition, alternative dispute resolution is not appropriate for all cases. The institutional design that the Directive promotes could also reduce the financial obstacle as well as the difficulties of proof.

1.2. DESIGNATION OF ENFORCEMENT AUTHORITIES FOR EACH MEMBER STATE

It is clear that the Directive, as the Proposal, opts resolutely for public enforcement, in the hands of public authorities, as opposed to private enforcement between buyers and suppliers. However, the Directive differs from the Proposal in several ways that are noteworthy. This is true as regards the institutional design (1) as well as concerning the competence of the enforcement authority (2). Despite some improvements, one may regret some lacks concerning institutional aspects as well as the powers of the authority.

1.2.1. The institutional design

It is laudable that Article 6.1 states that "*Member States shall ensure that each of their enforcement authorities has the necessary resources and expertise to perform its duties, and shall confer on it the following powers*". This requirement, strengthened in the final text[10] should be underlined as being the backbone when tackling UTPs. Beyond human and financial means, it can also raise the issue of whether the authority can identify priorities for action. Recital 28 indicates that "administrative priorities" might be considered provided that the authority "informs the complainant and give the reasons therefore".

10 Comp. Article 6 of the Proposal: "*Member States shall ensure that the enforcement authority is properly equipped and shall confer on it the following powers*".

The Directive is practically silent on the nature and the composition of the authority. It is interesting to observe that, contrary to the Proposal that refers to "a public authority", the Directive as finally adopted refrains from indicating such a feature.

Therefore, the choice should be left open to Member States which will be able to opt for an administrative authority or a judicial one. In the case of a collegial entity, it could be composed of judges or administrative officers only, or it could also welcome qualified experts such as academics, representatives of relevant economic sectors, which is the case in France with the CEPC. However, we could also imagine that the authority be constituted by only one person, such as the Minister for Economic Affairs in France.

In reality, some of the requirements of the Directive provide guidance on the nature of the authority designated: confidentiality of complaints as well as the power to investigate on its own initiative and to give priority to some complaints could lead to rather choose an administrative authority.

It is up to the Members State to decide whether they create ex nihilo an enforcement authority or whether they designate a preexisting authority.

Even if nothing is said about ways to challenge the decisions of dismissing the complaint or the conviction decision of the enforcement authority, a judicial review seems necessary, as well as the implementation of all the procedural safeguards. It is noteworthy that the Directive explicitly states, on the one hand, that the enforcement authority shall inform the complainant "within a reasonable period of time"[11], and on the other hand, that the exercise of its powers is subject to appropriate safeguards in respect of rights of defence".[12]

This leads to address another crucial issue, namely the separation between the investigation and the adjudication. In order to guarantee due process rights, the same entity should not investigate and decide over its own investigation.

There are two ways to deal with this issue: either the separation can be functional, where within the same entity two separate units are in charge; or the separation can be structural, when two different bodies are in charge of investigation and adjudication.

The Directive removes an issue that the Proposal raised, because of its drafting: Article 4 of the Proposal required all Member States to "*designate a public authority*". It was questionable whether the reference to a public authority meant only one. In this case, it could have been impossible for a Member State to set up a structural separation with two different entities. More broadly, the draft wording initially raised the question of whether a Member State could have more than one authority in charge of unfair trade practices, as regards material competence or territorial competence: it could become a problem for Member States such as France that have already several enforcement authorities as well

11 Article 5.4 and 5.5.
12 Article 6.2.

as for a federal State that could be compelled to have only one authority for the whole country.

Fortunately, the final text of the Directive enables Member States to designate "one or more authorities." Article 4.2 adds that in this case, it is necessary "to designate a single contact point for both cooperation among the enforcement authorities and cooperation with the Commission".

1.2.2. The competence of the designated authorities

As usual, it is worth considering both territorial and subject matter competence of the designated authorities.

Firstly, the Directive has discarded centralized enforcement via an enforcement body at EU level, for instance the European Commission. It is the same as regards a parallel application by competent Member States authorities and the European Commission as in competition law. Such a choice makes sense since there will remain many differences of substantive rules in Member States.

But this could be problematic when multiple injurers and/or multiple injured come from different MSs or when States outside of the EU are involved.

The Directive addresses partly the issue of cross-border practices. It sets a rule at Article 5.1 that gives complainants a choice. Contrary to the Proposal that designates only the "*enforcement authority of the Member State in which the infringer buyer suspected to have engaged in a prohibited trading practice is established*", the new provision states that suppliers may bring their cases to the enforcement authority of their own Member State, even if the alleged UTPs occurred elsewhere in the EU.

Recital 30 explains that they might use this second solution in preference to the first because they find it easier: in addition to the example of " linguistic reasons" given in the Directive, financial considerations may play a major role in this regard. However, Recital 30 adds that "in terms of enforcement, filing a complaint with the enforcement authority in which the buyer is established might be more effective". When choosing the authority to which they address complaints, plaintiffs should also take into account the level of protection granted by the legal systems in each of the involved Member States.

Nevertheless, this unique rule seems to be insufficient to resolve all the difficulties due to cross-border practices. In comparison with the Proposal, the Directive seems to reinforce the importance of cooperation among enforcement authorities. Pursuant to Article 8.1, "*Member States shall ensure that enforcement authorities cooperate effectively with each other and with the Commission, and that they provide each other with mutual assistance in investigation that have a cross-border dimension*". This provision is almost identical to Article 7.1 of the Proposal. But it is obvious that the two provisions, devoted respectively to the meetings between the enforcement authorities and to the website established and managed by the Commission, are more detailed and more demanding.[13] It is an open question whether it will be sufficient to address all the problems raised by cross-borders infringement. In this regard, Antitrust Law and Regulation 2003/1 could have served as useful model.

Secondly, *ratione materiae* competence is addressed by Article 4. Under this provision, the designated authority must "*enforce the prohibitions laid down in Article 3 at national level*". However, the authority can be entitled to enforce other fields of law, such as for instance Competition law. Indeed, the Directive permits to expand the mandate of a preexisting authority, *e.g.* national competition authorities.

One may regret that the Directive does not deal with the relationship between UTP legislation and competition law or other sets of rules.

The Explanatory Memorandum to the Proposal states that "UTP rules will be compatible with and complementary to the EU's competition rules" but does not provide any further information.

Even if dedicated to tackling UTPs, the authority may have to enforce, such as in France, much more rules than those laid down in Article 3, for instance the very famous French Book IV that contains many provisions. It could also be authorized to enforce contract law, going beyond UTP legislation. For example, the French CEPC, when assessing the lawfulness of a practice, applies not only UTP legislation but also, depending on the case, contract law, antitrust law, etc.[14]

2. THE EFFICIENCY OF TACKLING UNFAIR TRADE PRACTICES

Assessment of the effectiveness must be complemented with a review of the efficiency. In this aim, it is not sufficient to consider the measures that can be ordered by the designated authorities (A). Indeed, the enforcement mechanism cannot be based solely on them and comprise adjudication by civil and criminal courts (B).

2.1. THE MEASURES ORDERED BY THE AUTHORITIES IN CHARGE OF TACKLING UTPS

Article 6 provides the enforcement authorities with a range of measures dedicated to either deter *ex ante* UTPs (1) or address *ex post* consequences of UTPs (2).

---

13 Comp. Article 8.2 and 8.3 of the Directive with Article 7.2 and 7.3 of the Proposal.

14 See Article L. 440-1 of the French Commerce Code: "the advice from the Review panel deals with legal compliance of the practice or the documents in question".

2.1.1. *Preventing and deterring ex ante*

Article 10 ("Reporting") provides that the enforcement authorities "*publish an annual report about their activities falling within the scope of the Directive, which shall inter alia state the number of complaints received and the investigations opened or closed during the previous year. For each closed investigation, the report shall contain a summary description of the matter, the outcome of the investigation and, where applicable, the decision taken*". By informing buyers and suppliers about their activities, by way of annual reports, it aims to influence the behavior of undertakings and facilitate the adoption of good practices. Prevention requires information, or education so to speak.

However, deterrence grows also thanks to fines, either financial or reputational through the publication of a decision. Pursuant to Article 6.1 (f), the enforcement authority shall have the power to publish its decisions finding an infringement or imposing penalties and interim measures. The reputational sanctions might have a significant deterrent effect, especially when issued against retailers affected by consumers' behavior. This happens when they are public and reach a wide number of consumers.

Article 6. 1 (e) provides that the authority can "*impose, or initiate proceedings for the imposition of, fines and other equally effective penalties and interim measures on the author of the infringement*". It adds some criteria being specified that the penalties "*shall be effective, proportionate and dissuasive taking into account the nature, duration, recurrence and gravity of the infringement*". This list is not necessarily restrictive. However, there is no mention of the upper limit of the fine.

As stated in Recital 34, "the existence of a deterrent, such as (…) fines and other equally effective penalties" as well as the power "to publish investigation results, including the publication related to buyers that have committed infringements", may "encourage behavioral changes and pre-litigation solutions between the parties".

2.1.2. *Addressing ex-post UTPs consequences*

But the Directive aims at addressing ex-post UTP's consequences too; the authority shall have the power to order the termination of the prohibited practice. Pursuant to Article 5.7, where finding an infringement, the enforcement authority "*shall require the buyer to bring the prohibited trading practice to an end*". Interestingly, this is repeated in the provision dedicated to its powers. Article 6.1 (d) provides that the enforcement authority can "*take decisions finding an infringement of the prohibitions laid down in Article 3 and require the buyer to bring the prohibited trading practice to an end.*" It shows how crucial this power of injunction is.

Yet again the Directive leaves a great deal of flexibility for injunctions that could be ordered. One could question the space left to a cooperative approach between the authority and the perpetrators of UTPs. The issue is not addressed by the Directive even if it contains an Article 7 dedicated to alternative dispute resolution mechanisms. This provision as well as Recital 41 make it clear that it covers rather "voluntary alternative dispute resolution between suppliers ab buyers" than public dispute resolution mechanisms. However, it does not prevent from using such mechanisms.

For instance, we could imagine that the enforcer issues first recommendations and advices which are not legally binding and, if they are not followed, can exercise sanctioning powers. Likewise, and as it exists for anticompetitive practices or other rules concerning UTPs, it could be possible to provide the infringer with the possibility to submit commitments. These commitments could result in an undertaking to cease the infringement and to remove the consequences of the infringement.[15]

2.2. THE NECESSARY LINK WITH DECISIONS FROM CIVIL AND CRIMINAL COURTS

As effective and various as the measures adopted by the enforcement authority may be, it remains that many consequences of UTPs can only be tackled *via* judicial enforcement. Compensation for damages, restitution of unduly paid sums or invalidity of clauses in contracts are not at all covered by administrative enforcement and require civil judgments (1). Moreover, in some Member States, UTPs may also constitute criminal offences falling within criminal courts' competence. Unfortunately, the Directive does not cover these issues at all; despite several potential difficulties, it does not clarify the coordination between administrative and judicial enforcement, as regards civil decisions (1) as well as criminal ones (2).

2.2.1. Coordination between civil remedies

Without pretending to be exhaustive, it is worth pointing out that if nothing is planned, the risk of contradictory decisions cannot be excluded. If no coordination is in place, no consistency between the outcomes of simultaneous or sequential proceedings concerning the same UTP would be ensured: that means that the same practice could be considered a UTP for the purpose of

15 See F. Cafaggi & P. Iamiceli, Unfair Trading Practices in Food Supply Chain. Regulatory Responses and Institutional Alternatives in the Light of the New EU Directive European Review of Private Law 5-2019, 1075–1114, n° 47: "Cooperative enforcement should complement hierarchical enforcement".

administrative sanctions and not for that of civil remedies. There is undoubtedly a need to address this issue and to provide coordination.

But the question remains how this should be made. Could the Directive 2014/104 of 26 November 2014 on certain rules governing actions for damages under national law for infringements of the competition law provisions be a model or rather be avoided?

For instance, difficulties can arise from access to evidence held by the enforcement authority.

Another question is even more sensitive: should we recognize a binding-effect to authority's infringement decisions? Such a measure would greatly alleviate the burden of proof and allow the victims to prove the facts necessary to substantiate theirs claims. But such a rule is running counter to the independence of the judiciary.

2.2.2. Coordination with criminal sanctions

Maybe the most tricky issue is that of the relationships between the administrative measures and criminal decisions. In the cases where criminal fines apply, we could wonder about the application of the "ne bis in idem" principle and how to regulate it. For instance, it raises the question of whether it is possible to combine criminal and administrative sanctions.

Undoubtedly the Directive lacks provisions in this matter. It is the reason why some commentators consider that "coordination between national judiciaries and administrative authorities should be regulated in the process of implementation".[16]

3. CONCLUSION

Even if everything is not fully satisfactory, it should be borne in mind that legislating is a very difficult thing to do, the fact we have a Directive is probably a good thing, being a first step which should lead in the near future to other EU legislation. In other words, it takes time to tackle efficiently UTPs in B-to-B relationships. As the saying goes, "Rome was not built in a day"...

16 F. Cafaggi & P. Iamiceli, Unfair Trading Practices in Food Supply Chain. Regulatory Responses and Institutional Alternatives in the Light of the New EU Directive European Review of Private Law 5–2019, 1075–1114, n° 46.

CHAPTER 4

THE COMMON AGRICULTURAL POLICY AND THE DIRECTIVE ON UTPS IN THE AGRICULTURAL AND FOOD SUPPLY CHAIN

Ensuring a Fair Standard of Living for the Agricultural Community?

Tom VERDONK
PhD candidate, Consumer Competition Market, KU Leuven

1. INTRODUCTION

1. Throughout history, governments have often opted for a different approach for the agricultural sector than other economic sectors, introducing laws and policies specifically aimed at agricultural production and trade. An ancient example of this can be found in the Babylonian Code of Hammurabi. Although this Code is arguably best-known for containing the principle of *lex talionis* ("an eye for an eye, a tooth for a tooth"), a substantial share of the Code's laws dealt with agriculture.[1] These laws recognized the special status of food production, trade and consumption, and covered a wide variety of legal domains and themes relevant for the agricultural sector, including the regulation of prices[2], tort[3], finance[4], and insolvency.[5]

---

1 For an English translation of the Code of Hammurabi, see < https://en.wikisource.org/wiki/The_Laws_of_Hammurabi,_King_of_Babylonia>.

2 E.g., Law 257: "The rate of pay for a field laborer is 8 "gur" of grain annually for his services."

3 E.g., Law 55: "If anyone opens his canal for the purpose of irrigation [in a negligent manner] and thereby floods the fields [of his neighbors] shall be held to account to those neighbors and to pay them grain corresponding with their [the neighbors'] loss."

4 E.g., Law 50: "If anyone borrows money upon a cultivated grainfield or cultivated sesame field he shall receive the grain or sesame which is grown upon that field. He shall pay back to the person making him the loan the money borrowed, with interest."

5 E.g., Law 52: "In event anyone borrows money upon a field and fails to raise grain or sesame whereby to repay his creditors, his indebtedness is not extinguished."

2. While most of these laws could not stand the test of time[6], agricultural laws and policies do not necessarily belong to the past in the view of many legislators around the world. In the European Union (EU), for example, the Common Agricultural Policy (CAP) is exemplary with regard to the contemporary relevance of agricultural legislation and policies. In fact, since the very beginning of post-World War II European cooperation and economic integration, the Treaties have provided a legal basis for a common, unified policy for agriculture, and on the basis of this policy, a wide variety of measures have been introduced. The recently adopted Directive on unfair trading practices in business-to-business relationships in the food supply chain[7] (hereafter referred to as the Directive) is no exception in this regard, as its legal basis is found in one of the CAP's Treaty provisions, as set out in Article 39 of the Treaty on the Functioning of the European Union (TFEU).

3. Accordingly, plenty of references to Article 39 TFEU are found throughout the preamble, the explanatory memorandum, and the impact assessment of the adopted Directive. Although the legal basis of the Directive in itself provides fertile ground for discussion (as will be done in Chapter I of this book), it is also interesting to examine how the Directive relates to this vast but unique policy of the EU. Therefore, this chapter seeks to explore how the Directive that aims to tackle unfair trading practices between businesses in the food supply chain fits within the overall development of the EU's CAP. In order to do so, the second section provides a brief introduction to the CAP, discussing its historical background and its objectives and highlighting some of the CAP's main reforms during the past decades. The third section then further elaborates on one of the key objectives of the CAP, i.e. to ensure a fair standard of living for the agricultural community, which, as said, provides the legal basis for the Directive. Building on that, the fourth section evaluates the Directive against the background of the CAP. The fifth and final section shares a few final comments with regard to the Directive.

6 Examples of these are the numerous provisions with regard to slavery (e.g., Law 17: "Anyone capturing a male or female slave, and returning said male or female slave to his or her master, shall be compensated by the master to the extent of 2 shekels of silver."), and a common sanction for violation of various laws was the death sentence (e.g., Law 1: "Any person convicted of preferring charges against another person which he cannot substantiate shall be put to death.").

7 Directive (EU) 2019/633 of the European Parliament and of the Council of 17 April 2019 on unfair trading practices in business-to-business relationships in the agricultural and food supply chain [2019] OJ L111/59.

2. THE DEVELOPMENT AND OBJECTIVES OF THE COMMON AGRICULTURAL POLICY

2.1. HISTORY OF THE CAP

4. From the very beginning of post-World War II European economic cooperation and integration, the CAP has occupied a prominent position in the European Treaties.[8] Following the experiences of the war and prior to the inception of the Treaty of Rome, establishing the European Economic Community (EEC), European countries struggled with securing a stable food supply.[9] In order to resolve the difficult food supply situation, the first six original Member States of the EEC considered an agricultural policy necessary that would raise agricultural output, create self-sufficiency and secure farm incomes. The latter objective was prompted in part by low incomes of family farms, back then still accounting for a significant part of the European workforce.[10] Although agricultural sector's share of total employment was declining in all countries and was in the United Kingdom in 1955 already below five per cent, many other European countries still saw the percentage of workers working in agriculture as high as forty per cent. The observed income gap between family farms and workers from other sectors of the economy was therefore seen as a problem that had to be addressed.[11]

5. As discussions for further economic integration between the six countries – France, Germany, Italy, Netherlands, Belgium, and Luxembourg – in the 1950s commenced, it became soon clear that a common agricultural policy was essential. The aim of the inclusion of a common agricultural policy within the common market and customs union was twofold: economic and political. One the one hand, the exclusion of agriculture and food in the formation of a common market and customs union could not be justified *economically*, given the economic significance of food production and consumption at the time. On the other hand, inclusion of agriculture was *politically* important in order to find a compromise between the founding Member States, as they were concerned about how the common market would impact their national interests. Particularly, the competitiveness of

---

8 Cardwell, M. (2004), *The European Model of Agriculture*, Oxford University Press, Oxford, p. 7.

9 Danielsen, J. (2013), *EU Agricultural Law*, Kluwer Law International, Alphen aan den Rijn, p. 1.

10 Zobbe, H. (2001), 'The Economic and Historical Foundation of the Common Agricultural Policy in Europe', The Royal Veterinary and Agricultural University – Unit of Economics Working Papers 2001/12, available at <https://ageconsearch.umn.edu/bitstream/24212/1/ew010012.pdf>, p. 8.

11 Harvey D., 'What does the history of the Common Agricultural Policy tell us?' in McMahon, J. and Cardwell, M. (2015), *Research Handbook on EU Agriculture Law*, Edward Elgar, Cheltenham, pp. 6–7.

Germany's industry was considered a threat to the other Member States. In order to safeguard competition between the founding Member States on the common market, a common market for agricultural products was deemed necessary to counter the imbalance caused by Germany's economic strength, especially as France was the predominant agricultural producer within the European Economic Community.[12] In addition to this, there was a practical difficulty in excluding agriculture from being a part of an integrated market because it would have been a difficult exercise in practice to draw a clear line between agricultural and industrial products, as also identified by the Spaak Report.[13]

2.2. RELEVANT TREATY PROVISIONS

6. Therefore, the Treaty of Rome included the common agricultural policy (Articles 38 to 47). It also set out the five key objectives of this policy in Article 39, which have actually remained unchanged since 1958. Indeed, Article 39 of the Treaty on the Functioning of the European Union (TFEU) is identical in substance to Article 39 of the EEC Treaty:

> "*(a) to increase agricultural productivity by promoting technical progress and by ensuring the rational development of agricultural production and the optimum utilisation of the factors of production, in particular labour;*
> *(b) thus to ensure a fair standard of living for the agricultural community, in particular by increasing the individual earnings of persons engaged in agriculture;*
> *(c) to stabilise markets;*
> *(d) to assure the availability of supplies;*
> *(e) to ensure that supplies reach consumers at reasonable prices.*"

The second paragraph of Article 39 stresses the special nature of agriculture:

> "*In working out the common agricultural policy and the special methods for its application, account shall be taken of:*

12 Ibid., p. 7. See also Spaak Report, Chapter 4, Section 1: "*On ne peut concevoir l'établissement d'un marché commun général en Europe sans que l'agriculture s'y trouve incluse. C'est l'un des secteurs où les progrès de productivité qui résulteront du marché commun, c'est-à-dire de la spécialisation progressive des productions et de l'élargissement des débouchés, peuvent avoir les effets les plus importants sur le niveau de vie des producteurs aussi bien que des consommateurs. En outre, cette inclusion de l'agriculture dans le marché commun est une condition de l'équilibre des échanges entre les différentes économies des États membres*", available at <https://www.cvce.eu/content/publication/1997/10/13/4dd69921-433b-4bc0-acec-808f72fec9ae/publishable_fr.pdf>.

13 Zobbe, H. (2001), 'The Economic and Historical Foundation of the Common Agricultural Policy in Europe', The Royal Veterinary and Agricultural University – Unit of Economics Working Papers 2001/12, available at <https://ageconsearch.umn.edu/bitstream/24212/1/ew010012.pdf>, p. 4.

(a) *the particular nature of agricultural activity, which results from the social structure of agriculture and from structural and natural disparities between the various agricultural regions;*
(b) *the need to effect the appropriate adjustments by degrees;*
(c) *the fact that in the Member States agriculture constitutes a sector closely linked with the economy as a whole."*

7. In addition to Article 39 TFEU, other relevant Treaty provisions for the CAP are Articles 40 to 43 TFEU, establishing rules for the establishment and functioning of a common market for agriculture. The form of the CAP in order to attain the objectives of Article 39 is laid down in Article 40: a common organisation of agricultural markets is established through (a) common rules on competition, (b) compulsory coordination of the various national market organisation, and (c) a European market organisation. Moreover, the second paragraph of Article 40 states that all measures that are required in light of the CAP objectives are permitted and specifies a number of measures that can be particularly relevant, such as regulation of prices, aids for the production and marketing of the various products, storage and carryover arrangements, and common machinery for stabilising imports or exports. Article 42 prescribes the relationship between competition law and agricultural policy. Essentially, a derogation has been granted from competition policy principles for agricultural products and trade in such products.[14] Lastly, Article 43 sets out the legislative procedure for the CAP. Since the Lisbon Treaty the European Parliament has a right of co-decision in the field of agriculture.[15]

8. Alongside the specific CAP Treaty provisions, a number of other Treaty provisions may be relevant as well, since they lay down other objectives which are applicable to all EU policies and measures, including agricultural policy. Examples of such provisions are the provisions that promote environmental protection (Article 11 TFEU), animal welfare (Article 13 TFEU), cultural diversity (Article 167(4) TFEU), public health (Article 168 TFEU), and consumer protection (Article 169 TFEU). Those objectives have become increasingly important for agricultural production and food consumption, thus also affecting the implementation of CAP measures. To avoid any confusion, when referring to the CAP objectives as set out in Article 39 TFEU, these will be referred to as the 'traditional' CAP objectives.

---

14 For a more elaborate discussion on the relationship between agricultural policy and competition law, see Gerbrandy, A. and De Vries, S. (2011), *Agricultural Policy and EU Competition Law. Possibilities and Limits for Self-Regulation in the Dairy Sector*, Eleven International Publishing, The Hague. See also Regulation (EU) No 1308/2013 establishing a common organisation of the markets in agricultural products (CMO Regulation) [2013] OJ L347/672.

15 Danielsen, J. (2013), *EU Agricultural Law*, Kluwer Law International, Alphen aan den Rijn, p. 7.

9. These traditional objectives of the CAP are economic (Article 39 (a), (c) and (d) TFEU) and social (Article 39 (b) and (e) TFEU) in nature. The objectives do not only safeguard the interests of consumers, but they also have a strong focus on the protection of agricultural producers. Furthermore, no hierarchy between these objectives exists, though not all objectives of the CAP can be fully achieved at the same time.[16] In that regard, the European Court of Justice has held in its case-law that the EU legislator enjoys much flexibility when designing its agricultural policies and instruments, allowing it to take account of market trends and to set priorities. The ECJ has held that "*in pursuing the objectives of the common agricultural policy the Community institutions must secure the permanent harmonization made necessary by any conflicts between those objectives taken individually and, where necessary, allow any one of them temporary priority in order to satisfy the demands of the economic factors or conditions in view of which their decisions are made*".[17] Nevertheless, the ECJ has also held that "*although the Community legislature has a broad discretion with regard to the common agricultural policy, it is obliged to base its choices on objective criteria that are appropriate to the aim pursued by the legislation in question*".[18]

2.3. THE DEVELOPMENT OF THE COMMON AGRICULTURAL POLICY

10. As stated, the seven Treaty articles dealing with the CAP have remained basically unchanged in substance. The CAP itself, however, has taken many different shapes and forms during the past decades due to various reforms. Hence, in practice the wording of the objectives of the CAP in Article 39 TFEU has proven to be extraordinarily flexible. As a consequence, studying the CAP essentially involved studying CAP reforms. Unfortunately, this chapter does not lend itself for an elaborate discussion of these reforms. Instead though, a brief discussion of a few relevant aspects should suffice to describe the overall development of the CAP.

11. After the inception of the Treaty of Rome, the Stresa Conference was convened in 1958 to establish how the objectives of Article 39 of the EEC Treaty could be met. The Conference decided that European agriculture should be

[16] Barents, R. (1994), *The Agricultural Law of the EC*, Kluwer, Deventer, p. 36; Cardwell, M. (2004), *The European Model of Agriculture*, Oxford University Press, Oxford, p. 20; also already recognized in the judgment of 13 March 1968, *Beus v. Hauptzollamt München*, case 5/67, EU:C:1968:13.

[17] E.g., judgment of 5 October 1994, *Germany/Council*, C-280/93, EU:C:1994:367, para. 47.

[18] Judgment of 6 November 2014, *Robin John Feakins v The Scottish Ministers*, C-335/13, EU:C:2014:2343, para. 56.

supported through guaranteed prices rather than direct aids.[19] Subsequently, in 1960 it was established that instruments of the CAP had to be in conformity with three basic principles: unity of the market, Community preference, and financial solidarity. Ratified by the Council of Ministers in 1962, the principles had to be implemented through the common organisation of agricultural markets. From the outset of the CAP, the intention was not to merely create a common market for agricultural producers, but to go beyond that and to create a common agricultural *policy*.[20]

12. In terms of agricultural productivity, the CAP was very successful right from its inception. In fact, the instruments implemented by the CAP resulted in agricultural overproduction. Even more problematic was that despite increased spending and production, average farm incomes did not actually rise in the 1960s. In order to increase farms' incomes then European Commissioner for Agriculture Mansholt considered concentration of agricultural production a viable solution, but his plan found no support. Instead, multiple directives were adopted that aimed to modernize farms and to encourage cessation of farming and training of farmers.[21] This was the first reform of the CAP, and more would follow. In response to overproduction and in attempt to balance demand and supply, milk quotas were also adopted in 1984. The second CAP reform, approved in 1988, introduced market-related measures, including so-called agricultural stabilisers, which are maximum guaranteed quantities.[22]

13. The subsequent third reform of the CAP, the MacSharry reform of 1992, marked the first step from market support to producer support by reducing intervention prices and introducing land-based compensatory payments. Agenda 2000 continued this trend, while also creating a second pillar of the CAP for rural development policy, alongside the traditional agricultural policy. The 2003 Fischler reforms introduced the Single Payment Scheme, a system granting subsidies independent of volume, though direct payments were dependent on certain environmental and other public benefits (known as the cross-compliance

---

19 Harvey D., 'What does the history of the Common Agricultural Policy tell us?' in McMahon, J. and Cardwell, M. (2015), *Research Handbook on EU Agriculture Law*, Edward Elgar, Cheltenham, p. 8.

20 Article 38(4) TFEU.

21 Council Directive 72/159/EEC of 17 April 1972 of the modernization of farms, [1972] OJ L96/1; Council Directive 72/160/EEC of 17 April 1972 concerning measures to encourage the cessation of farming and the reallocation of utilized agricultural areas for the purposes of structural improvement, [1972] OJ L96/9; and Council Directive 72/161/EEC of 17 April 1972 concerning the provision of socio-economic guidance for and the acquisition of occupational skills by persons engaged in agriculture, [1972] OJ L96/15.

22 Harvey D., 'What does the history of the Common Agricultural Policy tell us?' in McMahon, J. and Cardwell, M. (2015), *Research Handbook on EU Agriculture Law*, Edward Elgar, Cheltenham, pp. 9–16.

system). The direct payments regime became further streamlined in the next couple of years, which ultimately also led to the abolishment of milk quotas in 2015. The sixth reform of the CAP (and the current one) included, among other measures, "greening payments', meaning that 30% of the direct income support will only be granted on the condition of certain environmental benefits.[23]

14. Overall, the CAP has thus seen a shift from market management, characterised by export funds and market price support, to producer support, in the form of direct payments, to a more market-oriented approach. In terms of budget, it is noteworthy that CAP expenditure over the years has taken a significant share of the EU budget, although this share has decreased quite sharply over the past 25 years, from 73% in 1985 to 41% in 2016. Most of the current CAP's budget goes to direct payments for farmers.[24]

3. ENSURING A FAIR STANDARD OF LIVING FOR THE AGRICULTURAL COMMUNITY

15. As mentioned in the introductory section, the EU legislator found the legal basis for the Directive that aims to tackle unfair trading practices in the food supply chain in the second traditional objective of the CAP, which is to ensure a fair standard of living for the agricultural community. Based on the wording of Article 39 TFEU, one would at first sight conclude that this objective is closely linked to the first objective. The use of the word 'thus' indicates that a fair standard of living for the agricultural community must be ensured by increasing agricultural productivity. Consequently, one could argue that the fair standard of living is to be realized by increased agricultural productivity as opposed through any income guarantee by direct payments or other measures. In other words, the second CAP objective indicates a result, to be attained mainly or even exclusively through the means mentioned in the first CAP objective.[25] However, according to some, this view is likely to be too narrow.[26] They argue it is clear that increasing per capita incomes of those working in agriculture depends not only on productivity growth but also on producer prices. Since both improving productivity and increasing per capita income are cited as a means of ensuring a

---

23 Harvey D., 'What does the history of the Common Agricultural Policy tell us?' in McMahon, J. and Cardwell, M. (2015), *Research Handbook on EU Agriculture Law*, Edward Elgar, Cheltenham, pp. 16–25.

24 For a recent overview, see <https://ec.europa.eu/agriculture/sites/agriculture/files/cap-post-2013/graphs/graph1_en.pdf>.

25 Barents, R. (1994), *The Agricultural Law of the EC*, Kluwer, Deventer, p. 34.

26 Van Rijn, T., 'Artikel 39 Vertrag über die Arbeitsweise der Europäischen Union' in Von der Groeben, Schwarze and Hatje (2015), *Europäisches Unionsrecht, 7. Auflage*, Beck, Baden-Baden, nr. 7.

decent standard of living, an active policy on prices and incomes is therefore not legally objectionable.[27]

16. However, this does not provide justifications for giving support to farmers in the first place. After all, why should the EU even be concerned with protecting a fair standard of living for the agricultural community? In that regard, the unpredictability that agricultural producers face is often referred to as a justification. Farmers are vulnerable, as their investments depend on economic, health, and weather conditions beyond their control. Accordingly, supporting farmers' incomes ensures (investments in) food production throughout the EU. This also benefits the final three traditional objectives of the CAP: market stabilisation, the availability of supplies, and reasonable consumer prices. Moreover, financial support for farmers pays for the provision of so-called public benefits, which are certain benefits which have no market value but are regarded as important in light of public interest. For instance, to receive a significant share of their CAP payments, farmers need to respect a set of basic rules related to environmental protection, animal welfare, and public health.[28]

17. In addition to this, EU institutions and Member States seem to have serious concerns over perceived persistently low incomes among European farmers. For example, according to a European Commission study published in 2018, the average agricultural income in the EU still amounted to only 55 per cent of the average wage in the total economy in 2016, and before that fluctuating between 45 and 64 per cent in the period 2007–2016.[29] Nonetheless, one must be careful with such comparisons. First, various statistical challenges make comparisons difficult. Secondly, these comparisons do not take into account factors related to the rural way of life which may impact a person's or household's standard of living. For instance, a farm household often lives in the building which also serves as the commercial premise for the farm operations and it can enjoy the consumption of self-produced goods. In other words, farm households' incomes do not necessarily *need* to match average wages of the total economy in order to obtain a reasonable or 'fair' standard of living.[30] Besides these issues, there could be doubt whether or to what extent farm household incomes actually lag behind those of the rest of the population. In some Member States, such as the Netherlands and Denmark, average farm household incomes are significantly

---

27 Ibid.; Barents, R. (1994), *The Agricultural Law of the EC*, Kluwer, Deventer, p. 34.

28 For an elaborate explanation of this so-called cross-compliance system, see <https://ec.europa.eu/agriculture/direct-support/cross-compliance_en>.

29 European Commission (2018), 'CAP post-2013: Key graphs & figures', available at <https://ec.europa.eu/agriculture/sites/agriculture/files/cap-post-2013/graphs/graph4_en.pdf>.

30 Van Rijn, T., 'Artikel 39 Vertrag über die Arbeitsweise der Europäischen Union' in Von der Groeben, Schwarze and Hatje (2015), *Europäisches Unionsrecht, 7. Auflage*, Beck, Baden-Baden, nr. 7.

higher than in others, and sometimes also higher than the national economy-wide average.[31]

18. Still, Article 39 TFEU does not define what constitutes a 'fair standard of living'; and it also does not suggest a comparison to other economic sectors to determine 'fairness'.[32] The Spaak Report, which served as the basis for the EEC Treaty, as mentioned earlier, saw as a key purpose for the CAP the maintenance of an adequate level of income for those agricultural enterprises, which reached a normal level of production. At that time, these farms were often family farms. This became the basis for the second traditional objective of Article 39 TFEU. Over the years, the European Court of Justice (ECJ) has developed case law from which important lessons can be drawn on what a fair standard of living means or, more precisely, the ECJ has made clear what it does not mean. Article 39(1)(b) is not to be interpreted as guaranteeing "a certain profit margin".[33] Furthermore, a 'fair' standard of living is not a "stable" standard of living.[34] This means that agricultural producers will need to accept periods of adjustment, even though another CAP objective is to stabilize markets.

19. In order to ensure a fair standard of living for the agricultural community, a number of instruments are relied on. The direct payments regime and the CMO Regulation are arguably among the most prominent ones.[35] The former grants farmers payments on the condition that they respect strict rules related to public benefits (plus additional payments may be made to young and small farmers), while the latter aims to establish a common organisation of agricultural markets by, for example, stipulating how producer organisations and their associations should operate and governing contractual relations in the agricultural sector. The CMO Regulation also provides exemptions from EU competition rules. In particular, the direct payments regime has been subject to heavy criticism. Due to the area-based allocation of entitlements, most of the direct payments go to the largest estate holders. As a result, roughly 25% of the direct payments are received by the 80% of the farms with the lowest incomes.[36] A common

---

31 European Commission (2018), Figure 11: Agricultural factor income (current) per annual work unit per country, 2017.

32 Van Rijn, T., 'Artikel 39 Vertrag über die Arbeitsweise der Europäischen Union' in Von der Groeben, Schwarze and Hatje (2015), *Europäisches Unionsrecht, 7. Auflage*, Beck, Baden-Baden, nr. 7.

33 Judgment of 14 January 1987, *Zuckerfabrik Bedburg*, 281/84, EU:C:1987:3.

34 Judgment of 19 September 2013, *Panellinios Syndesmos Viomichanion Metapoiisis Kapnou*, C-373/11, EU:C:2013:567.

35 See, respectively, Regulation (EU) No 1307/2013 establishing rules for direct payments to farmers under support schemes within the framework of the common agricultural policy [2013] OJ L347/608 and Regulation (EU) No 1308/2013 establishing a common organisation of the markets in agricultural products (CMO Regulation) [2013] OJ L347/672.

36 E.g., the British Queen is a prominent recipient of direct payments, which will – obviously – end with the UK's withdrawal from the EU; see The Guardian, 'The Queen, aristocrats and

critique in relation to the objective of ensuring a fair standard of living is that "CAP direct payments [will] only contribute to a "fair standard of living for the agricultural community" if one is prepared to believe that a farmer's need for income support grows in proportion to the amount of land that he/she farms."[37]

4. EVALUATION OF COMMISSION'S PROPOSAL

20. The CAP's objective to ensure a fair standard of living for the agricultural community, and thus to protect the welfare of agricultural producers as opposed to consumer welfare, is unique in terms of sector-specific regulation and really sets the agricultural sector apart from the rest of the economy. The Directive explains this objective of the CAP as a duty to protect farmers' profitability: unfair trading practices (UTPs) must be tackled because they jeopardise the profitability of agricultural producers and lead to downward pressure on their market income. By prohibiting certain practices, farmers' position vis-à-vis other market participants should be strengthened and hence they should be protected against the effects of competitive distortions passed on to them, which should increase their profitability.[38] Although income protection of agricultural producers has been the starting point of the Directive (and remains its legal basis), the scope of protection has not been limited to just agricultural producers. Introducing a system of differentiated levels of protection, the Directive will apply to certain UTPs which occur in relation to the sales of agricultural and food products by a supplier to a buyer, depending on the turnovers of the buyer and the supplier. Originally, the Directive proposed by the Commission would only protect supplying small and medium-sized enterprises (SMEs) against UTPs by buyers that were not SMEs. The adopted Directive, however, does not only protect SMEs but a wide range of suppliers, including those which have an annual turnover of 350 million euros.[39] Additionally, non-farming suppliers and manufacturers involved in the sale of agricultural and food products will also be protected by the Directive. Associations of agricultural producers, such as cooperatives, are also covered by the Directive.

Saudi prince among recipients of EU farm subsidies', 29 September 2016, available at <https://www.theguardian.com/environment/2016/sep/29/the-queen-aristocrats-and-saudi-prince-among-recipients-of-eu-farm-subsidies>.

37 Von Cramon-Taubadel, S. (2017), 'The Common Agricultural Policy and the Next EU Budget', BertelsmannStiftung, available at <https://www.bertelsmann-stiftung.de/fileadmin/files/user_upload/EZ_Reflection_Paper_2_Taubadel_2017_ENG.pdf>, p. 5.

38 Directive (EU) 2019/633 of the European Parliament and of the Council of 17 April 2019 on unfair trading practices in business-to-business relationships in the agricultural and food supply chain [2019] OJ L111/59, recital 7; European Commission, 'Proposal for a directive on unfair trading practices in business-to-business relationships in the food supply chain' COM(2018)173 final, p. 4, 28.

39 Article 1(2) of the Directive.

21. Leaving aside the discussion on the questionability of Article 39 TFEU as a legal basis for this, the widely expanded scope of the adopted Directive in comparison to the originally proposed Directive by the Commission is worrisome. As the Proposal had reached its next phase after being introduced by the Commission, the Council and the European Parliament reviewed it. While the Council's then agreed position only slightly expanded the scope of the proposal (mainly by including the Directive's applicability to agricultural products other than food)[40], some Members of the European Parliament (MEPs) were seeking to significantly expand it. On the same day as EU Member States reached an agreement on the Council's position, the Agriculture Committee of the European Parliament approved amendments to broaden to scope of the draft law. Arguably most remarkable, they wanted to include all actors in the food supply chain, and not only small and medium-sized producers and big buyers. In addition, they agreed on amendments to extend the list of prohibited UTPs.[41] The European Parliament approved the proposed amendments, and thus gave the Parliament's negotiating team a green light to start negotiating on the final wording of the Directive.[42] Ultimately, the EU institutions were able to reach a comprise, which is noteworthy in itself given the strong divergent positions of the Commission and the Parliament. Yet, at the same time it cannot be ignored that the adopted Directive clearly goes beyond the boundaries of agricultural policy.

22. Nevertheless, the Directive fits well within the overall development of the EU's CAP, characterised by a shift from a market management-oriented to producer-oriented to a more market-oriented approach. It does not aim to shield farmers from competitive forces, but merely to strengthen their autonomy in contractual relationships. Interestingly though, is that while the second traditional objective of the CAP is generally regarded a social objective, the Commission seemed to take the position in its original proposal that it is an economic objective. According to that proposal, UTPs arise from unequal bargaining powers between buyers and suppliers and must be addressed, because they can "put profits of affected suppliers under pressure and can result in a misallocation of resources, which reduces the efficiency of the food supply chain."[43] In other words, the Commission aimed to introduce regulation in

---

40 For a press release, see <https://www.consilium.europa.eu/en/press/press-releases/2018/10/01/better-protection-for-farmers-against-unfair-trading-practices-council-agrees-its-negotiating-position/>.

41 For an overview of the amendments, see <www.emeeting.europarl.europa.eu/committees/agenda/201810/AGRI/AGRI(2018)1001_1/sitt-8762379>; for a press release, see <www.europarl.europa.eu/news/en/press-room/20181001IPR14722/fairer-food-supply-chain-agriculture-meps-clamp-down-on-unfair-trading>.

42 For a press release and the procedure file, see <www.europarl.europa.eu/news/en/press-room/20181025IPR17307/food-supply-chain-a-step-closer-to-ending-unfair-trading>.

43 European Commission, 'Proposal for a directive on unfair trading practices in business-to-business relationships in the food supply chain' COM(2018)173 final, p. 28.

response to a market failure (closely) related to market power, to which farmers are falling victim. Either way, this has arguably more academic than practical relevance, as the Directive still aims to protect farmer's profitability.

23. Another interesting element of the Directive is that it would introduce a minimum common standard of protection across the EU. By taking a minimum harmonization approach, the Directive allows Member States to introduce or maintain rules that exceed the level of protection offered by the Directive. This process is also known as 'gold-plating'. Since significant differences between the profitability of farmers across the EU exist, as described in the previous section, this may actually not be undesirable. Gold-plating allows Member States to take into account regional characteristics when designing their UTPs legislation. At the same time, a minimum harmonization approach does not tackle the regulatory divergence between EU Member States, which the Commission considered an essential argument to introduce the Directive in the first place. As the Directive has been adopted, agricultural producers in different EU Member States will continue to face different regulatory regimes when dealing with UTPs against them.

24. In fact, around the time the Directive was originally proposed, it seems that such divergence would only get worse in the near to mid-future. In 2021 a new reform of CAP will be introduced, which was heavily debated before and after the Commission presented its legislative proposals in June 2018 and continues to be the subject of discussions as no decision has been made. One of the more controversial plans from the Commission for the post-2020 CAP is the theme of 'renationalization', meaning that Member States will enjoy more autonomy in determining their agricultural policy.[44] Clearly, it is highly debatable whether a uniform approach to UTPs or the agricultural sector at large will emerge anytime soon. Moreover, the new reform tends to further reduce direct payments, which will put more pressure on farmers' incomes. One could question whether the Directive will counterbalance this loss of income.

5. FINAL COMMENTS

25. This Chapter discussed how the Directive that aims to tackle UTPs in the food supply chain fits within the overall development of the EU's CAP. Generally, the Directive is not out of line with the development of the CAP, especially in light of the recent more market-oriented focus. However, it remains to be seen to

44 For an overview of the different legislative proposals on the CAP beyond 2020 presented by the European Commission on 1 June 2018, see <https://ec.europa.eu/info/food-farming-fisheries/key-policies/common-agricultural-policy/future-cap_en>.

what extent the instrument will actually be able to ensure a standard of living for the agricultural community, even more so if post-2020 direct payments would be further reduced under the new CAP reform. Clearly, a system to tackle UTPs in the food supply chain is far from enough to uphold agricultural incomes. Then again, the Directive is just one of many instruments available to ensure a fair standard of living for the agricultural producers. Finally, it is interesting to see that a similar close relationship between regulation of UTPs and agricultural policy is likely to develop in the United Kingdom. In September 2019, the UK Government introduced a new Agriculture Bill into the UK Parliament. Among other provisions, the draft bill includes a provision that gives the Government the power to make regulations "for the purpose of promoting fair contractual dealing by the first purchasers of agricultural products (...) in relation to contracts they make for the purchase of agricultural products from producers."[45] Hence, despite the UK's withdrawal from the EU, regulation of UTPs and agricultural policy will remain closely intertwined, at least in the near to mid future, in both the UK and the EU.

45 Bill 266 2017–19, see <https://services.parliament.uk/bills/2017–19/agriculture.html>.

CHAPTER 5

THE DIRECTIVE ON UTP IN THE AGRICULTURAL AND FOOD SUPPLY CHAIN – A GERMAN PERSPECTIVE

Jochen GLÖCKNER*
Prof. Dr. iur., LL.M. (USA); Chair for German and European Private and Business Law; Judge at the Higher Regional Court Karlsruhe

1. THE SCENE – REAL WORLD PROBLEMS AND THE LEGAL FRAMEWORK OF THE COMMISSION'S PROPOSAL

1.1. REAL WORLD PROBLEMS AS IDENTIFIED BY THE COMMISSION

Initially it was price spikes of agricultural products that caused the European Commission to put the food supply chain on their agenda.[1] It didn't take long though for the plunge in particular of milk prices to catch the attention of the public and politicians. During the height of the farmers' crisis in 2014/15 farmers dumped their milk in the city centers and protested in front of the EU institutions in Brussels.[2] During this phase the focus of attention shifted to certain trade practices affecting the relationship between farmers, co-operatives, food producers and retail chains.[3] They are made possible by a lack of bargaining

* While this chapter is based on the author's presentation at the Second UTP Roundtable at the KU Leuven on June 21, 2018, it has been updated to include the recent development.

1 Commission of the European Communities, Communication from the Commission to the European Parliament, the Council, the European Economic and Social Committee and the Committee of the Regions of 10–28–2009, A better functioning food supply chain in Europe, COM (2009) 591 final, p. 2.

2 Cf. <https://www.fwi.co.uk/business/photos-dairy-farmers-soak-brussels-streets-milk-price-protest>, site last accessed 09–18–2019.

3 European Commission, Communication from the Commission to the European Parliament, the Council, the European Economic and Social Committee and the Committee of the Regions of 07–15–2014, Tackling unfair trading practices in the business-to-business food supply chain, COM (2014) 472 final.

power of agricultural producers caused by various factors: first and foremost, of course, the nature of farm products makes a short term adaptation of production to market demand next to impossible. The recreation cycle combined with the exposure of production to natural circumstances beyond the control of the farmers like the weather or diseases on the one hand combined with the high concentration of the retail market all over Europe on the other typically results in a high degree of dependence of agricultural producers as opposed to retailers.[4]

While one may be tempted to doubt this thesis based on the fact that the food production industry likewise has become increasingly concentrated with global players like Nestlé (total yearly turnover of almost 80 bn EUR[5]), at least it seems plausible that extra costs caused by unfair trading practices "are passed back along the food supply chain to the weakest link which is often the farmer".[6]

Notwithstanding such distortions, from a perspective of Competition law the food market presents itself structurally just like any other market though: if it is reduced to three levels (agricultural producers, food producers, retailers) there is a vertical dimension of the market that is governed by contractual relationships in particular – the "food supply chain" as addressed in the UTP Directive. However, there remains a horizontal dimension determined by the competitive relationships within the same levels of production, i.e. competition between agricultural producers, between food producers and between retailers. While market structures for food products may be particular in many ways as described above, this fundamental structure is underlying even the food market. The consequences will be shown later.

1.2. REACTIONS OF THE DIRECTIVE ON UNFAIR TRADING PRACTICES IN BUSINESS-TO-BUSINESS RELATIONSHIPS IN THE AGRICULTURAL AND FOOD SUPPLY CHAIN

Despite the fact that the farmers' crisis turned out to become a major political issue, the European Commission initially remained quite reluctant to engage in legislative activity.[7] Ultimately, it was the European Parliament's resolution

---

4 Proposal of the Commission of 04–12–2018 for a Directive of the European Parliament and of the Council on unfair trading practices in business-to-business relationships in the food supply chain, COM (2018) 173 final, Explanatory Memorandum (hereinafter: Explanatory memorandum), p. 1.

5 Nestlé, Annual Review 2017, p. 1, quotes almost CHF 90 bn, <https://www.nestle.com/asset-library/documents/library/documents/annual_reports/2017-annual-review-en.pdf>, site last accessed 09–18–2019.

6 Explanatory memorandum, p. 2.

7 Report from the Commission to the European Parliament and the Council of 29 January 2016 on unfair business-to-business trading practices in the food supply chain, COM (2016) 32 final, p. 12.

of June 2016[8], that finally got the European Commission going and set the legislative process in action. On April 12, 2018 a proposal for a Directive on unfair trading practices in business-to-business relationships in the food supply chain[9] (hereinafter abbreviated as UTPD-P) was presented by the European Commission. It received preferential treatment by the Austrian presidency in the Council.[10] A political compromise was achieved in record time on December 19, 2018.[11] On April 31, 2019 the Directive (EU) 2019/633 on unfair trading practices in business-to-business relationships in the agricultural and food supply chain (hereinafter referred to as "UTP Directive"; "UTPD")[12] entered into force. Its main contents can be summarized briefly.

1.2.1. Minimum harmonization, Arts. 1(1), 9(1) UTPD

The trading practices business-to-business that are addressed by the UTP Directive typically either are integral elements of exchange contracts or are committed in the context of contractual relationships between businesses. The regulatory approach towards state and/or court intervention into business-to-business contracts varies widely among Member States; on the one hand some Member States have a proud tradition of abstention when it comes to limiting core elements of private autonomy. Others may have different traditions. So it comes as no surprise that the UTP Directive restricts itself to prohibit some very specific and evident forms of unfair trading practices[13], but permits the Member States to raise the level of protection. The Union Law instrument to achieve this goal is minimum harmonization, a principle that seemed almost forgotten after the change of the European Union's regulatory approach in the wake of the ECJ's judgement on tobacco advertising in 2000.[14] The principle of minimum harmonization is laid down in Arts. 1(1), 9(1) UTPD.

---

8 European Parliament, resolution of 7 June 2016 on unfair trading practices in the food supply chain, P8_TA(2016)0250, para. 46.

9 Proposal of the Commission of 04–12–2018 for a Directive of the European Parliament and of the Council on unfair trading practices in business-to-business relationships in the food supply chain, COM (2018) 173 final.

10 Austrian Presidency priorities discussed in committees, Press release 10–07–2018, Reference No: 20180710IPR07609, <www.europarl.europa.eu/pdfs/news/expert/2018/7/press_release/20180710IPR07609/20180710IPR07609_en.pdf>, site last accessed on 09–18–2019.

11 European Commission – Press release: Agreement on unfair trading practices in the food supply chain will protect all EU farmers, Brussels, 12–19–2018, IP 18/6790, Proposal for a directive of the european parliament and of the council on unfair trading practices in business-to-business relationships in the food supply chain – Confirmation of the final compromise text with a view to agreement, interinstitutional dossier 2018/0082 (COD), Doc.-Nr. 5061/19.

12 Directive (EU) 2019/633 of the European Parliament and of the Council of 17 April 2019 on unfair trading practices in business-to-business relationships in the agricultural and food supply chain, OJ 2019, L 111/59.

13 Explanatory memorandum, p. 3.

14 ECJ, 10–05–2000, C-376/98 – Federal Republic of Germany v. European Parliament and Council of the European Union – Advertising and sponsorship of tobacco products, 2000 ECR I-8419.

1.2.2. *Limited scope of application*

(1) Ratione materiae: only sales of agricultural and food products, Art. 1(2) UTPD

While it is perfectly clear that the market for agricultural and food products is affected by very specific imperfections relating both to the nature of the products and to the retail chain, the European Commission has not found it necessary even in its initial proposal to argue why the scope of application of the proposed directive should be limited to the supply chain of food products pursuant to Art. 1(2) UTPD-P. This limitation has not been questioned in principle. In the later phase of the legislation procedure the scope of application was extended to all agricultural products (*infra* 3.).

(2) Ratione personae: only sales in "Big-to-small" contracts, Art. 1(2) UTPD

Unfair trading practices were identified in particular as a result of the inferior negotiating power of suppliers due to their economic dependence on the large retail chains. That is why[15] the European Commission initially intended to limit the special prohibitions to cases, in which such practices occur in a relation to sales by a supplier that is a small and medium-sized enterprise (SME) to a buyer that is not an SME, Art. 1(2) UTPD-P. As for the concept of SME the Commission intended to make fruitful Recommendation 2003/361[16] which defines SME following absolute business figures, mostly in terms of turnover and number of employees.[17] During the legislation procedure it became obvious that such a criterion was not suited to mirror the concept of economic dependence. That being said the European legislator refrained from going all the way to an open requirement of economic dependence as a function of the relative positions of the respective undertakings, the UTP Directive now determines its scope of application depending on the relation of absolute turnover figures of buyer and supplier, Art. 1(2) UTPD.

1.2.3. *Specific provisions instead of a general clause, Art. 1(1) UTPD*

As a result of earlier studies and an impact assessment the European Commission already in its initial proposal refrained from making use of a general clause[18] comparable to the one contained in Art. 5 of the Directive on Unfair Commercial Practices[19] (hereinafter: UCP Directive, UCPD). Instead the

---

15 Explanantory memorandum, p. 9.

16 Commission Recommendation of 6 May 2003 concerning the definition of micro, small and medium-sized enterprises, OJ 2003, L 124/36.

17 Explanatory Memorandum, p. 8, rec. 7 s. 2, 3, Art. 1(2), 2 let. c UTPD-P.

18 Explanatory memorandum, p. 9.

19 Directive 2005/29/EC of the European Parliament and of the Council concerning unfair business-to-consumer commercial practices in the internal market and amending Council Directive 84/450/EEC, Directives 97/7/EC, 98/27/EC and 2002/65/EC of the European

Commission tried to gain political acceptance by narrowing down the positive obligations to some very essential and intuitive requirements. The Commission argued that some forms of trading practices were considered to be unfair "as such" or "by their nature" while others remained subject to the parties' contractual discretion.[20]

The two kinds of unfair trading practices are kept distinct by the two paragraphs of Art. 3 UTPD. Reading the Explanatory Memorandum and the considerations it becomes clear that the distinction does not really depend on whether particular practices are unfair as such and therefore cannot be justified by a contract.

In fact, the underlying rationale is rooted in law and economics. The Explanatory Memorandum rightly spelled out that practices foreseen in clear and unambiguous terms in the supply agreement before the transaction are likely to generate efficiencies and therefore should not be prohibited.[21] That is why their control should be limited as opposed to practices that occur after the transaction has started without being agreed in advance.[22] The final text of the UTP Directive has adopted this approach, cf. rec. 16 UTPD. Following this demarcation line the subsequent analysis will distinguish between conduct under the contract as governed by Art. 3(2) and conduct in breach of a contract as governed by Art. 3(1) UTPD.

1.2.3.1. Conduct under a contract, Art. 3(2) UTPD

Article 3(2) UTPD prohibits particular practices even though they may be based on a prior agreement. It is the return of unsold agricultural and food products to the supplier (let. a), the charging of payments as a condition for the stocking, displaying or listing of agricultural and food products ("shelf rents") (let. b), payments of the supplier for the promotion of agricultural and food products ("promotional contributions") (let. c) and payments of the supplier for the advertising and marketing of agricultural food products (let. d-f). However, such practices are deemed unfair only if they are not agreed upon in clear and unambiguous terms at the conclusion of the supply agreement.

1.2.3.2. Conduct in breach of a contract, Art. 3(1) UTPD

On the other hand Art. 3(1) UTPD prohibits another group of trading practices irrespective of whether they have been agreed upon: it is late payment for perishable agricultural and food products (let. a), the cancellation of orders of

Parliament and of the Council and Regulation (EC) No 2006/2004 of the European Parliament and of the Council, OJ 2005, L 149/22.

20 Explanatory memorandum, p. 9; rec. 12 s. 2 UTPD-P.

21 Explanatory memorandum, p. 9.

22 Explanatory memorandum, p. 9.

perishable agricultural and food products at overly short notice (let. b), unilateral changes of the terms of the supply agreement with respect to the frequency, timing or volume of the supply, quality standards or prices (let. c), the payment of the supplier for wastage of food products occurring after the passing of risk to the buyer (let. d, e), the buyer's refusal to confirm the terms of the agreement in writing (let. f), infringement of trade secrets (let. g), buyer's threats to retaliate for the use of contractual rights (let. g) and the buyer's demand of compensation for the costs of having to deal with consumer complaints irrespective of cause.

1.2.4. Battling the "fear factor", Art. 4, 6 UTPD

From the very beginning of the discussion it was obvious that most, if not all, of the trading practices considered to be unfair were infringing on either general Contract law or the binding force of the supply agreement. On the other hand the remedies afforded by Contract law are generally not considered to be sufficiently effective as they have to be enforced by litigation.[23] Suppliers with an inferior bargaining position thus may find themselves in a dilemma having either to accept the unfair trading practices or to take the risk of "winning their case, but losing their business". In shorthand this problem has been referred to as "fear factor".[24]

One of the main goals of the UTP Directive was to provide for remedies helping to overcome this fear factor.[25] Two instruments are foreseen to this purpose: firstly, the UTP Directive distrusts private enforcement. That is why enforcement has to be granted by authorities pursuant to Arts. 4, 6 UTPD. Secondly, as even enforcement authorities will not have sufficient information to act on their own initiative and a formal complaint may induce just as much repression as a private law suit, Art. 5 UTPD tries to offer confidentiality to the parties supplying the information necessary to enforce the law against infringing buyers.

1.2.5. Homogeneity, Art. 8 UTPD

Finally, even though the UTP Directive is not based on the internal market competence, but on Art. 43(2) of the Treaty on the Functioning of the European Union (hereinafter: TFEU) instead, the Explanatory Memorandum clearly shows the need for harmonized protection throughout the Union.[26] The UTP Directive

23 European Commission, Communication from the Commission to the European Parliament, the Council, the European Economic and Social Committee and the Committee of the Regions of 07-15-2014, Tackling unfair trading practices in the business-to-business food supply chain, COM (2014) 472 final, p. 7.

24 Explanatory memorandum, p. 2.

25 Explanatory memorandum, p. 2, 10.

26 Explanatory memorandum, p. 10.

aims at insuring homogeneity of both the evolution of law and the enforcement practices, rec. 36 – 39 UTPD. That is why a network of enforcement authorities has been created in Art. 8 UTPD that meet regularly, exchange information, discuss best practices and provide for mutual assistance in investigations that have a cross-border dimension.

2. BACKDROP UNDER EXISTING GERMAN LAW

Neither the Commission's proposal nor the UTP Directive have become an object of great discussion among German lawyers.[27] Of course, the reason for this is not the lack of unfair trading practices, but rather the fact that most of the concerns perceived by the European Commission and addressed in the UTP Directive have already been covered by established elements of German law and under various aspects: first and foremost, it is worth noting that German law has a tradition of subjecting even general terms and conditions (hereinafter: GTC) in contracts concluded by traders (usually referred to as "B2B") to a control of general fairness. Moreover, German Unfair Competition law not only relates to commercial practices committed in business-to-consumer relations, but encompasses conduct in business-to-business relations. Finally, German Competition law for over 45 years has expanded the scope of specific prohibitions of unilateral conduct to undertakings with relative market power limited to individual business partners or competitors. The following part will test these existing elements of German law against the requirements of the UTP Directive.

2.1. CONTRACT LAW REMEDIES

2.1.1. Conduct under the contract, Art. 3(2) UTPD

As already mentioned Contract law remedies are broadly available for the kind of conduct under the contract as governed by Art. 3(2) UTPD. The control of General Terms and Conditions with regard to their content has a broad scope of

27 The position taken by the German Bundesrat (the second chamber of parliament representing the Bundesländer) on June 8, 2018 was generally positive, BR-Drs. 116/18. The position of the Trade Association Germany (Handelsverband Deutschland) sought to narrow down the scope of application and objects against the use of enforcement authorities, <https://www.einzelhandel.de/index.php?option=com_attachments&task=download&id=9630>, site last accessed on 09-18-2019. The Centrum für Europäische Politik (cep) criticizes the proposal for not taking into consideration the existence of economic dependence, cepAnalyse no. 21/2018, p. 4. <https://www.cep.eu/fileadmin/user_upload/cep.eu/Analysen/COM_2018_173_Unlautere_Handelspraktiken/cepAnalyse_COM_2018__173_Unlautere_Handelspraktiken.pdf>, site last accessed on 09-18-2019.

application under German Contract law, in particular secs. 305 ff. of the German Civil Code (hereinafter: GCC[28]). Different from the scope of application of the Unfair Terms Directive[29], German Contract law has never limited the scope of application to business-to-consumer contracts. To be sure, scrutiny of content is deeper and offers a higher degree of protection, if GTC are used against consumers, cf. sec. 310(3) GCC. By the same token, scrutiny of content is limited, if GTC are used in B2B contracts, sec. 310(1) GCC. Most notably there is a black list of clauses that are considered to be typically unfair, unless used against traders, secs. 308, 309 GCC Nevertheless, German courts have tended even while not applying the black list in secs. 308, 309 GCC to B2B contracts directly, to make use of them as legislative indicators of unfairness in B2B contracts.[30]

Moreover, in B2B contracts the general requirement of sec. 307(1) s. 2 GCC applies that all GTC have to be clear and comprehensible. Of course, the standard of comprehensibility will vary in accordance with the typical addressees of the GTC, yet, if GTC are unclear or incomprehensible even for typical addressees in the business, they will be deemed ineffective pursuant to sec. 306 GCC independent of their subject. So, with regard to this requirement German control of GTC goes far beyond the control of conduct under Art. 3(2) UTPD.

Likewise, the fear factor is mitigated by the way control of GTC is exercised: the primary legal consequence of the use of any unfair or intransparent GTC is the ineffectiveness of the particular clauses pursuant to sec. 306 GCC. All of the provisions contained in Art. 3(2) UTPD relate to situations in which the buyer is enforcing his right to either receive return of the consideration paid (let. a), or payments for stocking, displaying or listing of agricultural and food products (let. b), or for sales promotions or marketing (let. c through f). Consequently, the fear factor has only little significance. At the time the buyer stipulates corresponding rights in GTC, the supplier is not forced to negotiate such clauses out of the contract and thereby wage war before even getting the contract. Instead, the (legally advised) supplier may lean back and wait to see whether the specific risks involved in such clauses materialize. If they do, it is for the buyer to bring his claims under the contract; the supplier is then in a comfortable situation to rely on the ineffectiveness of the pertinent clauses.

2.1.2. Conduct in breach of the contract, Art. 3(1) UTPD

Things become more complicated for the kind of conduct governed by Art. 3(1) UTPD. Late payment as governed by Art. 3(1) let. a UTPD is a breach of contract and gives rise to all typical remedies. Under German Contract law payment is

---

28 An English version of the provisions of the German Civil Code referred to in this contribution is available at < https://www.gesetze-im-internet.de/englisch_bgb/>, site last accessed on 09-18-2019.

29 Council Directive 93/13/EEC on unfair terms in consumer contracts, OJ 1993, L 95/29.

30 Federal Supreme Court, 09-19-2007, VIII ZR 141/06, BGHZ 174, 1, para. 12.

regularly due immediately, sec. 271 GCC. More specifically, the requirements of the Late Payment Directive[31] have been implemented in sec. 286(3) GCC. Under the current economic circumstances late payment of a solvent debtor is even highly attractive for the creditor as the default interest rate as laid down by sec. 288(2) GCC of 9% above the basic rate of interest is much higher than the rate of interest typically to be achieved on the capital markets.

The same holds true for the undue cancellation governed by Art. 3(1) let. b UTPD. Contract law for good reasons denies a general right for cancellation. This is the core of the principle of *pacta sunt servanda.* Only long term contracts concluded without a specific date of expiry can be terminated without justifying reasons. Apart from that long term contracts can be terminated only for compelling reasons, sec. 314 GCC, and single-time exchange contracts can be revoked only, if there has been a breach of contract by the other side and either a reasonable period of time for cure of that breach has lapsed, sec. 323(1) GCC, or it is inacceptable for the creditor to continue the performance of the contract, sec. 324 GCC. So in the absence of such a right of the supplier to terminate or revoke the contract any cancellation will be an (anticipatory) breach of contract, for which the supplier owes damages, sec. 280(1) GCC.

The unilateral change of terms governed by Art. 3(1) let. c UTPD is treated accordingly. There is no contractual right to unilaterally change the terms of a contract. The "changes" are simply invalid and the non-compliance of the buyer with the original terms of the contract will amount to a breach of contract ensued by all typical remedies including damages.

Finally, the shift of the passing of the economic risk for loss of products after the acceptance as governed by Art. 3(1) let. d UTPD is only possible on the grounds of a contractual agreement, as the law specifies at what time the risks of performance and counter-performance pass in exchange contracts.

So while the rights and duties of the parties under Contract law are fairly clear with regard to the conduct covered by Art. 3(1) UTPD, and the remedies will compensate adequately for the economic harm caused to the supplier, it is quite obvious that the enforcement of such remedies must remain weak whenever an inferior supplier encounters a buyer with superior bargaining power. At this point the fear factor as addressed by the European Commission's proposal comes into play.

Yet, one more issue seems not to be addressed by the UTP Directive. It appears unclear why the practices described under Art. 3(1) UTPD should be so egregious ("unfair by their very nature", rec. 16 s. 3 UTPD) that they have to be withdrawn from party autonomy. This is obvious for payment terms (let. a). There is nothing to be said against a supplier granting periods of payment longer than 30 days. Even the prohibition in Art. 3(1) let. a UTPD is based on

31 Directive 2011/7/EU of the European Parliament and of the Council on combating late payment in commercial transactions, OJ 2011, L 48/1.

the assumption that the parties may determine when payment is due. The same holds true for the fact pattern relating to the passing of risk (let. e). It might be possible that quality control upon delivery is difficult and expensive while payment in accordance with the amount of items useable for processing is substantially easier. In such cases it should be left to the parties to agree on the time of the passing of the risk.

2.1.3. *Remedies*

At the bottom line protection against unfair trading practices as described in Art. 3(2) UTPD is afforded by German Contract law to a considerable extent. As a consequence of the particular operation of control of GTC after the contract is concluded even the fear factor is being overcome. On the other hand, contract law remedies against conduct as governed by Art. 3(1) UTPD do not reflect the fear factor sufficiently.

2.2. UNFAIR COMPETITION LAW REMEDIES

Like in many of today's EU Member States Unfair Competition law has emerged in Germany at the beginning of the 20th century.[32] Different from many Member States, however, Unfair Competition law has not remained a specific business tort law. Already by the early 1930s scholars[33] pointed out that most cases of unfair competition, typically in the guise of misleading advertising, were in fact primarily prejudicing the opposite market side rather than competitors. 1965 saw the advent of representative actions against unfair competition brought by consumer associations.[34] Even after the entry into force of the UCP Directive the German legislator upheld the integrative approach to govern both B2C and B2B conduct within one single set of rules contained in the Act against Unfair Competition (hereinafter: AUC[35]).[36] To a large extent the core of the provisions

32 The first Act against Unfair Competition from 1896 was soon followed by the 1909 version that remained in force until 2004.

33 Most notably Eugen Ulmer, who later became the first Director of the Max-Planck-Institute for foreign and international Patent, Copyright and Competition law, cf. *Ulmer*, Wandlungen und Aufgaben im Wettbewerbsrecht GRUR 1937, 769, 772.

34 Act amending the Act against Unfair Competition, the Trademark Act and the Utility Model Act of July 21st 1965 (Gesetz zur Änderung des Gesetzes gegen den unlauteren Wettbewerb, des Warenzeichengesetzes und des Gebrauchsmustergesetzes), BGBl. 1965, I p. 625.

35 An English version of the Act against Unfair Competition is available at <https://www.gesetze-im-internet.de/englisch_uwg/>, site last accessed on 09–18–2019.

36 Government's proposal for an Act amending the Act against Unfair Competition (Entwurf eines Ersten Gesetzes zur Änderung des Gesetzes gegen den unlauteren Wettbewerb) of 08–20–2008, BT-Drs. 16/10145; Government's proposal for a Second act amending the Act against Unfair Competition (Entwurf eines Zweiten Gesetzes zur Änderung des Gesetzes gegen den unlauteren Wettbewerb) of 05–01–2015, BT-Drs. 18/4535, p. 9.

contained in the UCP Directive was simply extended in its scope of application to commercial practices business-to-business. This includes most notably aggressive commercial practices as governed by Arts. 8, 9 UCPD.

2.2.1. *Conduct under the contract, Art. 3(2) UTPD*

Unfair trading practices governed by Art. 3(2) UTPD will also entail remedies under Unfair Competition law. It is established case law that the use of ineffective GTC amounts to unfair competition under sec. 3a AUC.[37] As a consequence the use of intransparent GTC does not only entail Contract law remedies such as the invalidity of the respective clauses, but also the tort law remedies laid down in secs. 8, 9 AUC.

2.2.2. *Conduct in breach of the contract, Art. 3(1) UTPD*

Even in the absence of unfair contract terms unilateral measures that are in breach of contract and exercising any undue influence are considered aggressive commercial practices under sec. 4a AUC. As already mentioned, the scope of application of said provision is not limited to commercial practices business-to-consumer, but also serves to protect inferior business partners.[38] As the type of commercial practice addressed by this provision is typically committed along the lines of production or distribution and, consequently, in vertical relationships, there is no requirement of a competitive relationship between the party exercising undue influence and the victim. To the contrary, the scope of application of this provision is limited to a vertical relationship; the exercise of pressure within competitive relationships is not governed by sec. 4a AUC, but by sec. 4 AUC.

2.2.3. *Remedies*

The reinforcement of Contract law remedies by the remedies of Unfair Competition law appears highly attractive. This is not so much due to the availability of damages under sec. 9 AUC, as damages may also be sought for a breach of contract, as mentioned above. The bulk of the case law arising from litigation under the Act against Unfair Competition results from claims for injunctive relief as governed by sec. 8 AUC. Injunctive relief does not require intent or negligence and the misconduct of employees or even third-

37 Federal Supreme Court, 03-31-2010, I ZR 34/08 – Liability waiver on the internet, WRP 2010, 1475, 1476; Federal Supreme Court, 05-31-2012, I ZR 45/11, GRUR 2012, 949 – Abusive penalty; Federal Supreme Court, 12-14-2017, I ZR 184/15 – Replacement of clauses, GRUR 2018, 423.

38 *Köhler*/Bornkamm/Feddersen, UWG, 38th ed., 2020, §4a para. 1.1; Harte-Bavendamm/Henning-Bodewig/*Picht*, UWG, 4th ed., 2016, §4a paras. 11, 14.

party contractors is attributed pursuant to sec. 8(2) AUC. Injunctive relief may force the defendant to abandon entire business models, if these are deemed by the courts to be unfair. The scope of injunctive measures extends to measures of abatement including the publication of judgements at the expenses of the defendant.[39]

Claims for injunctive relief may not only be brought by the injured party pursuant to sec. 8(3) no. 1 AUC, but also by business and consumer associations just as well as by chambers of commerce pursuant to sec. 8(3) nos. 2–4 AUC. Giving standing to sue to these institutional plaintiffs takes away the fear factor to a considerable extent. The institutional plaintiffs will be considered to sue for the infringement of their own rights and do not have to lay open where the evidence presented has been gained. There is only one remaining downside as, arguably, injunctive relief does not provide for sufficient deterrence as might be provided by fines. On the other hand it is quite obvious that the negative publicity accompanying litigation and a negative outcome, let alone the publication of a negative judgement will be considered highly undesirable even for retail firms with a high bargaining power as opposed to their suppliers.

2.3. COMPETITION LAW REMEDIES

Finally, the scope of German Competition law is much wider with regard to unilateral conduct than the scope of European Competition law. While there is full primacy of European Competition law with regard to anti-competitive covenants pursuant to Art. 3(2) s. 1 Regulation no. 1/2003[40] and the German legislator explicitly chose to avoid a split of laws in this field[41], EU Competition law allows the Member States to apply stricter rules on unilateral conduct, Art. 3(2) s. 2 Regulation no. 1/2003.

The German legislator has made ample use of the leeway thus created. Sections 18 ff. of the Act against Restraints of Competition (hereinafter: ARC)[42] allow for a both wider and deeper control of unilateral conduct, as the prohibitions laid down in sec. 20 ARC do not require a dominant position within the meaning of Art. 102 TFEU or sec. 18 ARC. The specific prohibitions

39 Cf. already Federal Supreme Court, 06–29–1956, I ZR 176/54 – Regensburger Karmelitengeist, GRUR 1956, 558, 563. Today sec. 12(3) AUC expressly confers such a right implementing the Enforcement Directive.

40 Council Regulation (EC) No 1/2003 on the implementation of the rules on competition laid down in Articles 81 and 82 of the Treaty, OJ 2003, L 1/1.

41 Government's proposal for a Seventh act amending the Act against Restraints of Competition (Entwurf eines Siebten Gesetzes zur Änderung des Gesetzes gegen Wettbewerbsbeschränkungen) of 08–12–2004, BT-Drs. 15/3640, p. 22.

42 An English version of the Act against Restraints of Competition in the current version of the Ninth amendment, is available at <www.gesetze-im-internet.de/englisch_gwb/>, site last accessed on 09–18–2019.

created by sec. 20 ARC merely require a relative dominance of one undertaking with regard to another, dependent, undertaking. Already at this point it is worth noting though that the extension of the prohibition of abuse of a dominant position does not encompass exploitative abuses as the fact pattern laid down in sec. 19(2) no. 2 ARC is not included in the list of sec. 20 ARC. The main purpose of the extension is to keep the markets open.[43]

2.3.1. Conduct under the contract, Art. 3(2) UTPD

The forms of unfair trading practices described by Art. 3(2) UTPD can easily be conceived of as exploitative abuses. Even the wording of Art. 102 TFEU seems to have in mind such forms of abuse when it talks in let. a about "imposing unfair trading conditions". A parallel provision is contained in sec. 19(2) no. 2 ARC ("demands business terms"). On the basis of these provisions we find universal protection against the abuse of a dominant position by exploitative use of bargaining power in the course of contract negotiations. Moreover there is well-established case law in Germany that the use of GTC that are ineffective under secs. 305 ff. GCC amounts to an exploitative abuse under Competition law.[44]

Yet, the problem remains that in the context of the kind of unfair trading practices the European legislator intends to address there will hardly be any dominance as required by Art. 102 TFEU or sec. 19 ARC. Market dominance is typically defined as

> "a position of economic strength enjoyed by an undertaking which enables it to prevent effective competition being maintained on the relevant market by affording it the power to behave to an appreciable extent independently of its competitors, its customers and ultimately of the consumers."[45]

This definition conveys the concept of "absolute" dominance, irrespective of direction (horizontal or vertical) and number of market participants (as suppliers, customers or competitors) or their countervailing negotiating power. At this point our initial market analysis becomes relevant: as long as there is effective competition on the retail level – or on the food producer level, for that

43 Government's proposal for a Seventh act amending the Act against Restraints of Competition (Entwurf eines Siebten Gesetzes zur Änderung des Gesetzes gegen Wettbewerbsbeschränkungen) of 08-12-2004, BT-Drs. 15/3640, p. 21; Government's proposal for an Eighth act amending the Act against Restraints of Competition (Entwurf eines Achten Gesetzes zur Änderung des Gesetzes gegen Wettbewerbsbeschränkungen) of 05-31-2012, BT-Drs. 17/9852, p. 20, both refer to an important role in terms of economic policy and protection of SME.

44 Federal Supreme Court, 01-24-2017, KZR 47/14 – VBL-Gegenwert II, WRP 2017, 563, para. 35.

45 ECJ, 02-13-1979, 85/76 – Hoffmann-La Roche & Co. AG v Commission of the European Communities, 1979 ECR 461, para. 38.

purpose – there is no independence of any single retailer or of any single food producer and, consequently, no single market dominance.

The requirements of joint dominance, in particular the existence of structural links[46], are likewise not met. It must be ascertained whether economic links exist between those undertakings which enable them to act together independently of their competitors, their customers and consumers.[47] Even on the most concentrated food retail markets this is not the case. So there remains a considerable gap for cases without market dominance.

This is where sec. 20 ARC becomes relevant. As already noted above this provision – in effect since 1973[48] – extends the scope of control of unilateral conduct to cases where there is only a "relative" market power vis-à-vis particular suppliers or customers. Relative market power is defined by sec. 20(1) ARC as a dependence of small or medium-sized enterprises as suppliers or purchasers of a certain type of goods or commercial services as a consequence of the lack of sufficient and reasonable possibilities of switching to other undertakings.

Such dependence may be based either on grounds lying within the product (1). A shop for sports equipment may depend on supply of skis, tennis rackets or apparel from a well-renowned producer.[49] Dependence may also be caused by grounds lying in the dependent undertaking itself and its business relationship (2). Thus a distributor who has been specializing in products of one particular supplier over many years may not only have acquired special expertise on these products, but may also find it hard to sell and work on other products making it difficult to substitute to distributing other products. Moreover, dependence may be based on scarcity of the products (3). The seminal case was provided by the first oil crisis when the vertically integrated fuel producers chose to supply only their own network of gas stations with car fuel, but refused to supply independent gas stations.[50] Finally, dependence may be caused by demand (4), either if suppliers adapt their products to the buyers' needs in a way they cannot market them elsewhere or as a consequence of the retail function of the buyer. Supplies to the large super market chain stores will typically belong to the latter group if they amount to more than 10% of the sales of a supplier, even if an individual analysis of mutual dependencies is always warranted.[51]

---

46 ECJ, 04-27-1994, C-393/92 – Almelo, 1994 ECR I-1508, para. 42.

47 ECJ, 03-16-2000, joined cases C-395, 396/96 P – Compagnie maritime belge SA, 2000 ECR I-1365, para. 39.

48 The mediate predecessor of sec. 20 ARC – following sec. 20(2) ARC 1999 – was sec. 26(2) s. 2 ARC 1973, cf. Art. 1 no. 12 let. c of the Second act amending the Act against Restraints of Competition (Zweites Gesetz zur Änderung des Gesetzes gegen Wettbewerbs-beschränkungen) of 08-03-1973, BGBl. 1973, I p. 917.

49 As in the leading case Federal Supreme Court, 11-20-1975, KZR 1/75 – Rossignol, NJW 1976, 801.

50 Cf. Kartellgesetznovelle – Materiellrechtliche Vorschriften und Erläuterungen aus dem Bericht des Wirtschaftsausschusses des Bundestages, WRP 1973, 376, 385.

51 Federal Supreme Court, 01-23-2018, KVR 3/17 – Wedding rebates, WRP 2018, 556, paras. 42 ff.

Even though the special protection afforded by sec. 20 ARC has been limited to SME ever since 1989, it is generally agreed that the quality of an SME is a function of its relative significance on a particular market. Absolute terms such as number of employees or turnover are irrelevant. It is worth noting that the Federal Supreme Court found a decision of the Federal Cartel Office flawed, in which the Federal Cartel Office had reasoned the quality of an SME only on the basis of turnover thresholds, but failed to assess the market situation. Whether an enterprise is small or medium-sized has to be assessed in every single case on the basis of the facts, taking into consideration the peculiarities of the relevant market including the horizontal relationship to competitors with regard to customers and under particular circumstances also the vertical relationships to customers with countervailing buying power.[52]

During the last 45 years the concept of relative market power has been hammered out by the German competition authorities and courts. While on the one hand it is obvious that the existence of relative market power has to be ascertained in every single relationship and may result in different outcomes for different products even within the same business relationship[53], the concept of "relative market power" itself does not seem to be more problematic to apply than the concept of absolute market dominance.

In the cases pertinent for unfair trading practices covered by the UTP Directive one would have to apply the principles governing relative market power based on demand, in particular if suppliers depend on buyers as a consequence of the high shares of the buyers in the retail market. It is no wonder that control under Competition law currently is the instrument of choice to combat unfair trading practices.

On the other hand the extension of protection afforded by sec. 20 ARC is limited to specific forms of abuse, most notably forms of exclusionary abuse and discrimination pursuant to secs. 20(1), 19(2) no. 1 ARC. Exploitative abuses as governed by sec. 19(2) no. 2 ARC are not included. This is not a mistake, but a well-founded decision taken by the legislator. It is no secret that the body of case law under the prohibitions of exploitative abuses in general is extremely slim, to put it mildly. The reluctant use of Competition law in cases of exploitative abuses has to do with fundamental assumptions on the functioning of markets: any and all competitive activity is about the possibility to command prices exceeding costs, and any state measure trying to curb those prices based on the argument that they are unfair or excessive risks to disturb the most fundamental working condition of the market economy.

---

52 Federal Supreme Court, 09–24–2002, KVR 8/01 – Adaptation of conditions, WRP 2002, 1436, 1439.

53 Cf. *Loewenheim*, in: Loewenheim/Meessen/Riesenkampff/Kersting/Meyer-Lindemann, Kartellrecht, 3rd ed., 2016, sec. 20 GWB paras. 13 ff.

Notwithstanding this, already in 1980 the German legislator included a prohibition of so-called *tapping* that is governed today in secs. 20(2), 19(2) no. 5 ARC.[54] The figurative term "tapping" (in German "anzapfen") relates to the picture of hitting a tap into a barrel to gain unlimited access to its resources. In the 1960s and early 1970s the newly emerged supermarket chain stores had gained superior purchasing power and made use of this purchasing power by squeezing their suppliers, typically in the guise of asking for side performances instead of exercising direct price pressure on the suppliers. The famous "list of sins" issued by the German Ministry of Economic Affairs[55] in 1974 and the Joint Declaration of the Organizations of the Commercial Economy to Maintain Competition on the Merits[56] of 1976 did not remain unheard. In the Fourth amendment to the ARC in 1980 the predecessor of the provision cited above was enacted to cover trading practices relating to "industrial fringe benefits" demanded by retailers from suppliers[57], e.g. "entrance fees", "listing fees", "shelf rental fees", "shop window rental fees", "promotion fees", "special rebates" for special occasions etc. These have returned in some of the unfair trading practices identified by the European Parliament.[58] The current provision declares the conduct abusive, if an undertaking or an association of undertakings in relation to the undertakings which depend on them,

> "requests other undertakings to grant it advantages without any objective justification; in this regard particular account shall be taken of whether the other undertaking has been given plausible reasons for the request and whether the advantage requested is proportionate to the grounds for the request.."

Again, secs. 20(2), 19(2) no. 5 ARC cover many forms of business conduct more than Art. 3(2) UTPD. However, the effectiveness of the German provisions was hampered in the past by a certain reluctance of the courts to interfere with contractual relationships. In particular the judgement rendered by the Higher

54 The mediate predecessor of sec. 19(2) no. 5 ARC – following sec. 20(3) ARC 1999 – was sec. 26(3) ARC 1980, cf. Art. 1 no. 8 let. c of the Fourth act amending the Act against Restraints of Competition (Viertes Gesetz zur Änderung des Gesetzes gegen Wettbewerbsbeschränkungen) of 04-26-1980, BGBl. 1980, I p. 458.

55 "List of Sins", Federal Ministry of Economics of 11-15-1974 (Beispielskatalog von Tatbeständen, die zu Wettbewerbsverzerrungen führen können, Bundeswirtschaftsministerium, 15. November 1974), WRP 1975, 24.

56 Safeguarding Protection on the Merits, Joint Declaration of Organizations of the Commercial Economy (Sicherung des Leistungswettbewerbs, Gemeinsame Erklärung von Organisationen der gewerblichen Wirtschaft), WuW 1976, 17.

57 Government's proposal for a Fourth act amending the Act against Restraints of Competition (Entwurf eines Vierten Gesetzes zur Änderung des Gesetzes gegen Wettbewerbsbeschränkungen), of 27 September 1978, BT-Drs. 8/2136, p. 25.

58 European Parliament, resolution of 7 June 2016 on unfair trading practices in the food supply chain, P8_TA(2016)0250, F. indents 11, 12.

Regional Court Düsseldorf[59] over EDEKA's demands of so-called wedding rebates following the acquisition of more than 2,000 Tengelmann retail shops made this reluctance very clear.

The German legislator has reacted promptly: expressly citing the EDEKA judgement[60] the Ninth amendment of the Act against Restraints of Competition in 2017 made it clear that the simple demand of any undue advantage was sufficient and no specific causal nexus between the relative dominance and the particular contractual agreement had to be established. Moreover, the test of the negative requirement "without objective justification" was simplified by adding the requirement that reasons for the additional advantage be given.

Only a few months later the Federal Supreme Court ruled on appeal over the Higher Regional Court's EDEKA judgement and quashed it.[61] Even for the old law the Federal Supreme Court found that there was neither an unwritten requirement of discrimination nor a need for any specific causal nexus for the application of sec. 19(2) no. 5 ARC. Adding to that, the Federal Supreme Court established a positive assumption against any objective justification in cases of either obvious discrepancy of performances or of demands of contributions to shop modernizations without any relation to the exchanged contract as such.

2.3.2. *Conduct in breach of a contract, Art. 3(1) UTPD*

The principles described above apply in full to the types of conduct governed by Art. 3(1) UTPD. Sections 19(2) no. 5, 20(2) ARC also catch anticipatory breaches of contract, if these are the expression of independence due to a form of relative market power. As early as 2002 the Federal Supreme Court has held that there is an assumption of a lack of objective justification for retroactive changes of supply terms.[62]

2.3.3. *Remedies*

The remedies available may appear to some as the strongest arguments for taking legislative action against unfair trading practices in the ambit of Competition law: not only has there been a healthy branch of private enforcement of secs. 19, 20 ARC in Germany over decades. In addition there is public enforcement through highly reputed competition authorities, most notably the Federal Cartel

59 Higher Regional Court Düsseldorf of 11–18–2015, VI-Kart 6/14 (V) – Edeka wedding rebates, WuW 2016, 23.

60 Government's proposal for a Ninth act amending the Act against Restraints of Competition (Entwurf eines Neunten Gesetzes zur Änderung des Gesetzes gegen Wettbewerbs-beschränkungen), BT-Drs. 18/10207, p. 52.

61 Federal Supreme Court, 01–23–2018, KVR 3/17 – Wedding rebates, WRP 2018, 556.

62 Federal Supreme Court, 09–24–2002, KVR 8/01 – Adaptation of terms and conditions, WRP 2002, 1436.

Office (Bundeskartellamt). While enforcement under Unfair Competition law may seem tainted with a certain lack of deterrent power, this cannot be said with regard to the enforcement of Competition law: not only is there a possibility to hand down fines as laid down in sec. 81(2) no. 1 ARC, but also the amount of fines makes them a very credible element of deterrence.[63]

As regards the fear factor the enforcement by competition authorities for long has become used to granting confidentiality to the complainants as far as possible without infringing on procedural rights of the offending undertaking. The so called "horse and rider" problem[64] has been solved by granting the competition authority the right to initiate proceedings even without any formal complaint. Moreover even for legal redress confidentiality is maintained by sec. 70(4) s. 3 ARC.

3. SUMMARY AND CRITIQUE

3.1. CONSERVATIVE APPROACH OF THE UTP DIRECTIVE

At the bottom line the European legislator has chosen a fairly conservative approach to unfair trading practices which is somewhat in line with the Commission's initial reluctance to take legislative action in the first place. The scope of application of the UTP Directive is limited to unfair trading practices in the agricultural and food supply chain and even on this narrow field the UTP Directive is not trying to mimic the regulatory approach of the UCP Directive, despite their very similar headlines.

3.2. LIMITED NEED OF ADAPTATION OF GERMAN LAW

With regard to the main topic of this contribution it should be easy to see why the Commission's proposal so far has been received quite favorably in Germany[65]

63 There is an marked move towards an enforcement of Unfair Competition law by administrative authorities, cf. Art. 1 Nr. 5 of the Directive (EU) 2019/2161 of the European Parliament and of the Council of 27 November 2019 amending Council Directive 93/13/EEC of 5 April 1993 and Directives 98/6/EC, 2005/29/EC and 2011/83/EU of the European Parliament and of the Council as regards better enforcement and modernisation of Union consumer protection rules, *OJ* 2019, L 328/7.

64 The metaphor goes back to medieval times when combatants were hidden by their armour. In these days they were required to name the horse and the rider when entering a tournament.

65 Federal Minister of Agriculture *Klöckner* reportedly welcomed the initiative, topagrar online of 04-12-2018, < https://www.topagrar.com/management-und-politik/news/eu-vorschlag-gegen-unfairen-handel-stoesst-auf-offene-ohren-9429384.html>, site last accessed 09-18-2019.

and not prompted immediate reactions neither by businesses nor by lawyers.[66] In substance, i.e. in respect of the rules for commercial conduct, the UTP Directive does not go beyond what is offered by German law already, be it in the guise of Contract, Unfair Competition or Competition law. As a consequence, the need for adaptation of German law appears very limited at a first glance. On the other hand, the combination of the various elements of the proposal – in particular the straightforward prohibitions combined with the need for administrative enforcement – may prove to be a string causing the German legislator to stumble anyhow.

Even though the European Commission has never elaborated on the structural and dogmatic layout of implementing provisions, it is clear that an enforcement based on private initiative and civil lawsuits is insufficient. It comes as no surprise that the Commission quite openly encourages the expansion of the competencies of competition authorities.[67] Fortunately, during the last amendment of the Act against Restraints of Competition an expansion of the competencies of the Federal Cartel Office has already been discussed. On the basis of sec. 32e(5) ARC the Federal Cartel Office may conduct a sector enquiry where it has reasonable grounds to suspect substantial, permanent or repeated infringements of consumer protection law provisions which, due to their nature or scale, harm the interests of a large number of consumers. A further expansion has already been prepared by the Federal Ministry of the Economy by mandating expert studies in preparation of the upcoming 10th amendment to the Act against Restraints of Competition that were published in late August and early September 2018.[68] An implementation within the Act against Restraints of Competition has become less self-evident by the last changes that came into the UTP Directive, in particular the overly detailed drafting of the prohibitions and the rules on the personal scope of application.

66 Most reactions were generally supportive, but urging modifications to the setup of the prohibitions, in particular the Resolution of the Bundesrat, position taken on June 8, BR-Drs. 116/18; or the position taken by the Centrum für Europäische Politik, cepAnalyse no. 21/2018, p. 4.

67 Explanatory memorandum, p. 11, 14.

68 On administrative enforcement of consumer law *Podszun/Busch/Henning-Bodewig*, Behördliche Durchsetzung des Verbraucherrechts?, <https://www.bmwi.de/Redaktion/DE/Publikationen/Studien/behoerdliche-durchsetzung-des-verbraucherrechts.pdf?__blob=publicationFile&v=10>, site last accessed on 09–18–2019; on the modernisation of control of unilateral conduct of dominant undertakings *Schweitzer/Haucap/Kerber/Welker*, Modernisierung der Missbrauchsaufsicht für marktmächtige Unternehmen, <https://www.bmwi.de/Redaktion/DE/Publikationen/Wirtschaft/modernisierung-der-missbrauchsaufsicht-fuer-marktmaechtige-unternehmen.pdf?__blob=publicationFile&v=15>, site last accessed on 09–18–2019.

3.3. SOME OBSERVATIONS

So while there seems to be no fundamental concern about the prohibitions required by the UTP Directive in Germany, the UTP Directive deserves some observations with regard to its substance.

3.3.1. Does a prohibition of unfair trading practices really come as a "free lunch"?

The first, but certainly not the least important, point of criticism relates to the presentation of the UTP Directive and its economic consequences by the Commission. The idiom "there is no free lunch" adequately describes the underlying problem. According to the Commission unfair trading practices cause damages to the amount of 4.4 bn EUR per year.[69] On the other hand the Commission states that the regulation of unfair trading practices comes at no extra costs for consumers.[70]

This is another point where our initial analysis of the structure of the relevant markets should make us skeptical. While the Commission's empirical assumption that the bargaining power is spread very unevenly along the food supply chain[71] certainly has its merits we should take just as seriously that we do find a highly competitive retail market all over the EU Member States. Even though the food product retail market has already reached a very high degree of concentration[72] market structure has by no means petrified. To the contrary, there is cut-throat competition[73] and with very low profit margins[74] there is still a tendency towards further concentration.[75] This evidence makes it very likely that the economic benefits gained by retailers with relative market power to the detriment of their dependent suppliers will be passed on to consumers. Consequently, the Commission's argument that a partial harmonization of

69 Explanatory memorandum, p. 10.

70 Explanatory memorandum, p. 10.

71 Explanatory memorandum, p. 2.

72 Explanatory memorandum, p. 2.

73 Observers may remember that US retailer Wal*Mart was entering the German market in the end-1990s with a very aggressive pricing policy. Following a price war based on sales under costs that even made it to the highest German competition court, Federal Supreme Court, Federal Supreme Court, 11–12–2002, KVR 5/02 – Wal*Mart, WRP 2003, 770, Wal*Mart left the German market in 2006 and reportedly lost US$ 1 bn during this endeavor, Frankfurter Allgemeine, Wal-Mart verlässt Deutschland, 07–28–2006, <www.faz.net/aktuell/wirtschaft/unternehmen/einzelhandel-wal-mart-verlaesst-deutschland-1356926.html>, site last accessed 09–18–2019.

74 For the German market the Monopoly Commission in 2010/11 found earnings before income tax (EBIT) of less than 1–3%, Monopoly Commission, Main Report 2010/11, BT-Drs. 17/10365, p. 347.

75 As the spectacular takeover of Tengelmann by Edeka in 2017 on the basis of a ministerial permission pursuant to sec. 42 ARC shows.

unfair trading practices is expected to have limited effect on consumers[76] is not very convincing. In the same vein the BEUC, a major consumer rights NGO, has pleaded that the AGRI commission's resolution be tabled to the plenary of the European Parliament. BEUC fears that due to the "amendments introduced by the AGRI committee, there is a serious risk that consumers could be prevented from wider choices and better prices".[77]

It is the fundamental task of any legislator to take normative elements into account when deciding who should benefit economically from certain performances. It may and even should be a good decision to let the farmers enjoy the benefits of their work instead of saving the consumers' pennies. However, a clear stance of the European legislator seems more credible than a questionable promise that a decision in favour of the farmers should come at no extra costs for consumers.

3.3.2. *Horizontal or sectoral approach?*

The sectoral approach the Commission has chosen is arbitrary in scope and will prove to be difficult to handle. The definition of agricultural and food products in Art. 2 let. d UTPD in combination with an annex is extremely wide, but as a consequence subjects contractual relationships to the particular prohibitions of the UTP Directive, for which the structural imperfections of the markets as described above just do not exist.

On the other hand market imperfections may lead to the possibility of unfair trading practices also beyond the lines of the agricultural and food supply chain. Industrial relationships between car producers and suppliers of components spring to mind. A relative dominance of the buyer is just as obvious as in cases of the supply of food products.

Looking at the jurisdiction cited by the UTP Directive (Art. 42(2) TFEU) one is tempted to assume that the scope *ratione materiae* has been kept narrow not even as a consequence of the relationship between the European Union and the Member States and to avoid opposition from the Member States, but that the UTP Directive has been limited to agricultural products rather as a consequence of the internal competencies, powers and political interests within the Commission – the core provisions of the UTP Directive are not Competition law by their nature.

76 Explanatory memorandum, p. 10 f.

77 BEUC, Letter to the MEPs of 10–19–2018 Re: Unfair Trading Practices – AGRI Committee report harms consumers: Please vote to reject request to enter trialogue negotiations, <https://www.beuc.eu/publications/beuc-x-2018-091_unfair_trading_practices-agri_committee.pdf>, site last accessed on 09–18–2019.

3.3.3. *Ratio: sufficient consideration of economic dependence by turnover relation requirement?*

With respect to the purpose of the UTP Directive to compensate for the relative imbalance of bargaining power any limitation of its scope of application recurring to absolute (turnover) figures is bound to fall short.[78] The compromise found in Art. 1(2) UTPD that makes use of the difference of absolute turnover figures not only puts on display poor legislative technique, but also fails to achieve its self-set goals. The European legislator assumes that relative market power can be estimated appropriately when looking at the annual turnovers of the market participants (rec. 14 s. 2 UTPD). The legislator admits that this is but a guess, but stressed that market participants were put in a position to foresee their respective rights and duties under the UTP Directive (rec. 14 s. 3 UTPD).

However, it is hard to understand why the pertinent turnover figures should support any – irrebuttable(!) – assumption of limited bargaining power in the first place. Pursuant to Art. 1(2) let. c UTPD a supplier with an annual turnover of 49m EUR would have to be protected against a buyer with an annual turnover of 51m EUR. The promised advantage in terms of legal certainty will be brought to bear only in favour of powerful buyers which are told exactly which suppliers to avoid in order not to be subject to the prohibitions of the UTP Directive.

3.3.4. *Substantive gaps in the proposal*

In the course of the legislative procedure little effort was made to create a structurally solid foundation of this extended control. One important aspect has been identified in rec. 16 s. 2 UTPD: in order to reduce the risk of limiting of the use of fair and efficiency-creating agreements

> "it is appropriate to distinguish between practices that are provided for in clear and unambiguous terms in supply agreements or in subsequent agreements between parties and practices that occur after the transaction has started without having been agreed beforehand, [...]".

Unfortunately, the binding part of the UTP Directive as laid down in Art. 3 UTPD does not mirror this very clear and convincing approach. The efficiency argument supporting the theory of harm can be made to the detriment of all

78 It deserves mentioning that the Federal Supreme Court found a decision of the Federal Cartel Office flawed because the Federal Cartel Office had assessed an undertaking to be a small or medium-sized enterprise solely on the basis of its annual turnover, but had failed to take into consideration the market conditions. Whether or not an undertaking is small or medium-sized has to be assessed on a case-by-case analysis with due consideration of the particular market, the undertaking's relations to competitors in respect of customers and in particular cases also the vertical relationship to customers with countervailing market power, Federal Supreme Court, 09-24-2002, KVR 8/01 – Adaptation of conditions, WRP 2002, 1436, 1439.

unclear or ambiguous terms, not only to the particular terms laid down in Art. 3(2) UTPD.

Moreover, the UTP Directive does not explain why contractual rights agreed upon in clear and unambiguous ways should be prohibited under Art. 3(1) UTPD. The explanation that certain trading practices are "unfair by their very nature", rec. 16 s. 3 UTPD, is not convincing. This is obvious for payment terms (let. a). Agreements on payment terms are a well-proven instrument to set an incentive to invest and to test new markets. Even the legislator's own argument – the creation of efficiencies – justifies the use of longer payment terms as the specific costs of the term can easily be calculated. The same holds true for the fact pattern relating to the shift of risk (let. d). Why should the parties not agree to shift any risk? This may be a rational and efficiency-enhancing choice.

The only issue justifying to overstep the lines set by the parties acting in exercise of their contractual autonomy is the factual lack of this autonomy. In many instances the supplier will bite the bullet and sign a clear and unambiguous contract only due to the economic pressure exercised by the buyer. This is why the line of argument of exploitative abuses as unilateral conduct needs to be continued even if the exercise of power is directed at contractual stipulations. The provisions in Art. 3(1) UTPD do not make it very clear that the crucial element justifying a special form of control is the unilateral exercise of undue pressure. Such pressure may materialize either before the conclusion of a contract[79] and often find its results in unfair contract clauses or during the performance of a contract.

3.3.5. *Public enforcement of Contract law?*

The last observation is made from a rather methodological perspective. All of the unfair trading practices addressed by the UTP Directive arise out of contractual relationships. While it is very understandable that the Commission as a consequence of the fear factor – which has been correctly identified as standing in the way of the enforcement of contractual rights in many instances – sees a need to include other enforcement mechanisms, the compulsory use of state authorities should make our alarms ring.

There is a long-standing and good tradition of separation of Contract law and administrative requirements at least in Civil law jurisdictions and there is no need to do away with this separation altogether. When battling the fear factor the baby shouldn't be thrown out with the bath water. The German example shows that in particular the control of GTC can work quite well without state administrations. The UTP Directive's calling for an enforcement authority is

79 Resolution of the Bundesrat, position taken on June 8, 2018, BR-Drs. 116/18, para. 11; AGRI committee of 10-10-2018, Draft European Parliament Legislative Resolution, Amendments 14, 88, A8-0309/2018.

clearly adapted to the almost simultaneous revision of the CPC Regulation[80] that also increases state involvement in Consumer law enforcement and the amendments proposed in the "New deal for consumers", calling for penalties for infringements of the UCP Directive, the Consumer Rights Directive and the Unfair Terms Directive.[81] Their leitmotiv is the strong reliance on state control of and intervention into markets. Yet, it is highly doubtful whether the rollback of liberalization initially triggered by the European Union itself in the 1980s and 90s is either adequate or desirable.

Where the European Commission acts as an enforcement authority, in particular with regard to the Union's common rules on competition in Arts. 101 ff. TFEU, it does so very successfully, but also based on a more than adequate endowment, both in terms of finances and of workforce. The European legislator's confidence in the performance of enforcement authorities may be based on this role model. Yet, it appears somewhat over-optimistic. The creation of new gate keepers and possibly a panoply of agencies with less than transparent jurisdictions may do more harm to market integration and competition than it may do good to the farmers.

Maybe, it would make more sense to address some of the market imperfections instead: the crucial problem of producers of agricultural and food products is that the retailers are the gatekeepers with regard to the shelf space as the bottleneck in the food supply chain. If it were made easier for agricultural producers, i.e. farmers, to market their products directly to the consumers[82], this would not only raise awareness of consumers for the origin and value of the produce and the way it comes into existence and ultimately finds its way onto their lunch and dinner tables ("farm to fork", cf. rec. 5 s. 2 UTPD)[83], but also contribute to less traffic, pollution and emission of dangerous chemicals. Phytosanitarian rules effectively hindering farmers from directly selling dairy or meat products to consumers just as much as administrative obstacles and bureaucratic efforts required to directly sell fresh agricultural produce from the farm should be revised. Less or better regulation might prove a better way to help farmers than more regulation.

---

80 Regulation (EU) 2017/2394 of the European Parliament and of the Council of 12 December 2017 on cooperation between national authorities responsible for the enforcement of consumer protection laws and repealing Regulation (EC) No 2006/2004, OJ 2017, L 345/1.

81 Art. 1(5), 2(10), 3 Proposal for a Directive of the European Parliament and of the Council amending Council Directive 93/13/EEC of 5 April 1993, Directive 98/6/EC of the European Parliament and of the Council, Directive 2005/29/EC of the European Parliament and of the Council and Directive 2011/83/EU of the European Parliament and of the Council as regards better enforcement and modernisation of EU consumer protection rules, COM (2018) 185 final.

82 European Economic and Social Committee, Improving the food supply chain, opinion given by Peter Schmidt as rapporteur on 09-19-2018, NAT/734, para. 5.8.

83 Council conclusions, Healthy Nutrition for Children: The Healthy Future of Europe, OJ 2018, C 232/1, para. 36 let. m.

CHAPTER 6
FRENCH REGULATORY EXPERIENCES WITH THE CONTROL OF UTPS

Denis Voinot
Professor University of Lille
René Demogue Research Team – CRD&P

1. INTRODUCTION

Will the Directive (EU) 2019/633 of the European Parliament and of the Council on unfair trading practices in business-to-business relationships in the agricultural and food supply chain[1] invite the French public authorities to reconsider the current French legal framework[2] to tackle unfair trading practices ("UTPs")?[3] There is no clear answer.

On the one hand, reading the Directive, it seems that the forthcoming EU legal framework will not provoke another "revolution". Firstly, it can be observed that the EU directive has a more narrow scope than the French regime, since the latter is not limited to the food sector. Secondly, it seems that the current French regime is already in compliance with the directive, because it consists of general rules, such as the criterion of "*significant imbalance*"[4], which could probably be used to tackle the UTPs specifically addressed in the Directive.

On the other hand, the EU directive could perhaps constitute an opportunity to clarify the French regime torn between competition law and contract law, whose legal nature is not so clear and which is difficult to understand without regard to the economic and legal context (1.). Any clarification of the current French UTP regime should take into account the narrow relation between UTPs and trade negotiations (2.), as well as the specific role of the *Commission for the Examination of Commercial Practices* (CEPC) within the French UTP regime (3.)

1 *OJ* L 111, 25.4.2019, p. 59–72.
2 A. Fortunato, *Clauses et pratiques restrictives de concurrence*, thèse Lille 2, 2016.
3 See. A. Fortunato, «Proposition de directive européenne sur les pratiques commerciales déloyales entre professionnels: conséquences pour le droit français», *AJ Contrat*, May 2018, n°5, p. 224.
4 Article L. 442-6, I, 2° Commercial code; see *infra*.

2. ECONOMIC AND LEGAL CONTEXT

France has a complex legal framework to tackle UTPs, which cannot be understood without a short description of the specificity of the economic and legal context.

Economic context. Economically, it is essential to consider the important place of the retailers in food and non-food supply chains. In general, retailers such as Carrefour, Auchan, Leclerc, etc. have an important power to negotiate annually with their suppliers and to eventually purchase products at a certain price. This negotiation power is ensured by the recourse to central purchasing departments. Not all suppliers have equal bargaining power vis-à-vis these retailers. Trade negotiations often lead to troubles between stakeholders about fair benefits allocation[5] and more specifically to troubles between producers and suppliers on one hand and retailers (often engaging in UTPs) on the other.

Legal context. Facing this economic context, French public authorities have developed many rules to tackle UTPs. Recently, the reform of general contract law has made it possible to punish economic duress and dependence (Article 1143 Civil code) and also to avoid unfair non-negotiable terms in standard-form contracts (Article 1171 Civil code). Book 4 of the Commercial code – pricing freedom and competition – consists of rules to punish classical anti-competitive practices like concerted actions (Article L. 420–1 Commercial code) or abuse of a dominant position (Article L. 420–2 Commercial code).

Yet, the main B2B legal framework tackling UTPs can be found in Title 4 of this code, entitled "Transparency, restrictive competitive practices and other prohibited practices" and specifically prohibiting many UTPs. Until 2019, the Commercial Code did not use the expression "unfair commercial practices" *tel quel*. It is safe to say that Title 4 pursues "predominantly an objective different from that of protecting competition on the market"[6], although this does not mean that there is no consideration at all for the market.[7] The main purpose of Title 4 is to ensure a better balance in trade relations between producers and suppliers on the one hand and retailers on the other.[8] Since the entry into force of the Ordinance of 24 April 2019 reforming Title IV of the Commercial Code, a new chapter entitled "Unfair business-to-business commercial practices" was introduced which modernises and simplifies the rules tackling UTPs.

5 See Le Monde – 20 June 2018 – «La grande distribution fait son beurre sur le dos des agriculteurs».

6 Council Regulation (EC) No 1/2003 of 16 December 2002 on the implementation of the rules on competition laid down in Articles 81 and 82 of the Treaty, point (9).

7 See Cour de Cassation, July 8, 2008, 07–16761. For the Court the economic ministry lawsuit of the Article L. 442–6, III of the commercial code is "an autonomous action to protect the market and competition".

8 See Constitutional Council Decision n° 2018–749 QPC, November 30, 2018. Concerning the constitutionality of Article L. 442–6 Commercial Code, the Council concluded "the Parliament sought to aim balance relationships between trade partners"

3. UTPS AND TRADE NEGOTIATION

Trade negotiation. Apart from this, it is essential to point out that there is an important link between recurrent trade negotiations and the regulation of UTPs in Title 4 of the Commercial Code. The expression "trade negotiation" is enshrined in various Articles of Title IV of Book IV of the Commercial Code.[9] Trade negotiations between suppliers and retailers are essentially tariff negotiations and typically lead to purchase contracts for products at a certain price. The meaning of tariff negotiations is that the price is being negotiated by the contracting parties from one year to the next. But in the meantime many contractual arrangements, which may have financial implications for the parties, may be added.

These annual tariff negotiations are subject to a special and long-standing attention from the French public authorities. In this regard, the French transparency requirement is quintessential. For the parties, transparency means communication of general terms of sale to purchasers (Article L. 441-1 Commercial code), mandatory terms in invoices (Article L. 441-9 Commercial code) and mandatory annual agreement (Article L. 441-3 Commercial code). The deal must be formalised and must include certain mandatory terms (price rebates, initial price before negotiation, final negotiate price, etc.). The aim of these rules is to allow the administration to verify that the free negotiability of the price was effective and did not result from UTPs.

Unfair Trading Practices. The Commercial code consists of two categories of UTPs. First of all, there is a list of automatically null and void contract terms. For instance, any person engaged in production, distribution or service activities must not benefit from retroactive discounts, rebates or commercial cooperation agreements, or automatically more favourable conditions granted to competing companies by the contracting partner.

Secondly, there is a list of 3 practices, according to which the perpetrator may be held personally liable (Article L. 442-1 Commercial code; *ex* L. 442-6). The first prohibited practice is to obtain or attempt to obtain from the other party an advantage that does not correspond to any consideration or is manifestly disproportionate to the value of the consideration granted (Article L. 442-1, I, 1° Commercial code).[10] Another prohibited practice is the sudden termination

9 D. Voinot, "La négociation des contrats de la grande distribution", *AC Contrats d'affaires, Concurrence, Distribution*, 2016/7, p.316.

10 G. Chantepie, «Le déséquilibre significatif au miroir de la Cour de cassation», AJCA 2015, p. 218; J.-L. Fourgoux, J. Riffault-Silk, M. Chagny, D. Tricot et C. Pecnard, «Approches plurielles du déséquilibre significatif», *Concurrences* n° 2-2011. – M. Béhar-Touchais, Que penser de l›introduction d›une protection contre les clauses abusives dans le Code de commerce?: *RDC* 2009-3, p. 1258; De la sanction du déséquilibre significatif dans les contrats conclus notamment avec la grande distribution: Rev. Lamy concurrence 2008, n° 17, p. 45. – M. Chagny, Une (r)évolution du droit français de la concurrence? À propos de la loi LME du 4 août 2008: JCP G 2008, I, 196. – M. Cousin, La négociabilité des tarifs et des conditions

of an established commercial relationship (Article L. 442–1, I, 3° Commercial code).

Yet, the most well-known prohibited practice pertains to subjecting, or attempting to subject, the other party to obligations that create a "*significant imbalance*" in the rights and obligations of the parties (Article L. 442–1, I, 3° Commercial code)[11] – introduced originally in 2008.[12] The same criterion of "significant imbalance" appears in the Consumer code (Article L. 212–1) and in the Civil code (Article 1171) and now also in *Directive (EU) 2019/633 on unfair business-to-business trading practices in the agricultural and food supply chain.*[13] But there is an important difference between the Civil and Consumer codes on the one hand and the Commercial code on the other hand. In both Civil and Consumer laws, the evaluation of the unfair nature of terms does not involve the definition of the main purpose of the contract nor the adequacy of the price. Yet, there is no similar carve-out in the Commercial law's control system. The generality of the prohibition of "*significant imbalance*" in the Commercial code was unsuccessfully contested by retailers as non-constitutional in 2011.[14] Afterwards, in the *Le Galec* case, the French Court of Cassation held that the provisions of paragraph 2 of paragraph I of Article L. 442–6 (now L. 442–1)

de vente après la LME: quels garde-fous?: JCP E 2008, 2288. – J.-L. Fourgoux, Concurrence: la loi du 4 août 2008 de modernisation de l'économie, une révolution prometteuse mais ténébreuse: Gaz. Pal. 2008, 2, doctr. p. 2887. – D. Ferrier et D. Ferré, La réforme des pratiques commerciales (loi n° 2008–776 du 4 août 2008): D. 2008, p. 2234. – C. Lucas de Leyssac et M. Chagny, Le droit des contrats, instruments d'une forme nouvelle de régulation économique?: RDC 2009–3, p. 1268. – M. Malaurie-Vignal, Le nouvel article L. 442–6 du Code de commerce apporte-t-il de nouvelles limites à la négociation contractuelle?: Contrats, conc. consom. 2008, chron. 5. – R. Saint-Esteben, L'introduction par la loi LME d'une protection des professionnels à l'égard des clauses abusives: un faux ami du droit de la consommation: RDC 2009–3, p. 1275.

11 G. Chantepie, Le déséquilibre significatif au miroir de la Cour de cassation, AJCA 2015, p. 218; J.-L. Fourgoux, J. Riffault-Silk, M. Chagny, D. Tricot et C. Pecnard, Approches plurielles du déséquilibre significatif: Concurrences n° 2–2011. – M. Béhar-Touchais, Que penser de l'introduction d'une protection contre les clauses abusives dans le Code de commerce?: RDC 2009–3, p. 1258; De la sanction du déséquilibre significatif dans les contrats conclus notamment avec la grande distribution: Rev. Lamy concurrence 2008, n° 17, p. 45. – M. Chagny, Une (r)évolution du droit français de la concurrence? À propos de la loi LME du 4 août 2008: JCP G 2008, I, 196. – M. Cousin, La négociabilité des tarifs et des conditions de vente après la LME: quels garde-fous?: JCP E 2008, 2288. – J.-L. Fourgoux, Concurrence: la loi du 4 août 2008 de modernisation de l'économie, une révolution prometteuse mais ténébreuse: Gaz. Pal. 2008, 2, doctr. p. 2887. – D. Ferrier et D. Ferré, La réforme des pratiques commerciales (loi n° 2008–776 du 4 août 2008): D. 2008, p. 2234. – C. Lucas de Leyssac et M. Chagny, Le droit des contrats, instruments d'une forme nouvelle de régulation économique?: RDC 2009–3, p. 1268. – M. Malaurie-Vignal, Le nouvel article L. 442–6 du Code de commerce apporte-t-il de nouvelles limites à la négociation contractuelle?: Contrats, conc. consom. 2008, chron. 5. – R. Saint-Esteben, L'introduction par la loi LME d'une protection des professionnels à l'égard des clauses abusives: un faux ami du droit de la consommation: RDC 2009–3, p. 1275.

12 Modernization of the Economy on August 4, 2008.

13 Point 1.

14 See Constitutional Council Decision n° 2010–85 QPC January 13, 2011.

of the Commercial Code do not exclude that "*significant imbalance may result from an inappropriateness of the price to the good sold*" and thus authorise "*a judicial review of the price, provided that it does not result from free negotiation and characterises a significant imbalance in the rights and obligations of the parties*". To understand this quite daring solution, it is really important to point out the complex economic reality of recurrent trade negotiations, which lead not only to an agreed price but to a contractual set of rights and obligations in which prices are often customised by suppliers and to which the most varied rebates are applied. In addition to that, the price of ancillary services provided by the distributor to its suppliers and the numerous contractual requirements for the implementation of the contract (service rate clause, end-of-year rebate clause, return clause of goods damaged by consumers, etc.) may have multiple financial consequences. This is the reason why the judgment of the Court of cassation must be approved in a case where a procurement centre was accused of having imposed the payment of a year-end rebate without real return on a large number of suppliers. But retailers considered that such an interpretation could result in giving a new impact to Article L. 442–1, I, 2° (ex. L. 442–6, I, 2°) of the Commercial code. As a consequence, recently, the Constitutional Council re-examined the constitutionality of this rule and decided these "*impugned provisions allow the judge to rely on the price to characterise the existence of a significant imbalance in the obligations of the trading partners*". This does not mean that the judge has a general power to check the price in any circumstances, but it means that he has such power only when there has been no real negotiations between trade partners who have been reluctant to negotiate prices in accordance with the trade negotiation legal framework in the Commercial code (Article L. 441–1, L. 441–3 and L. 442–1 Commercial code). In other circumstances, i.e. when there has been no real trade negotiation, it shall be more difficult to bring the case to court to check the price.

4. SANCTIONS FOR UTPS IN TITLE VI OF THE COMMERCIAL CODE

The detection of UTPs by the *Commission for the Examination of Commercial Practices*.[15] An essential role in the French UTP regime is played by the *Commission for the Examination of Commercial Practices*[16] (CECP). It is a public authority composed of 24 members including 74% of retailers and suppliers. The CEPC has the task of giving opinions or making recommendations on various issues: commercial or advertising documents, including invoices and contracts covered by industrial and commercial confidentiality, and also

15 Article L. 440–1 commercial code.

16 Article L. 440–1 Commercial code; see. https://www.economie.gouv.fr/cepc

practices involving commercial relations between producers, suppliers and retailers. Importantly, the CEPC does not have the power to order or to punish perpetrators of UTPs. Although a wide range of authorities[17] (see *infra*) or persons can refer cases to the Commission, typically producers, suppliers or retailers make requests to the CEPC.

The success of the CEPC could be explained by a number of factors. First, recourse to the CEPC is relatively informal and free of charge and, on top of this, the anonymity of applicants is safeguarded. Secondly, as the opinions of the CEPC are published, they often do act as a source of inspiration or as a best practice for professionals. So, the Commission plays the role of a regular monitoring centre for commercial practices, invoices and contracts that are being referred to the Commission by producers, suppliers or retailers. Thirdly, each year the CEPC publishes a report that is submitted to the Government and the Parliament. It consists of a detailed analysis of the number and nature of violations of the provisions of Title 4 that have been punished by administrative or criminal sanctions as well as of civil decisions on transactions that engage the liability of their perpetrators.

Action by a person with legitimate interest. Any person who provides proof of legitimate interest can introduce a request before a court to obtain compensatory damages or nullity of terms. Proceedings can be brought before eight competent civil or commercial specialized district courts; appeal is possible before the Paris Court of Appeal only. Nevertheless, actually litigation will mainly depend on the status of the business relationship. It is easier to press charges when the business relationship has come to an end than when it is still ongoing. Moreover, Article L. 442-1, I°, 3° (ex. L. 442-6, I, 5°) of the Commercial code provides for personal liability of the perpetrator who is "*abruptly breaking off an established business relationship, even partially, without prior written notice commensurate with the duration of the business relationship and consistent with the minimum notice period determined by the multi-sector agreements in line with standard commercial practices*". This is certainly the most used rule of Title IV of the Commercial code. But when there is still an ongoing trade relationship, the "fear factor" (fear for commercial retaliation, etc.) represents an important barrier to take legal action against those who engage in UTPs.

Action by public authorities. A final crucial element of the French UTP regime is the possibility of public authorities (the Public Prosecutor's Office, the Minister responsible for Economic Affairs, and, in certain circumstances,

---

17 The minister responsible for economic affairs, the minister responsible for the economic sector concerned, the president of the Competition Authority, any legal entity, in particular professional associations or trade unions, approved consumer associations, boards of commerce or chambers of agriculture.

the President of the Competition Authority) to initiate legal proceedings before civil or commercial courts. A wide range of sanctions is of avail. So, during these proceedings, the Public Prosecutor's Office and the Minister responsible for Economic Affairs may ask the court to order any UTP to be ceased. They may also request a civil fine of up to 5 million euros; this fine may even be increased to three times the amount of the total sums unduly paid or may be proportionate to the benefits from the breach or 5% turnover realized in France. On top of these civil sanctions, the aforementioned public authorities may, for all the unfair practices, request a declaration of nullity of the illegal clauses or contracts. Moreover, they can claim compensation for the loss suffered and, if necessary, the recovery of the mistaken payments (Article L. 442–1, I, 3° Commercial Code). For instance, in the *Le Galec* case, the judge pronounced a fine of 2 million euros and 61 million euros for the mistaken payments to share between hundreds of suppliers and producers. It must also be noted that victims do not have to sue and sometimes they do not even know that public authorities have brought a claim in their place. This is possible because the French Court of Cassation has ruled that this action is of a special legal nature: it is "*an autonomous action to protect the market and competition*". In addition to that, it is also the only way to effectively address the "fear factor".

5. CONCLUSION

To conclude, while French law on unfair B2B commercial practices seems to comply with the new EU directive 2019/633, some questions remain. This is the case, for example, of the scope of the European directive, which is at least theoretically intended to apply to public actors. In this respect, French law is not very clear, particularly since the 2019 reform. The next steps (transposition of the Directive, law ratifying the Ordinance) will undoubtedly provide an opportunity to clarify certain obscure points.

CHAPTER 7

THE REGULATION OF UTPS IN THE FOOD SUPPLY CHAIN IN THE UNITED KINGDOM*

Mateja Durovic
Reader in Contract and Commercial Law, King's College London

1. INTRODUCTION

The adoption of the EU Directive on unfair trading practices in the agricultural and food supply chain has brought gross significant positive changes in the regulation of agricultural and food supply chains in the European Union. The United Kingdom was one of the EU Member States which has already before regulated this field, although in a more restrictive manner than the one provided by the Directive. During the last decade, the main legal instrument in the UK has been the Groceries Supply Code of Practice which has established a general fairness principle of commercial practices in the food supply chain.[1] The Groceries Supply Code of Practice ("GSCOP" or "Code") is a legal code that sets out the features of 'fair dealing' principle in cases when retailers purchase groceries products for re-sale. It is a government backed Code of practice which was adopted in 2009 and came into force in 2010. Its main function is to prohibit retailers' unfair commercial practices directed towards the suppliers.[2]

The principal reason behind the adoption of the Code was to sanction the previously existing and widely spread retailers' engagement in the unfair commercial practices which had been negatively affecting the suppliers. For example, these abuses were noticeable in cases when the retailers were pushing undue risk and unexpected costs onto the suppliers. Eventually, this led to the reduction of suppliers' incentive to invest and innovate, affecting negatively the entire market. The previously existing legal framework aimed to secure fairness

* Mateja.durovic@kcl.ac.uk.

1 Groceries Supply Code of Practice 2009, Available at: https://www.gov.uk/government/publications/groceries-supply-code-of-practice/groceries-supply-code-of-practice.

2 Paragraph 2 GSCOP.

of commercial practices at the UK market turned out to be ineffective and insufficient to protect adequately the suppliers, and the GSCOP was eventually designed to remedy these shortcomings and provide a high level of protection to the suppliers.[3] Accordingly, since the adoption of the GSCOP, it has been possible to observe a continuous improvement of protection of suppliers in food supply chains in the last years in the UK.[4]

2. DEVELOPMENT OF THE FOOD SUPPLY CHAIN FAIRNESS RULES

The groceries industry in the UK has been a comparative European example of an industry sector which has had a long history of supervision by the state authority in charge of securing competition and fairness at the market. Already in 2000, the Competition Commission (the predecessor of the current UK Competition and Markets Authority) carried out an investigation into the groceries sector which revealed two competition-distorting features: 'price-flexing' and unfair behavior towards the suppliers. These two practices were subsequently supposed to be regulated and limited through the adoption of the Supermarkets Code of Practice (SCOP).

The SCOP entered into force in 2000, but its vague terms made it difficult to tell whether the code has been breached.[5] Likewise, the SCOP was a sort of voluntary code which decreased its effects in practice. Furthermore, the SCOP failed to afford the adequate level of protection. There were instances where the excessive risks and costs were passed onto the grocery suppliers. In these cases, it was pointed out that the SCOP was not breached 'due to the fact that, in most cases the SCOP regulates a practice (e.g. requires that the retailer undertake the practice reasonably) rather than prohibiting it outright or because the SCOP does not sufficiently address a poor practice'.[6]

Unlike the SCOP, the GSCOP clearly clarifies and addresses retailer practices that transfer excessive risk and prohibits practices where necessary, rather than regulating that they are undertaken reasonably.[7] The UK model of regulation of fairness of unfair trade practices in the food supply chain has also influenced

3 Competition Commission Report, 'The Supply of Groceries in the UK, Market Investigation' (2008) (CC Report, 2008 Report), para [3], page 6.

4 Groceries Code Adjudicator, *Annual Report and Accounts 1 April 2017 – 31 March 2018,* June 2018, p.5. available at: https://assets.publishing.service.gov.uk/government/uploads/system/uploads/attachment_data/file/718541/GCA_Annual_Report_and_Accounts_2017-18_web_accessible_version.pdf.

5 Department for Business Innovation & Skills, 'Groceries Code Adjudicator. Impact Assessment.' May 2013 (BIS Impact Assessment), para [37], page 14.

6 BIS Impact Statement, [40], 15.

7 BIS Impact Assessment, [54], 17.

development in other common law jurisdictions as it was the case with Australia.[8]

3. THE SCOPE OF APPLICATION OF THE GSCOP

The main goal of the GSCOP is to guarantee certain level of fairness in the supply chain and protect suppliers. This has been defined by a far reaching and general paragraph 2 of the GSCOP which imposes a universal principle of fairness. All other provisions of the Code are to be read in line with this general fairness duty. The present fairness obligation is exclusively a one-way duty, imposed only on the retailers while acting with their suppliers. This is because the main goal of the GSCOP is to protect small and medium enterprises (SMEs) as a weaker party in contractual relationship while acting as direct suppliers of the large enterprises which are much more powerful than the SMEs.

The application of the Code is always mandatory (unlike its predecessor SCOP). Its application can never be limited or excluded in any manner. The GSCOP is binding for all of the so called 'Designated Retailers' under the Code. The notion Designated Retailers encompasses any retailer with an annual turnover exceeding £1bn with respect to the retail supply of Groceries in the United Kingdom, and which is designated in writing by the Competition and Markets Authority. As it stands, ten companies in total fulfil this condition and are thus covered by the Code. These are all major supermarkets operating on the UK Market: Asda, Co-op, M&S, Morrison's, Sainsbury's, Tesco, Waitrose, Aldi, Iceland and Lidl UK.

These big retailers are specifically bound by the GSCOP because they control a significant portion of the market, with the 'Big Five' in 2000 or 'Big Four' now, following the Safeway and Morrison's merger, control 90% of the one-stop shopping market[9], and they 'pay, on average, between 4 and 6 percent less than the mean' price for their groceries'.[10] It is such a prominent market position that, in the eyes of the former Competition Commission, justifies limiting the application of the GSCOP to the largest retailers as it was pointed out that there were very few cases of unfair commercial practices in practices which involved a grocery retailer with an annual turnover of less than £1 billion.[11] On the other

8 C. Beaton-Wells and J. Paul-Taylor, Codifying Supermarket-Supplier Relations A Report on Australia's Food and Grocery Code of Conduct, 2017, Vii., available at https://law.unimelb.edu.au/__data/assets/pdf_file/0006/2463135/Deidentified-draft-Code-Report-with-chapter-breaks_LATEST_010917.pdf.

9 Paul W. Dobson, 'Exploiting Buyer Power: Lessons From the British Grocery Trade' (2005) 72(2) Antitrust Law Journal 529, 541.

10 CC Report 2008, [5.22], 88.

11 CC Report 2008, [11.411], 256.

side of the suppliers' chain, there are more than ten thousands suppliers which are being protected by the Code.

It could be argued that such an approach preserves the 'balance' between 'properly governing the industry' and 'avoiding over-regulation.'[12] It seems that this approach is aimed to preserve the cornerstone of any commercial relationship in a market economy that is freedom of contract, intervening only when the contractual terms are not actually negotiated because of retailers' buyer power.[13] In essence, the Competition Commission found that '*all* large grocery retailers, wholesalers and buying groups have buyer power in relation to at least some of their suppliers'[14], and that effectively it is the suppliers that are weaker parties in that particular relationship.

The scope of GSCOP covers food (other than that sold for consumption in the store), pet food, drinks (alcoholic and non-alcoholic, other than that sold for consumption in the store), cleaning products, toiletries and household goods. Contrary to this, from its application are excluded petrol, clothing, DIY products, financial services, pharmaceuticals, newspapers, magazines, greetings cards, CDs, DVDs, videos and audio tapes, toys, plants, flowers, perfumes, cosmetics, electrical appliances, kitchen hardware, gardening equipment, books, tobacco and tobacco products.

It is important to note that the protection offered by the GSCOP applies exclusively to the direct supply relationships. Contrary to this, the indirect supply relationships are not covered, which is something that substantially limits application, as it excludes a number of entities or persons requiring protection.

4. PROHIBITED PRACTICES BY THE GSCOP

Some of the practices which are prohibited include diverse forms of practices which resemble the unfair contract terms prohibited in consumer contracts prohibited by applicable mandatory consumer legislation, whose aim is similarly to protect the weaker party.[15] This is, for example, the case with the GSCOP prohibiting any retrospective changes to terms of supply.[16]

As to the particular provisions contained in the code, the overarching duty of fair dealing of paragraph 2 of the Code was included to facilitate interpretation and dispute resolution (by setting a standard to which reference can be made)[17], as well as to strike a balance between the need to curtail the unreasonable

12 BIS Impact Assessment, [54], 18.
13 EU Green Paper, 6.
14 CC 2008 Report, [9.82], 172 (emphasis added)
15 Part 2 of UK Consumer Rights Act 2015,
16 Paragraph 3(1) GSCOP.
17 CC Report, 2008, [11.314], 238.

behavior by the retailers with the need for commercial flexibility, which a general duty of fair dealing appears to strike.[18]

The requirement that supply agreements be made in writing, originates from the fact that the Competition Commission found that many details or sometimes entire contracts would be made orally, which 'may make it more difficult to establish whether terms of supply have been changed retrospectively'.[19] The scope of the Code can be explained by reference to the market structure and the market characteristics as viewed by the Competition Authorities, not by citing a substantive requirement of fairness or eliminating unfair contractual practices.

Moreover, practices such as delay in payments are also prohibited. Accordingly, the retailer has always to pay a supplier for the delivered groceries in line with what has been agreed by the contract, and, in any case, at latest within a reasonable time after the date of the Supplier's invoice.[20] Similarly, requirement of any payment for shrinkage is not allowed. The Code prohibits any kind of provision under which the supplier would make payments to the retailer in the name of compensation for the shrinkage.[21] In addition to this, a number of practices connected with the promotion of products which might enable the retailer to abuse its bargaining position over the supplier are prohibited. Accordingly, a retailer is not allowed to request from the supplier predominantly to fund the costs of any promotion.[22]

5. SUPPLIER AS THE ONLY PROTECTED PARTY

The question is why it is exclusively the suppliers that are protected by the Groceries Supply Code of Practice. The short answer is because the suppliers are weaker than the retailers, as retailers possess 'buyer power'. Buyer power is defined as: 'a form of market power that a grocery retailer may have with respect to its suppliers that allows the grocery retailer to extract better terms from its suppliers than would otherwise be the case'.[23] Buyer power allows the retailer to 'obtain a better deal from its suppliers in terms of prices, product quality or purchasing terms… A supplier is likely to earn a smaller profit margin on goods sold to a grocery retailer with buyer power than those sold to grocery retailers that do not have buyer power'.[24]

In a nutshell, the possession of buyer power over the suppliers 'allows retailers to impose excessive risks and unexpected costs on suppliers, which

18 *Ibid*, [11.416], 257.
19 CC Report, [11.328], 240.
20 Paragraph 5 GSCOP.
21 Paragraph 7 GSCOP.
22 Paragraph 13(1) GSCOP.
23 CC Report 2008, 155.
24 CC Report 2008, [9.2], 156.

reduces suppliers' incentive or ability to invest and innovate. This could lead to reduced capacity, reduced product quality and fewer new product offerings, and ultimately, to a detriment to consumers.'[25] The notion of buyer power seems to be essentially focused on discrepancy between the relative economic dependency of suppliers and retailers on each other. On that view, buyer power arises from the ability to 'credibly threaten to impose a "long-term opportunity cost"' which, if carried out, would 'be significantly disproportionate to any resulting long-term opportunity cost to itself'.[26]

To illustrate, if Tesco bumps product X off the shelf it could lose 1% profits (especially so, given that there is a cohort of grocery suppliers eager to provide substitutes to product X) whereas, X's producer stands to lose 10% or 50% of their profits. The position of the retailer vis-à-vis a branded goods supplier allows the retailer to pose a 'twofold' threat as it can undermine the supplier's branded products. For example this can be done by placing them in less well-located shelf positions, raising their retail prices, or even substituting them for its own-label products (which can be given the appearance of offering better value to consumers).[27]

It is hard to dispute that the buyer's power in that sense introduces a significant imbalance between the parties which is reflected in contract terms forcing the supplier to compensate the retailer for shrinkage, non-attributable (to the supplier) wastage, share promotion costs for wrong prognostics, delay payments or retrospectively change the terms to deduct from invoices. The question then becomes: what are the origins of the buyer power? There are four main elements that can be identified: market structure, nature of the industry, role of the retailers vis-à-vis the suppliers, and the contractual disparity of power.

The increasing consolidation of retailers[28] creates a situation of 'significantly different levels of bargaining power and economic imbalances in individual trade relations between the actors in the chain'.[29] This is contrasted with the 'supply-side' where there are large numbers of suppliers (from manufacturers through primary producers, fresh food wholesalers, such as packers and processors to multinationals). There are approximately 311,000 farm holdings, 3,600 fresh food intermediaries and 6,600 food and drink manufacturers in the UK.[30]

When the grocery-retail market becomes an oligopoly there are several adverse outcomes for the suppliers: firstly, it means that there is a very large

25 CC Report 2008, [9.5], 157.

26 Dobson, 533.

27 Ibid., 539.

28 Ibid., 544.

29 European Commission, 'Communication From the Commission To The European Parliament, The Council, The European Economic And Social Committee And The Committee of Regions. Tackling Unfair Practices in the Business-to-Business Food Supply Chain' (2014) Com(2014) 472, 2.

30 BIS Impact Assessment, [14], 10.

number of suppliers of varying size competing against each other for limited shelf-space at the retailers' shops; secondly, there are few alternative retailers that could take an equivalent volume of product from the supplier, and it is likely that other retailers will have settled supplier contracts and allocated shelf-space, which means that it is immensely difficult for suppliers to secure alternative outlets if they are de-listed by one retailer, which gives the large retailer a very effective weapon.[31] Thus market consolidation amongst the retailers reduces the bargaining power of grocery producers, but also intermediaries.[32]

In the future, with the proposed acquisition of Asda by Sainsbury, the consolidation among the large grocery retailers will only progress, with Tesco and Asda/Sainsbury controlling 60% of the market, which means that the bargaining position of UK Grocery Suppliers will only deteriorate. This means that a more comprehensive protection is needed. Already from the Grocery Code Adjudicator's investigation into Tesco in 2016 and the recently announced investigation of Co-op shows that supermarkets continue to breach the GSCOP, which could hint that reform is badly needed.

Grocery producers must 'make investments in an uncertain commercial environment'[33], deciding on whether to invest and innovate or not based on predictions as to the future performance. When the large retailers 'transfer excessive risks or unexpected costs to their suppliers through practices involving retrospective adjustments to supply agreements or giving rise to moral hazard on the part of the grocery retailer, this is likely to lessen suppliers' incentives to invest in new capacity, products and production processes'.[34] The position is made even worse, by the fact that (typically) producers do not have a lot of spare resources to invest as they do not receive a "fair share" of the final retail price. In 2012, from a £1.18 retail price for 4 pints (2.3 litres) of semi-skimmed milk, only 57 pence (or 25 pence per litre) reached the farmer, to be set against 68 pence production costs, while by contrast the retailer mark-up was some 34 pence'.[35]

This means that an ill-timed investment could be even more detrimental, increasing the reluctance of suppliers to innovate, and increasing the likelihood of it being averse to the consumers' interests. Lastly, the production methods mean that suppliers operate under high fixed costs and so cannot afford to lose major contracts, which again makes them adamant on avoiding being de-listed by any of the major retailers.[36] The very essence of the grocery market, which is a result of it being based on trade of perishable, seasonal products places the

31 Dobson, 534.

32 CC Report 2008, [9.27], 162.

33 CC Report 2008, [9.40], 164.

34 CC Report 2008, [9.41], 164.

35 Michael N. Cardwell, 'Farmers, Milk Prices and Rural Indignation' (2015) 5(1) Oñati Socio-legal Series 51, 56.

36 Dobson, 560.

advantage firmly with the retailers, allowing them to impose unfair terms onto the suppliers.

Next, the position of the grocery retailers in the market allows them to exercise the buyer power against the retailers. Dobson observes how the retailers are customers, suppliers and competitors to the suppliers. They are customers in the sense that they purchase groceries from them. They are suppliers in the sense that they provide the essential shelf-space, the only way through which the suppliers can reach the consumer. They are competitors to the extent that they promote own-label products in competition with and as a possible replacement for manufacturer branded goods.[37]

The retailers will also often demand branded product development plans so that they can plan their own-label rival products for launch at or about the same time… and use "copycat packaging".[38] Consequently, the retailers have the ability to control branded product manufacturers' access to market, the prices at which those branded goods are sold and their rates of sale (through shelf position and size), as well as the availability of opportunities for in-store communications and promotions, and to demand access to commercially-sensitive marketing and product information ahead of a product's launch, which could then be used by those retailers in the development of their own-label products.[39]

Moreover, one could argue that it is actually the grocery retailers that are the weaker party. Approaching this issue simplistically, after all the retailers' business depends on being able to obtain and re-sell 'groceries' from the suppliers. Surely, that puts the suppliers in the position of power? In the UK concurred in principle pointing out that 'the buyer power of even the largest grocery retailers may be offset by the market power possessed by suppliers of the most prominent branded goods'[40], which suggests that the suppliers (especially prominent ones) may possess sufficient market power to 'cancel-out' any buyer power and ameliorate any imbalance. However, it is pointed out that the CC's comments pertain only to the 'prominent' suppliers, suggesting that in fact the manufacturers or suppliers of non-prominent-branded groceries are the most vulnerable to UTPs having to face immense buyer power of the retailers with no market power of their own to combat it.

The strong consumer loyalty to stores outweighs the loyalty towards individual products, which means that if the consumer's preferred good is not available to them at a given retailer's, instead of going to a different shop to get that preferred good, they will buy a substitute good at that preferred shop.[41] In that context, 'respective market shares mean little. A supplier with a high market share in the supply market will still be economically

37 Dobson, 531.
38 Young, 4–5.
39 CC Report 2008, [9.73], 171.
40 CC Report 2008, [9.21], 161.
41 Dobson, 536.

dependent on a retailer that commands only a modest market share of the retail market because of the supplier's relative lack of external opportunities… The critical issue is that retailers with buyer power can credibly threaten to cause substantial damage to a supplier's profits if negotiations break down and its products are delisted.[42] Furthermore, it has been pointed out that the role played by the retailers as 'gate-keepers', controlling both suppliers and consumers, gives them an ability to abuse such a position and dominate both (as both sub-groups rely on each other).[43] In such a landscape '[e]ven the very largest brand producers will find it difficult to avoid the exercise of retailer buyer power. All producers rely on the same few retailers as a necessary intermediary for them to reach final consumers for most of their sales'[44], and it is even harder for smaller suppliers.

The CC in the UK, also observed that the largest suppliers are capable of offsetting the buyer power exerted by the retailers, and that should 'suggest that certain suppliers could be excluded from the ambit of the GSCOP' but that they ran into the problem of demarcating the 'cut-off' line beyond which the GSCOP would not protect a supplier, and concluded that 'in order to be meaningful, any such criteria would need to be applied to a supplier's dealings in individual products and with individual grocery retailers which would entail significant practical difficulties. These practical difficulties were such that we decided that the GSCOP, as with the SCOP, should apply to the relevant retailers' dealings with all their suppliers'.[45]

6. THE ASSESSMENT OF THE EXISTING FRAMEWORK

As of its adoption, the Code has both been praised and criticized. The criticism will be addressed first. The GSCOP is a Code of Practice, which under s 5 of the 2009 Order must be incorporated into every Supply Agreement. The fact that a Supply Agreement must be incorporated does not mean that the bargaining strength is equal. The buyer power may still be used, just not in the ways prohibited by the Code. Furthermore, as evident from the Groceries Code Adjudicator (GCA) Investigation the buyer power was used to unduly delay payments to suppliers. The "fear factor" is still present, even if the GCA may actually accept anonymous tips and evidence during an investigation.

The GCA admitted in the 2016–2017 annual report that 'the proportion of suppliers who said they would not raise an issue with the GCA or were unsure

42 Dobson, 536.
43 Nicholson and Young, 7–8.
44 Dobson, 537.
45 CC Report 2008, [11.290], 233.

whether they would do so remained static at 53%. Fear that this could have an impact on the relationship with the retailer or they would suffer retribution remained the top factors behind this response'.[46] In 2016–2017 there were no disputes referred for arbitration under the Groceries Code Adjudicator Act 2013, and no new investigations were initiated. The Survey carried out by the GCA indicated that there was growing awareness amongst the suppliers about the GCA but that 'a majority of suppliers still expressed scepticism as to whether they would raise an issue with the GCA'.[47]

On the example of the milk sector, the GSCOP failed to help the producers during the milk crisis, when the producers were forced to protest against the low shares of prices received, because 'only about 3% of milk producers are in fact direct suppliers to the retailers, and the code is not binding on the intermediaries. Furthermore, the GCA cannot interfere in price, and it was the low price that was harmful'.[48] Cardwell in turn pointed out that even if GSCOP applies so as to protect a supplier from an onerous contract or term, it does not guarantee a fairer price, or contract with another large retailer. The situation is likely going to get worse with growing consolidation, and as the Code remains in force for longer, the retailers will find more and more loopholes.

Despite being criticised, the GSCOP has also been praised. It was pointed out that the GSCOP is a 'positive move forward', with its soft measures and structural obligations 'present subtle pressure to act in a compliant manner'.[49] The GCA report observed that there has been a change in the approach taken by the regulated retailers in the period since the appointment of the GCA in 2013, and there has been a general improvement in Code compliance'[50], though it is hard to assume that the GCA could have concluded that the introduction of the office of the adjudicator had no or negative effect.

The GSCOP has also been praised by the European institutions, notably the Commission in the Draft Directive expressed that '[e]xperience from the enforcement of UTPs by the UK Grocery Code Adjudicator shows that an effective protection regime can reduce the occurrence of UTPs and improve effective redress against them'. This is especially relevant bearing in mind how many of the EU Member States have much less developed system of protection against the unfair commercial practices in the food supply chains than the UK.

---

46 Groceries Code Adjudicator, 'Annual Report and Accounts 1 April 2016 – 31 March 2017', 21.

47 Anthony Seely, 'Supermarkets: The Groceries Code Adjudicator' House of Commons Briefing Paper Number 6124, 12 November 2015, 30–31.

48 Seely, 32–33.

49 Justine Stefanelli and Philip Mardsen, 'Models of Enforcement in Europe for Relations in the Food Supply Chain (2012) British Institute of International and Comparative Law, 13.

50 GCA Report, 24.

7. THE GROCERIES CODE ADJUDICATOR AND ENFORCEMENT OF THE CODE

Enforcement of the provisions of the Code and securement that the retailers comply with the GSCOP certainly represent two most important challenges. This is why the Groceries Code Adjudicator (GCA), as an independent regulator, was eventually established through an Act of Parliament in June 2013.[51] The main task of the GCA is to ensure that the ten largest UK supermarkets comply with the GSCOP, i.e. that they deal with their direct suppliers lawfully and fairly as pointed out by Paragraph 2 of the Code.

Besides its principal supervisory role, the GCA has been set up to strengthen the entire supply chain benefiting in such a manner not only the suppliers, but also retailers and consumers. The GCA helps strengthening the supply chain and bring further innovation to the groceries sector benefiting suppliers, retailers and customers.[52]

The introduction of the Adjudicator also helped insofar as it gave the suppliers someone to contact in case of unfair practices. Ms Christine Tacon CBE has become the first Adjudicator. Since her appointment, she has initiated two investigations into the big retailers for the alleged breach of the Code. These were the Tesco investigations in 2016 and Co-op in 2018. In that sense, it can be observed that the GCA is a kind of a Supermarket ombudsman.

The GCA has been given a number of powers. First, it can arbitrate in the individual disputes between a supplier and a trader. Second, it can investigate complaints of non-compliance with the Code. Third, it is entitled to give advice on the application of the GSCOP. Eventually, the GCA has power to issue recommendations and fines.

It is possible to observe that the GCA has adopted a modern regulatory approach, working collaboratively with the retailers to respond to issues raised by suppliers and others and bring about beneficial change in sector. The focus is on the collaborative approach, where the idea is to set up a friendly and collegial environment for business operations on both the sides: the side of the suppliers and the side of retailers. The GCA can launch investigations where there is a suspicion on the ground of (confidential) complaints that one or more retailers have breached the Code. That is something that the GCA has done twice so far: in case of Tesco in 2016 and in case of Co-op in 2018.

The enforcement is done through the issuance of recommendations, publication of information and fines. Imposition of a fine, based on the retailer's turnover, similar like in case of breach of competition law rules, had only been subsequently introduced in April 2015. Accordingly, the GCA has now the power to fine the major UK supermarkets up to 1% of their annual turnover, not just

[51] UK Groceries Code Adjudicator Act 2013.

[52] *Ibid.*

their grocery turnover. That penalty is something that has not yet been used in practice by the GCA. For example, in case of the GCA first official investigation, the Tesco case, the eventual imposition of this fine could have meant a fine of up to £690 million which is an extremely high amount of money.

The first statutory review of the performance and effectiveness of the GCA was performed in 2016 by the UK Department for Business, Energy & Industrial Strategy. Its results were published in 2017.[53] The published report has, overall, praised the results of the work of the Adjudicator, pointing out that it represents a modern regulator. However, it has been pointed out that more work needs still to be done in order to ensure high level of fairness at the market.[54]

The GCA publishes regular annual reports in which it presents and assesses its work and achievements and sets up plans for the future.[55] Moreover, the GCA also publishes a newsletter in which it identifies the major issues related to the compliance with the Code, current situation with its implementation and future plans.[56] What is important is that the GCS in its newsletter praises the efforts of individual retailers whose level of compliance with the GSCOP has improved.

The GCA is also dedicated to help the suppliers with providing information on compliance officers in each of the ten supermarkets whose task is to secure that the supermarkets comply with the GSCOP. Moreover, the GCA has also secured that each of the ten supermarkets has got special suppliers' helpline that the suppliers may easily use to contact the supermarkets. With that aim, the GCA has published in September 2018 a contact list with the names of all ten compliance officers and contact details of the retailers' hotlines.[57] The main idea behind the introduction of these helplines was to reduce concern of the suppliers about potential damaging of their relationship with the retailers by chasing payment disputes.

Similarly, securing adequate training of the all relevant stakeholders about the content of the GSCOP is one of the essential pre-requisites for its proper implementation in practice. In order to facilitate the trainings, in October 2018, the GCA published a list of the persons and entities offering trainings on the GSCOP.[58] It is important to note that the entities and persons contained on this

---

53 Department for Business, Energy & Industrial Strategy (UK), Statutory Review of the Groceries Code Adjudicator 2013–2016, July 2017, available at https://assets.publishing.service.gov.uk/government/uploads/system/uploads/attachment_data/file/629020/gca-statutory-review-2013-16.pdf.

54 *Ibid.*, 4.

55 Https://assets.publishing.service.gov.uk/government/uploads/system/uploads/attachment_data/file/718541/GCA_Annual_Report_and_Accounts_2017-18_web_accessible_version.pdf.

56 Https://assets.publishing.service.gov.uk/government/uploads/system/uploads/attachment_data/file/722422/Newsletter_Edition_16_final.pdf

57 Https://www.gov.uk/government/publications/code-compliance-officer-contact-details

58 Https://www.gov.uk/government/publications/groceries-code-training-providers/directory-of-gscop-training-providers

list are not endorsed by the GCA, but the main purpose of the list is to provide in a fully transparent manner the stakeholders with the names of all potential trainers.

8. THE TESCO CASE AS THE FIRST CASE OF INVESTIGATIONS CARRIED OUT BY THE GCA

The GCA was involved in several arbitration disputes on the ground of the GSCOP. However, due to their confidential nature, the details of these arbitration proceedings are not publicly known. The first public action of the GCA was launching the investigations into one of the major UK supermarkets, Tesco, in 2016. The investigations were directed to verify complaints concerning the alleged breaches of several paragraphs of the GSCOP: paragraph 5 (no delay in payments), paragraph 12 (requirements for additional payments for placement) and paragraph 2 (principle of fair dealing). Eventually, the Adjudicator confirmed that in case of any disagreement as to the goods supplied or the conformity thereof with the specifications Tesco would deduct or defer the payment, and sometimes even where a debt was acknowledged by Tesco, it would take them 12 months or over to pay the amounts due to the supplier.[59]

Furthermore, the Adjudicator found that the Tesco software would commit errors that resulted in suppliers being overcharged or underpaid, and when the mistake was pointed out to Tesco it would take them unreasonably long to remedy.[60] The GCA pointed out that 'the frequency and scale of the issues identified go beyond what [she] consider[s] to be an acceptable level of errors and resulted in business practices which were unfair.[61] In practice, what Tesco would do was to duplicate invoices, defer payments to meet its own margin targets, and even use the debt as a bargaining tool when discussing future relationship with the suppliers.

As it was discovered by the Adjudicator: 'Sometimes suppliers felt that they achieved a good deal out of these negotiations. Others felt under pressure to accept the terms put forward by Tesco in order to ensure they received something in return for money that they had feared they would not recover.'[62]

It is important to emphasize that Tesco was one of the largest, or in many cases even the largest customer for the suppliers. The majority of the suppliers indicated that Tesco accounted for even more than a quarter of their overall business. The impact of delay in payments on the suppliers' businesses was amplified by the importance of the Tesco relationship. This meant that the suppliers were more

59 GCA Investigation Report (2016), [20.2], 22.
60 Ibid, [22.1], 22.
61 Ibid, [22.6], 24.
62 Ibid, [31.9], 32.

heavily dependent on Tesco to maintain their current financial position and their future prospects than they might otherwise have been. This has placed Tesco in a powerful negotiating position with these suppliers which demonstrates very well the presence of inequality of bargaining powers between Tesco on the one side, and suppliers in the food supply chains, on the other side.[63]

The investigation has discovered that in one instance a supplier had sought a board level decision not to pursue a debt it believed it was owed from Tesco because the supplier was given the impression by Tesco that its future business with Tesco was at risk if it pursued the debt.[64] Moreover, the GCA found evidence of Tesco asking for "investment" from suppliers in exchange for benefits to be agreed with the supplier or as part of wider negotiations about meeting margin targets at the end of trading periods.[65]

In summation, the GCA concluded its report with pointing out that Tesco had acted in breach of Article 5 GSCOP, and against only the spirit but not the letter of Article 12 GSCOP, and against the general duty of fair dealing in Article 2 GSCOP.[66] As a remedy the GCA decided to make only recommendations.[67] However, the question to be raised here is whether the recommendations represent sufficiently efficient and dissuasive and why no other sanctions have been imposed on Tesco.

In TESCO case, the GSA issued following five recommendations:

1. Tesco should pay suppliers in line with the terms of the supply agreement.
2. Tesco should not make unilateral deductions.
3. Suppliers must be given at least 30 days to challenge any proposed deduction.
4. Tesco (and therefore all of the retailers) must provide the supplier with an explanation of the proposed deduction with reference to the terms of the supply agreement.
5. Where a supplier challenges a proposed deduction, Tesco must not deduct the disputed sum from the supplier's trading account or otherwise from money owed to the supplier for goods supplied.

9. THE CO-OP CASE AS THE SECOND CASE OF INVESTIGATIONS CARRIED OUT BY THE GCA

Following the Tesco investigations, in 2018 the GCA decided to launch its second investigation in order to better understand whether and in what amount there

63 Ibid, [37], 35.
64 Ibid, [40.2], 36.
65 Ibid, [46.1], 39.
66 Ibid, [44.2]-[44.3], 38.
67 Ibid, [57.1], 49.

has been breach of the Code, this time by the Co-op. This time the investigations has covered the Co-op for alleged breaches of the GSCOP by its de-listing practices as provided by paragraph 16 GSCOP (Duties in relation to De-listing) as well as through benchmarking and depot quality control charges as provided by paragraph 3 GSCOP (Variation of Supply Agreements and terms of supply) in the period between Summer 2016 and at least Summer 2017.[68] Both of these paragraphs are to be read in line with the general principle of fair dealing as set up by paragraph 2 GSCOP. The Co-op case is still pending and no information on it has been available so far.

10. CONCLUSIONS: THE NEED FOR REFORM OF THE EXITING LEGAL FRAMEWORK IN THE UK?

Despite all positive changes that the GSCOP has brought to the regulatory framework of the UK food supply chains, it seems that there is still need for further improvements. The effective measures to prevent unfair business-to-business commercial practices and the resulting detriments to both small-scale producers and consumers should be strengthened. The GCA has released the results of its survey into retailer compliance with the Code. The results show a downward trend in the number of suppliers reporting breaches of the Code which is certainly a very positive impact of the GSCOP. However, although this has been heralded as a positive indication of compliance by retailers, the results confirm that many suppliers continue to have concerns about the commercial consequences of complaining.

Another issue is that there is a presence of the lack of training amongst suppliers about the rights attributed to them under the Code and how these are to be protected. It was reported that "predatory practices" have driven more than 150 groceries producers out of business in 2017 which is a very high number. Therefore, it would be good to broaden the scope of competences of the GCA so that it can investigate allegations of unfairness at any stage of the supply chains that serve our supermarkets. Moreover, what should be done is to general broaden the scope of the GSCOP.

Moreover, as it stands now, the GCA's office has a permanent staff of only 4.7 FTE (Full Time Equivalent), while the Adjudicator herself works only three days a week. Bearing in mind that the GCA is intended to regulate the commercial practices of such huge ten retailers which cover their relationships with more than ten thousand suppliers around the UK and overseas, this institutional capacity seem to be inadequate and it is something that should be addressed and improved in the future.

68 'GCA Launches Investigation Into Co-Operative Group Limited', GCA 08.03.2018 (<https://www.gov.uk/government/news/tacon-launches-investigation-into-co-operative-group-limited>)

In that context, the recent adoption of the European Directive on unfair trading practices in the agricultural and food supply chain might certainly be used as a model for the reform of the current UK rules. Formally speaking, the effects of this Directive on the UK legal system are still unknown due to the UK decision to leave the European Union ("Brexit"). Initially, the UK withdrawal from the European Union had been scheduled for March 2019, but was eventually postponed for October 2019. The future relations of the UK with the European Union and the effects that the EU Law will have not yet been determined at the moment of finalisation of this chapter (June 2019). In any case, even if the UK leaves the European Union with the so called "no deal", this new EU Directive should be used as a model for the reform and improvement of the existing, rather limited UK legal framework for protection of fairness of commercial practices in the food supply chain.

CHAPTER 8

THE SUPPLY CHAIN INITIATIVE

Its Origins, Purpose and Activities

Michael HUTCHINGS*
Chair of the SCI

Since this article was written, the members of the Supply Chain Initiative decided to bring the initiative to an end. This decision was taken in large measure as a result of the adoption of the EU Directive on Unfair Trading Practices (Directive 2019/633). Once the Directive is implemented in national legislation, a number of the practices and examples covered by the SCI Principles of Good Practice (see paragraph 2.1 of this article) will be governed by law. The Directive notes that the Commission "endorsed a set of principles of good practice in vertical relations in the food supply chain, which was agreed by a majority of the operators in the food supply chain. Those principles became the basis for the Supply Chain Initiative launched in 2013" (Recital 3). The Directive also notes (Recital 41) that national legislation implementing the Directive can sit alongside voluntary governance measures "such as national codes of conduct or the Supply Chain Initiative". While the SCI no longer operates across the EU, a number of codes of conduct and voluntary platforms designed to reduce unfair practices, together with dispute resolution mechanisms, will continue to operate in a number of individual EU countries.

1. INTRODUCTION

The food supply chain is a complex, extremely efficient and diverse construct throughout Europe and equally all over the world. The multitude of actors from various sectors of different sizes and interests, often with unequal market power,

* Mr Hutchings is an English lawyer specialised in competition and EU law. He was a partner with the law firm Lovell White Durrant (now Hogan Lovells) for 15 years and managed its Brussels office in the mid-1980s. He has been working as an independent lawyer since 1996. He has extensive experience of working with companies and trade associations in the grocery sector and was closely involved in the UK competition inquiry that led to the adoption of the Groceries Supply Code of Practice and the appointment of the Groceries Code Adjudicator.

represents a challenge to ensuring consistent and good trading practices in the sector.

To address this challenge, the Supply Chain Initiative (SCI) was officially launched in September 2013 by 8 EU-level associations representing the food and drink industry (FoodDrinkEurope), the branded goods manufacturers (AIM), the retail sector (the European Retail Round Table – ERRT, EuroCommerce, EuroCoop and Independent Retail Europe), the European Association of Craft, Small and Medium-sized Enterprises (UEAPME, now called SMEunited) and agricultural traders (CELCAA). It is managed by a Governance Group, with an Independent Chair[1] and the SCI's remit is defined by the Rules of Governance and Operations.

The SCI aims to improve supply chain relations between trading partners. It is a voluntary initiative, designed to encourage parties to solve trading disputes in a non-adversarial manner that would enable the relationship to continue. Companies operating at any point along the food and drink supply chain can join the initiative, irrespective of their size and their geographical location in the EU or whether they are buyers or sellers of food and drink products. When joining the initiative, companies commit to fair trading practices by integrating the Principles of Good Practice into their day-to-day operations, complying with process commitments and monitoring their application in practice. The SCI requires that companies address disputes in a fair and transparent manner whilst reassuring the complaining party that it will not be subject to retaliation.

1.1. THE INDEPENDENT CHAIR OF THE SCI

In 2017, the Governance Group of the SCI appointed Mr Michael Hutchings as its Independent Chair. This appointment resulted from a commitment made at the High-Level Forum for a Better Functioning of the Food Supply Chain[2] in December 2016.

The role of the independent Chair is:

- to chair meetings of the Governance Group, which supervises the management and operation of the SCI.
- to act as a recipient for confidential complaints, which involves facilitating the handling of aggregated disputes with a cross-border dimension in a fully confidential setting. He has a duty to establish facts, to hear parties involved, and to settle disputes as appropriate.

1 Governance Group of the SCI, http://supplychaininitiative.eu/governance-group
2 High Level Forum for a Better Functioning Food Supply Chain, https://ec.europa.eu/growth/sectors/food/competitiveness/supply-chain-forum_en

- to issue guidance and recommendations of general interest and promote good practice in dialogue with the Governance Group, to promote fair dealings in the supply chain on specific topics with the full support of the sectors.
- to represent and promote the SCI to policy makers and other external audiences, to raise awareness about the SCI and his role as independent Chair, as well as to encourage more efficiency within the supply chain.

2. THE ROLE OF THE SCI IN PROMOTING GOOD TRADING PRACTICES IN THE FOOD SUPPLY CHAIN

2.1. PRINCIPLES OF GOOD PRACTICE

The Principles of Good Practice are the foundation of the SCI. Their purpose is to promote the respect of fair practices and discourage the exercise of unfair ones in the supply chain. They were developed in 2011 in the framework of a multi-stakeholder dialogue involving 11 organisations representing the various sectors in the food supply chain including farmers, processors, brands, SMEs, wholesalers and retailers.[3]

The High Level Forum for a Better Functioning Food Supply Chain of the European Commission warmly welcomed these Principles in November 2011 and subsequently, a Framework for their implementation and enforcement was adopted in January 2013. Following the Commission's recommendations in a report on unfair trading practices in the food supply chain[4], the rules were reviewed in 2017 to strengthen the SCI dispute resolution mechanism and to formally establish the role of an independent Chair. Since the end of 2018, the Rules of Governance and Operations are available in a total of 23 EU languages.[5] The translations have kindly been carried out by the European Commission as a result of a High Level Forum meeting.

The impact of setting a standard by means of these Principles has been significant. They are increasingly used as a point of reference across Europe in

3 European Brands Association (AIM), European Council of Young Farmers (CEJA), European Liaison Committee for Agricultural and Agri-Food Trade (CELCAA), Liaison Centre for the Meat Processing Industry in the European Union (CLITRAVI), Copa-Cogeca (representing farmers and their cooperatives in Europe, European Retail Round Table (ERRT), EuroCommerce (representing retail and wholesale in Europe), European Community of Consumer Co-operatives (Euro Coop), FoodDrinkEurope (representing the food and drink industry in Europe), European Association of Craft, Small and Medium-sized Enterprises (UEAPME; now SMEunited) and Independent Retail Europe (representing groups of independent retailers; formerly UGAL).

4 Commission report on unfair trading practices in the food supply chain – COM(2016) 32 final.

5 SCI Rules of Governance and Operations: https://supplychaininitiative.eu/about-initiative/rules

the private sector as well as by EU institutions, where they are an important reference point for instance in the agricultural markets task force.[6]

Principles of Good Practice
Contracting parties shall act in strict compliance with applicable laws, including competition law.

General Principles:

1. CONSUMERS: Contracting parties should always take into account consumer interests and the overall sustainability of the supply chain in their B2B relations. Contracting parties should ensure maximum efficiency and optimisation of resources in the distribution of goods throughout the supply chain.
2. FREEDOM OF CONTRACT: Contracting parties are independent economic entities, respecting each other's rights to set their own strategy and management policy, including the freedom to determine independently whether to engage or not in any agreement.
3. FAIR DEALING: Contracting parties should deal with each other responsibly, in good faith and with professional diligence.

Specific Principles:

1. WRITTEN AGREEMENTS: Agreements should be in writing, unless impracticable or where oral agreements are mutually acceptable and convenient. They should be clear and transparent, and cover as many relevant and foreseeable elements as possible, including rights and procedures of termination.
2. PREDICTABILITY: Unilateral change to contract terms shall not take place unless this possibility and its circumstances and conditions have been agreed in advance. The agreements should outline the process for each party to discuss with the other any changes necessary for the implementation of the agreement or due to unforeseeable circumstances, as provided in the agreement.
3. COMPLIANCE: Agreements must be complied with.
4. INFORMATION: Where information is exchanged, this shall be done in strict compliance with competition and other applicable laws, and the parties should take reasonable care to ensure that the information supplied is correct and not misleading.

6 "Improving market outcomes – enhancing the position of farmers in the supply chain", report of the agricultural markets task force to Commissioner Hogan, November 2016.

5. CONFIDENTIALITY: Confidentiality of information must be respected unless the information is already public or has been independently obtained by the receiving party lawfully and in good faith. Confidential information shall be used by the recipient party only for the purpose for which it was communicated.
6. RESPONSIBILITY FOR RISK: All contracting parties in the supply chain should bear their own appropriate entrepreneurial risks.
7. JUSTIFIABLE REQUEST: A contracting party shall not apply threats in order to obtain an unjustified advantage or to transfer an unjustified cost.

For more information: http://www.supplychaininitiative.eu/about-initiative/principles-good-practice-vertical-relationships-food-supply-chain

2.2. INCLUSIVE APPROACH

Since its launch in 2013, 417 companies from across the entire EU have registered with the SCI. Taking into account the subsidiaries of international groups, 1,208 operating companies are currently signed up.[7] Registered companies are present in all 28 EU Member States and cover farming, wholesalers, retail and manufacturing.

Registration also includes non-EU companies operating in the EU. In some national dialogues, companies are represented by their national associations. The above count does not include all these companies.

Non-registered companies, notably SMEs, benefit from the wider application of the SCI and the principles of good practice by registered larger businesses. Furthermore, the SCI provides simpler rules for medium or small-sized firms. Small sized firms need not register at all to be able to benefit from the complaints procedure that the SCI offers.

Distribution of membership across the supply chain

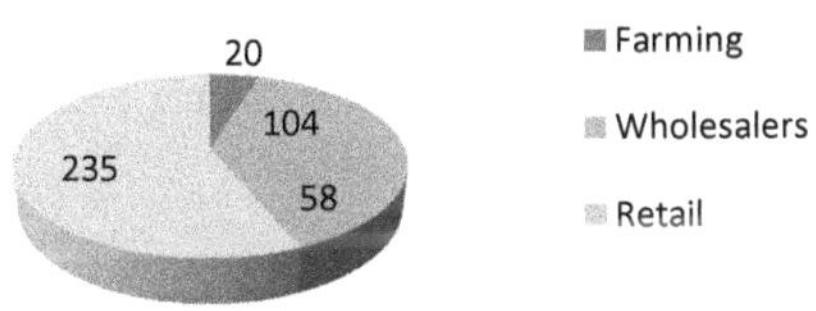

[7] Figures from June 2019

2.3. COMMITMENT AND MEASURING SUCCESS

Companies who signed up to the SCI agree to take part in a short annual compliance survey. This is not compulsory for micro and small companies that are subject to simplified requirements in this regard.

The aim of the survey is to monitor progress on the ground and to serve as a basis for evaluating compliance with the SCI Principles of Good Practice. The survey is conducted once per year by an independent party and responses are submitted anonymously.

The results of the 2018 survey showcase the positive impact of the SCI on day-to-day practices. For instance, 9 out of 10 companies trained all or some of their staff members on the Principles of Good Practice. Training staff is indeed an important element in triggering a culture change, so that good practices are implemented on all levels and do not simply remain a political commitment.

Similarly, it is important to communicate on implemented standards to business partners so that good practices spread and are respected more widely. Also in this area we have seen positive results. 84% of the registered companies communicated their registration to their business partners at national and/or group level.

Satisfaction with the SCI remains high among registered companies with 7 out of 10 respondents reporting a good level of satisfaction with the SCI. Companies considered that the SCI has helped them to improve daily communication with their trading partners (43%), improve their internal company processes (24%) and deal with disputes (21%).

The SCI acknowledges that there are areas for improvement, in particular 25% of respondents stated that their business partners are not registered with the SCI and 6% of respondents regretted that the SCI has not helped them solve disputes for breaches of the Principles of Good Practice with their business partners.

Based on these insights the SCI seeks to promote its activities and added-value more broadly to attract further companies, in particular by raising awareness about its revised dispute resolution mechanism.

2.4. TRIGGERING CHANGE – THE SCI DISPUTE RESOLUTION MECHANISM

Disputes are generally best dealt with at national level, and to date, all disputes have been resolved at that level. National rules and regulations take precedence over the SCI Rules of Governance and Operations and the SCI offers a complement to existing regulations and solutions where no mechanism exists.

The approach to disputes and the way they are addressed is however influenced by the SCI. The 2018 survey shows that 20 companies had been faced with an alleged breach of at least one of the Principles of Good Practice. 16 companies resolved the issue informally. In 4 cases, the companies were not able to solve the issue informally, and 1 company from the retail sector subsequently lodged 3 complaints with trading partners, which related to the following breaches of Principles of Good Practices: predictability, compliance and justifiable request.

Disputes can either occur at individual level or involve a number of players, in which case they are referred to as aggregated disputes.

For individual disputes companies can resort to a number of dispute resolution options:

- commercial track
- contract options
- internal dispute resolution
- mediation or arbitration
- judicial methods

The choice of dispute resolution mechanism lies with the complaining company unless this would infringe national law. By registering with the SCI, companies accept to solve their disputes related to the application of the Principles by any of these options.

Importantly, commercial retaliation against any company for using these mechanisms is a serious breach of the Principles of Good Practice. This is a fundamental standard that the SCI stands for and in fact only 3% of companies claimed that the fear for retaliation was an issue in the last survey.

A group of companies or an association acting on their behalf may submit an aggregated complaint to the Chair of the SCI, who will then verify that the request has substance and merit, has a cross-border impact and ensure that all national options have been exhausted. Along the entire process, the Chair guarantees the anonymity and confidentiality of the parties and information involved. This is a key feature in encouraging complainants to raise issues with the SCI.

If the complaint is indeed receivable, the parties are heard by the Chair of the SCI and, if justified, the party allegedly in breach is asked to comply or explain. The case may also be referred to an external mediator or arbitrator if deemed in the best interest of all parties involved. So as to ensure that key learnings of any case are shared to the benefit of the entire sector, guidance and recommendations may be developed by the Chair.

Graphical overview of the SCI dispute resolution mechanism:

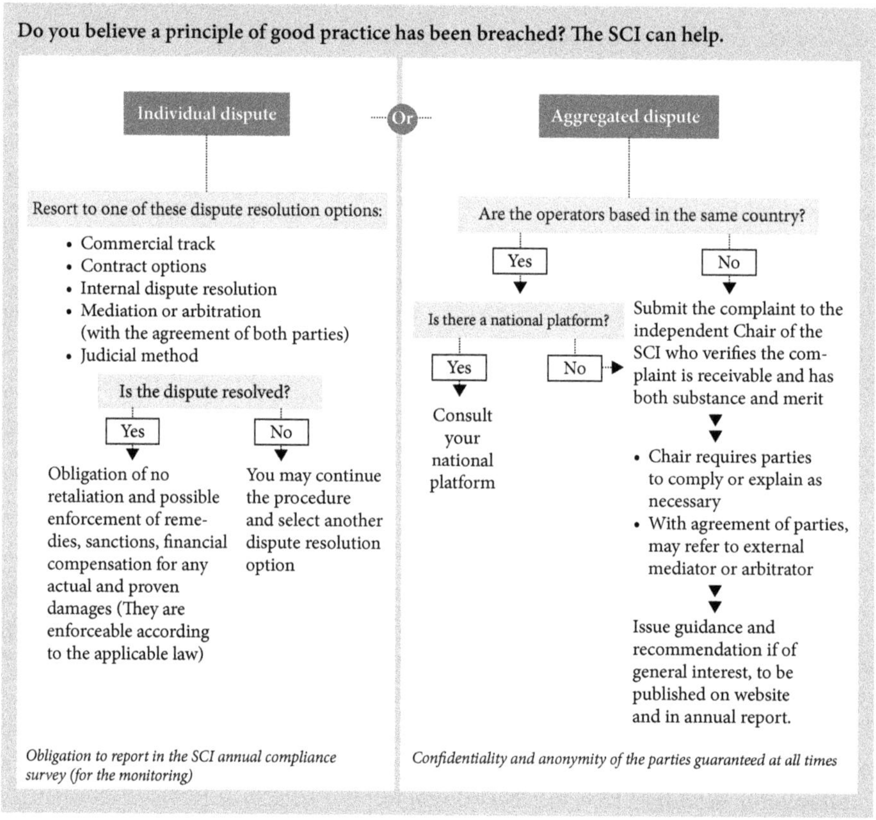

2.5. IMPACT AT THE NATIONAL LEVEL

The SCI acts like a catalyser for national change and encourages the establishment of national platforms. A national platform is a structure set up for the purpose of implementing the Principles at national level and to be the first point of reference to handle disputes.

Over the past years, six national dialogue platforms were established in Europe based on the SCI. These are located in Belgium, the Netherlands, Finland, Portugal, Germany and Slovakia. Furthermore, a wide range of initiatives and similar platforms exist in most European countries. Many used the SCI Principles of Good Practice as a basis for national legislation or codes of conduct.

All national efforts are adapted to their local specificities so as to maximise impact and effectiveness.[8] In some countries voluntary initiatives and legislation are combined as is the case in Spain for instance; in countries like Finland the national platform takes a more legal approach and does not require registration; and in other countries like Belgium, the national platform is based on mediation and takes a broader approach. In some countries like the UK, the regulator can enforce compliance with the rules by imposing substantial fines.[9]

3. FUTURE OUTLOOK

The SCI has grown rapidly in its five years of existence and its positive impact has been widely acknowledged. It will continue to provide a forum for representatives of the various sectors in the food supply chain to meet together and thereby improve trading relations, ultimately triggering a genuine culture change for the benefit of all players in the food supply chain.

---

8 National supporting initiatives, http://supplychaininitiative.eu/regionalnational-supporting-initiatives

9 UK Groceries Code Adjudicator https://www.gov.uk/government/organisations/groceries-code-adjudicator

CHAPTER 9

TACKLING UTPS – BELGIAN FARMERS THOUGHTS ABOUT THE BELGIAN EXPERIENCE WITH SELF-REGULATION

Pieter VERHELST
Member of the Executive Committee of Boerenbond (Belgian Farmers' Union)

Bert MEULEMANS
Boerenbond (Belgian Farmers' Union)

1. FARMERS' THOUGHTS ABOUT UNFAIR TRADING PRACTICES

In late fall 2015, Boerenbond, the Belgian farmers organisation representing Flemish farmers, conducted a survey among its members on unfair trading practices (UTPs). A structured questionnaire was sent out to a representative sample of 2.303 farmers, with an eventual useful response rate of 27%. Responses were re-weighted to restore representativeness.

First, farmers where asked to describe how they see unfair trading practices. They experience the imbalance between price received and quality required as the main injustice in the agri-food chain and strongly associate it with unfair trading practices. To bring this reported feeling in line with the specific discussion on unfair trading practices, farmers were asked to indicate if they had encountered any of the unfair trading practices listed. Their answers show that unfair trading practices are a common reality and are characterised by unilaterality and post deal changes. They indicate to have to bear the downside of the quantity, quality and price uncertainty while their contractual partners tend to secure the upside. Farmers perceive the risk of being confronted with UTPs higher downstream the value chain. Asymmetry in bargaining power and the lack of detail in commercial agreements seem to be the root causes of unfair trading practices.

1.1. UNFAIR TRADING PRACTICES' ASSOCIATIONS – PRICE AND QUALITY

Farmers were asked to write down spontaneous associations with the term 'unfair trading practices'. Associations around the price received for their products come out as the main element. 77% refers to pricing. Farmers describe how they compare prices received with their costs or with the price consumers have to pay for the product at retail level. The perception among farmers is that they have to sell their products at cost or below cost, while the other actors in the chain can make a profit and retailers fight a price war to the detriment of the farmers. Farmers see themselves as the weakest link in the agri-food chain, unable to forward costs while they have to pay the price full cost. A minority (9%) goes even further as they believe that price arrangements are made within the chain, setting prices at a level that only allows 'mere survival' of the farmers.

Other members (29%) refer in their answer to the quality aspect of agri-food products. Reference is made to a lack of objective quality controls. Others refer to the international dimension stating that higher quality requirements, stricter controls, heavier environmental and other conditions (e.g. labour costs) they have to follow do not bring added-value and even distort the level playing field and fair competition to the detriment of farmers.

It is clear from those open answers that farmers situate unfair trading practices at the macro level, in the market, rather than on the micro level, in individual commercial relations. They tend to refer to market failures and the weak position of the farmer in the chain resulting in unfair pricing. They experience the imbalance between price received and quality required as the main injustice in the agri-food chain and strongly associate it with unfair trading practices.

1.2. UNFAIR TRADING PRACTICES ARE A FARMERS' REALITY

1.2.1. Type and occurrence of listed unfair trading practices

To have a more precise understanding on the precise nature of unfair trading practices farmers are confronted with and to bring their experiences back to the commercial reality and in line with the discussion on UTPs at political level, farmers were provided a list of 18 trading practices commonly identified as potentially unfair. Farmers were asked whether they encountered one or more of those listed practices in the last five years.

Almost seven out of eight farmers indicated one or more practises. Only 13,5% did not select any of the listed practices. 20,4% checked one or two practices, 28,1% three to five and 38% even six or more (see Figure 1).

Figure 1. Number of listed UTPs encountered by farmers in the last five years

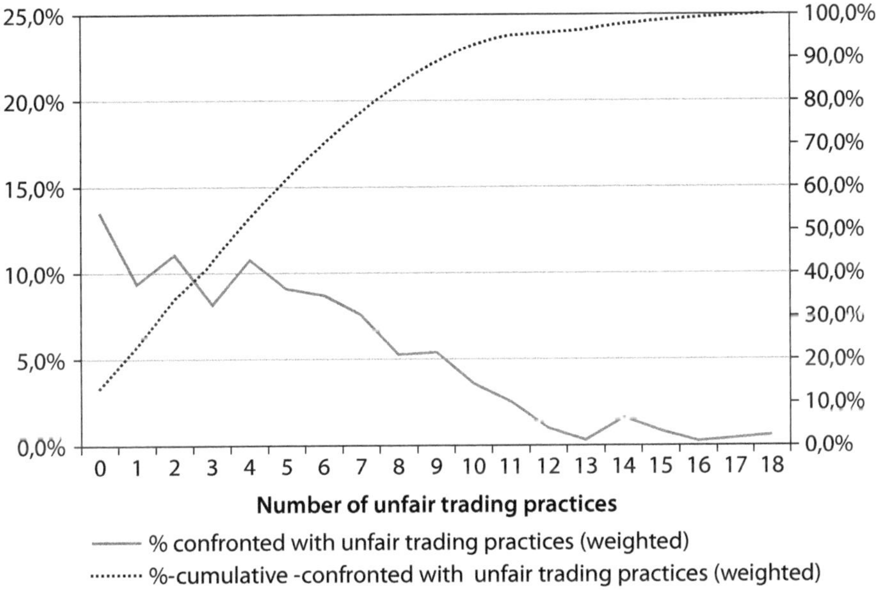

The most frequently reported UTPs (see Table 1) are, in order: unilateral price adjustment, unilateral imposed contract terms, improper quality assessment and unreasonable pricing of additional services (reported by 37% to 48%). Subsequently reported by over one in four: unilateral changes to quantity, non-disclosure of crucial information, unilateral changes to payment terms, failure to pay the agreed price, price adjustment out of proportion to the deviation from agreed quantities or quality and forced contribution to actions or activities outside the company. Further reported by one in five: careless handling of products, inaccurate quantification, refusal to confirm an agreement in writing, mandatory purchase or delivery of additional goods or services, unilateral termination of a contract (or threatening to), incorrect product information. Finally reported by one in ten: unjustified awarding of a public contract and carelessly handling confidential information.

Table 1. Reported unfair trading practices encountered in the last five years

	%
Unilateral upward or downward price adjustment without reasonable explanation	48
Unilaterally imposed contract terms	42
Improper quality assessment	41
Unreasonable pricing of additional services	37
Unilateral changes to the quantity to deliver	28
Non-disclosure of crucial information	28
Unilateral changes to the agreed payment terms	28
Failure to pay the agreed price	28
Price adjustment (up or downward) out of proportion to the deviation from agreed quantity or quality	27
Forced contribution to promotions, renovations or other activities outside the own company	26
My product was carelessly handled or stored by the buyer	22
Inaccurate quantification (number, weight, litre, ...)	22
Refusal to confirm an agreement in writing	21
Mandatory purchase or delivery of additional goods or services	20
Unilateral termination of a contract (or threatening to)	19
Incorrect product information	18
Unjustified awarding of a public contract	10
Confidential or secret information concerning my product was carelessly handled by a (potential) buyer	10

Two main characteristics prevail: unilaterality and post deal changes. As in the open end question, price and quality surface as the main elements. This closed end question further adds discussions on quantity, information bias, not respected payment terms and contracting issues to the picture. Farmers feel they do not have a say and that agreements are not respected. They indicate to have to bear the downside of the quantity, quality and price uncertainty while their contractual partners tend to secure the upside.

1.2.2. Where do unfair trading practices occur?

Farmers were asked to indicate for different marketing channels their perception on the level of risk of being confronted with unfair trading practices. The perceived risk to be confronted with UTPs is higher downstream the value chain (see Table 2).

Table 2. Perceived risk of UTPs

	– (1)	±	?	+ (2)	(1)-(2)
Buyers	16%	28%	15%	41%	-25%
Suppliers	29%	45%	8%	18%	11%
Difference	13%	17%	-7%	-23%	

– Lower risk; ± average risk;? no opinion; + higher risk;

Table 3 shows that the perceived risk of encountering UTPs is the lowest for direct sales channels, a situation where the farmer is in control of the sale. Also delivering to an individual retailer is perceived as being a low risk, a one-on-one situation where there is a certain balance. Risk is perceived as high when selling to wholesalers, retailers, food industry or in integrated farming models, situations where the level of control of the sale is low and the negotiation balance is skewed.

Farmers indicating that they use a specific sales channel usually report a lower perceived risk on UTPs for that specific channel (see Table 3). This is especially the case for farmers indicating that they sell directly to (individual) retailers. Remarkably, only food industry scores lower in this case compared to the overall perceived risk on UTPs.

Table 3. Perceived risk of UTPs across sales channels, overall and among farmers using the indicated sales channel

	% all			% only sellers			Comp.
	–	+		–	+		
	(1)	(2)	(1)-(2)	(3)	(4)	(3)-(4)	(3–4)-(1–2)
Direct selling to consumers	58%	1%	57%	67%	0%	67%	10%
Individual retailers	41%	9%	32%	52%	1%	52%	19%
Public authorities	30%	16%	14%	32%	7%	26%	12%
Fruit and vegetables cooperatives	24%	17%	7%	39%	22%	16%	9%
Cooperatives in animal production	21%	20%	1%	33%	22%	11%	10%
Integrated farming	5%	47%	-42%	5%	41%	-36%	6%
Food processing industry	5%	54%	-49%	3%	59%	-56%	-7%
Retailers	7%	64%	-58%	17%	58%	-41%	16%
Wholesalers	3%	67%	-64%	3%	67%	-64%	0%

– Lower risk; + higher risk;

Familiarity with a sales channel, level of control on the sale and balance in the relation influence the perceived risk of encountering unfair trading practices.

1.3. IMBALANCE IN THE FOOD CHAIN

The consolidation throughout the agri-food chain differs from link to link. Although bigger, consolidated companies face stiff competition among each other, they are eventually better placed to negotiate contract terms with a broad range of smaller suppliers by playing them of against one another. Seasonal peak production, the perishability of the product and the wide variability in production conditions and productivity add to the pressure on the farmers side. The significant imbalances in bargaining power within the food chain are one of the root causes of unfair trading practices.

The primary processing stage in the supply chain generally consists of larger enterprises in key sectors such as dairy, meat, cereals and sugar. This stage is to a large extent controlled by cooperatives, in particular in northern Europe, instrumental as rebalancing act. However, a sizeable share of agricultural commodities is processed by secondary processors into consumer products. The structure of the industry is mixed with some very large consumer brand processors as well as SMEs for specialised and/or perishable products. In many sectors, the market is dominated by one or two large processing companies setting the scene. The retail end of the supply chain consists increasingly of large retail chains but small chains and independent retailers also continue to exist. The stages of processing (especially secondary processing) and retail in the food supply chain are, in terms of value added, generally characterised by a high degree of concentration. In comparison, farmers (and to some extent primary processors) are fragmented, notwithstanding producer cooperation and policy measures encouraging it.[1]

The LARA 2016[2] describes the agri-food chain in the Flemish region. 24.000 farmers deliver agricultural products to 4.500 food companies forwarding their food products over 3.600 wholesalers and through 5 buying offices to 13 retailers and 2.232 food stores, supplying 2,7 million households and 6,4 million consumers (see Figure 2). The agri-food chain is hence often characterised as an hourglass.

1 Improving market outcomes. Enhancing the position of farmers in the supply chain. Report of the Agricultural Markets Task Force, November 2016.

2 Platteau J., Van Gijseghem D., Van Bogaert T. & Vuylsteke A. (reds.) (2016) Voedsel om over na te denken. Landbouw- en Visserijrapport 2016, Departement Landbouw en Visserij, Brussel.

Figure 2. Concentration in the agri-food chain, Flanders, 2014 (LARA, 2016)

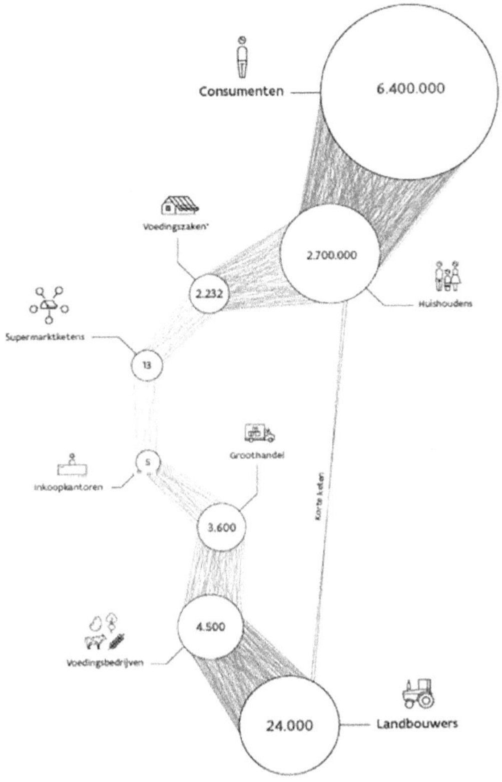

This specific structure results in an asymmetry in bargaining power that may lead to unfair trading practices, as larger and more powerful actors seek to impose contractual arrangements to their advantage, either through better prices or through improved terms and conditions.[3] This reading is in line with the farmers' perception that imbalanced relations increase the risks of unfair trading practices.

1.4. DEFINING UNFAIR TRADING PRACTICES

Based on the above analysis the following definition of unfair trading practices emerges:

An unfair trading practice usually arises from an imbalance of power in a commercial negotiation leading to a skewed distribution of costs, risks and

3 A better functioning food supply chain in Europe, Communication from the Commission. COM(2009) 591, November 2009.

benefits between the parties, eventually perceived as being unfair by one of the parties.

They can occur ex ante and find their way in a formal contract but more commonly arise ex post when an agreement is interpreted in one way or another. The latter is more often the case when a formal written agreement is lacking, or does not provide the necessary details.

2. TACKLING UNFAIR TRADING PRACTICES

Giving the high frequency of reported UTPs among farmers, the next question is how to tackle them. Farmers favour a double approach, by government and industry.

Strong market regulation at the European Union (EU) level through the Common Agricultural Policy (CAP) long predominated any concerns on unfair trading practices. Consecutive reforms of the CAP brought the issue of unfair pricing back on the farmers agenda, but also set the scene for collective bargaining, rebalancing negotiation power around the table, and self-regulation, specifying and formalising agreements. Both aspects are instrumental in avoiding unfair trading practices.

In response to this evolution, the Belgian Supply Chain Initiative has set at a horizontal level an agenda and established a framework for this self-regulation of the agri-food chain. Its code of conduct provides guidance on fair commercial relations. Enforceability is organised through a dispute settlement mechanism. Broad guidelines for sectoral inter-professional agreements and a methodology to demarcate generic from specific requirements, set the agenda for and facilitate further sectoral concertation and agreements.

The UTP Directive (EU) 2019/633 eventually draws a clear bottom line at EU level. Although it supersedes quite some elements of the industry led code of conduct and even goes beyond that, it leaves enough room for complementarity.

2.1. THE FARMERS EXPECTATION

The questionnaire conducted by Boerenbond among its members tested different approaches to tackle unfair trading practices. Farmers were asked to indicate who is best placed to tackle UTPs: governments, the sector or jurisdiction. They clearly stress the need for some kind of policy response to tackle UTPs. Most farmers believe that a double approach is needed by government and industry (41%). A pure government led approach, based on enforceable legislation and enforcement by public inspection bodies is backed by 29%. Support for just legal redress or a voluntary chain approach is far lower, only supported by one in seven.

In any case, UTPs have to be reported first, before they can be tackled. Table 4 indicates that almost three-quarters of the farmers discuss it with their colleagues when they are confronted with UTPs. Half of them confront the supplier or buyer directly. Only one in five or six contacts its own professional organisation, a lawyer or a third party. A small minority addresses public authorities or goes to court.

Table 4. Channels used to discuss or report UTPs

	%
Colleague	74
Supplier	49
Buyer	49
Professional organisation	22
Lawyer	15
Another third party	14
Public authority	9
Court	6

The questionnaire further assessed trust (on a scale from 1 to 10) in the different channels to discuss or report UTPs (see Table 5). The own professional organisation is trusted most with an average of 7,28 followed closely by an independent ombudsman (7,19). The difference between the high trust in and the low reporting towards the own professional organisation is remarkable. However, in more generic terms, rebalancing negotiations and discussing fair conditions is at the heart of the discussions among farmers within the farmers organisation. Hence, individual cases do not come up that easily through the farmers organisations, but they are well placed to signal commonly felt issues, which can be catalogued as aggregated disputes. Mediation by the Belgian Supply Chain Initiative (BE SCI – see 2.3.1) scores satisfactory (6,17), closely followed by dialogue with the concerned company (6,07). A lawyer getting in touch with the company (5,24) or mediation by public authorities (5,02) scores averagely. Mediation through an ombudsman within the concerned company, arbitration by public authorities or a court settlement is not highly trusted.

Table 5. Trust in different channels to report UTPs, on a scale from 1 to 10

	Average
Mediation through the own professional organisation	7,28
Independent ombudsman	7,19
Mediation through the BE SCI	6,17
Dialogue with the concerned company	6,07
Lawyer getting in touch with the concerned company	5,24
Mediation by a public authority	5,02
Ombudsman within the concerned company	4,76
Dispute settlement by a public authority	4,56
Court settlement	4,20

Although farmers report in response to the questionnaire a high occurrence of UTPs, the number of actual complaints is very low to non-existent (see also 2.3.1.2). The questionnaire tried to find the reasons behind this (see Table 6). When asked why UTPs are not reported more actively, an image arises of despondency in combination with the question "Is this not more trouble than it is worth?". Two-third says it is a hopeless battle and more than half refers to the time and cost of a procedure. Other elements are the lack of anonymity, fear for retaliation through less favourable terms, the lack of a clear way to file complaint and fear of losing a customer. No doubt that the feeling of despondency is linked with the farmers perception that unfair pricing is linked to fundamental market and system failure and a fundamental imbalance in market power.

Table 6. Reasons not to report UTPs

	%
It is a hopeless battle	66
It takes too long to reach any result	59
The cost of a procedure is too high	54
It is impossible to file anonymous complaint	37
Out of fear for less favourable terms	36
I don't know where to file complaint	35
Out of fear to lose a customer	32
A colleague with the same experience discouraged me	22
Out of fear to lose a supplier	10

2.2. FROM MARKET REGULATION 1.0...

The EU had strong agriculture market regulation through the Common Agricultural Policy, setting guaranteed prices. Giving the observation that farmers closely link the perceived fairness of pricing with UTPs, politically decided guaranteed prices based on a cost calculation predominate any concerns on unfair trading practices on the farmers side.

Consecutive reforms of the CAP resulted in ever less government involvement in agricultural markets bringing farmers closer to hard market realities. This entailed more and higher price volatility and brought the negative effects of the weaker farmers' position in the food chain to the forefront. Price uncertainty, stiffer competition and mounting pressure from a on European level consolidating downstream agri-food chain brought the issue of unfair pricing back on the farmers agenda, which can be linked to UTPs.

2.3. OVER MARKET REGULATION 2.0...

Although the EU backed down from what could be seen as old school market regulation 1.0, solely managed by public authorities, it established a toolbox of instruments that could be seen as market regulation 2.0, managed by the supply chain itself through self-regulation.

Figure 3. Market regulation 2.0 toolbox for self-regulation

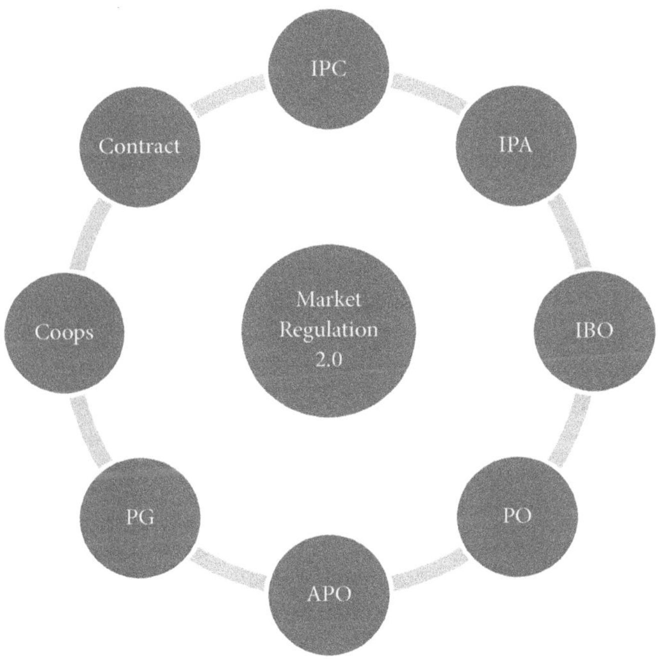

The toolbox (see Figure 3) provides instruments from the collective level down to the individual level ranging from horizontal inter-professional concertation (IPC) and eventual inter-professional agreements (IPA) over sectoral inter-branch organisations (IBO), cooperatives (Coops) or producer organisations (PO) and their associations (APO) or the junior league producer groups (PG) and finally contracts at the individual farmers level.

The toolbox can be characterised as a set of Matryoshka dolls. Self-regulation at the more collective level frames self-regulation at the lower level and eventually predetermines many contractual elements beforehand and at a higher, more balanced level of negotiation.

Specifically the sectoral instruments where broadly embedded in the CAP single Common Market (CMO) Regulation EU 2013/1308 setting a framework for inter-branch Organisation in articles 157–158, for producer organisations and their associations in articles 152–156 and for contractual relations in article 168. The EU framework hence allows and even encourages vertical self-regulation to a certain degree and clearly defines the precompetitive context.

2.3.1. Belgian Supply Chain Initiative

Within this market regulation 2.0 framework, the Belgian supply chain initiative (BE SCI), known as "het ketenoverleg", can be situated at the level of horizontal inter-professional concertation with the ambition to reach horizontal inter-professional agreements framing further self-regulation at sectoral level.

The BE SCI emerged from an ad-hoc crisis situation. In 2009, falling dairy prices, partially linked to the reform of the CAP, led to farmers' protests. Part of the protest focused on retailers, resulting in blocking distribution centres. To avoid further escalation representatives of farmers' organisations, food industry and retail started informal bilateral talks. Together they put pressure at the political level but they also acknowledged that part of the solution could be found within the chain. Food industry and retail understood that in order to ensure their much needed supply security farmers need a reasonable price. In the short run the dialogue resulted in a short term surcharge on drinking milk collected at retail level and redistributed at the level of dairy farmers. In the longer run the partners continued their dialogue and developed it to a solid platform to discuss common problems and challenges based on an open and balanced relation assuring so called social harmony and stability within the agri-food chain, thereby contributing to common sustainable growth. This resulted in common agenda setting, within the chain and at political level, and in a framework for further self-regulation at sectoral level.

The BE SCI is a voluntary, private initiative from representative organisations in the agri-food chain. It is a 'sui generis' construct as it falls outside the EU legal framework for cooperation within the agri-food chain as laid down in the single

Common Market (CMO) Regulation (EU) 2013/1308. However, it is comparable to the European supply chain initiative (EU SCI), established on 1 April 2013, a few years later than the BE SCI.

The BE SCI gathers representatives of the different federations throughout the agri-food chain:

- The feed sector represented by the Belgian Feed Association BFA
- The agriculture sector represented by AGROFront, i.e. Boerenbond and Algemeen Boerensyndicaat for the Flemish region and Fédération Wallonne de l'Agriculture FWA for the Walloon region
- The food industry represented by Fevia
- The branded goods manufacturers represented by BABM
- The SME food, trade and retail sector represented by Unizo for the Flemish region and UCM for the Walloon region
- The retail sector represented by Comeos

The BE SCI is broader in scope than the EU SCI as it also involves representatives of the feed and agriculture sector.

The BE SCI reconfirmed its mission in 2016: self-regulation on fair trading practices by establishing and enforcing a framework for transparent, fair and balanced pricing throughout the agri-food chain, knowing that the government withdraws from market regulation.

The functioning of the BE SCI and its ambition to set the agenda and to establish a framework for further self-regulation is summarised in Figure 4.

By developing a code of conduct the BE SCI has set a basic horizontal framework providing guidance to all actors in the food chain on fair commercial relations (see 2.3.1.1). The BE SCI manages and promotes affiliation to the code and organises its enforceability through a dispute settlement mechanism (see 2.3.1.2). Recognizing the broad and basic nature of the code and the need for more sector specific details to deal with disputes, the BE SCI developed broad guidelines for sectoral IPA's, setting the agenda for and facilitating further sectoral concertation that can eventually result in sectoral IPA's and even standard contractual terms (see 2.3.1.3). As discussions on quality and other requirements are often recurring in disputes, the BE SCI developed a methodology to clearly demarcate generic requirements from specific requirements (see 2.3.1.4). Eventually, it is up to inter-branch organisations to define the generic requirements for their sector. Finally, as the BE SCI wants to be a platform to discuss common problems and challenges it has dealt with a number of relevant issues on an ad hoc basis such as the Russian ban on European agri-food product, societal discussions on animal welfare, food and health, food waste and other sustainability issues.

By establishing together, on an equal footing, this horizontal framework and agenda, unfair trading practices can be dealt with and can be avoided as it promotes fair dealing and facilitates fair, balanced and transparent agreements at the appropriate sectoral inter-professional or commercial level. However, it must be clear that the BE SCI is explicitly limited to the broader horizontal level. It is up to each sector to bring in the necessary specificity and detail and eventually up to the individual contracting parties to respect agreements in the framework of self-regulation, to determine the commercial aspects of the deal in terms of quantity and quality required and price agreed and to determine their own commercial strategy in terms of added-value creation and risk management.

Figure 4. BE SCI – agenda and framework for self-regulation

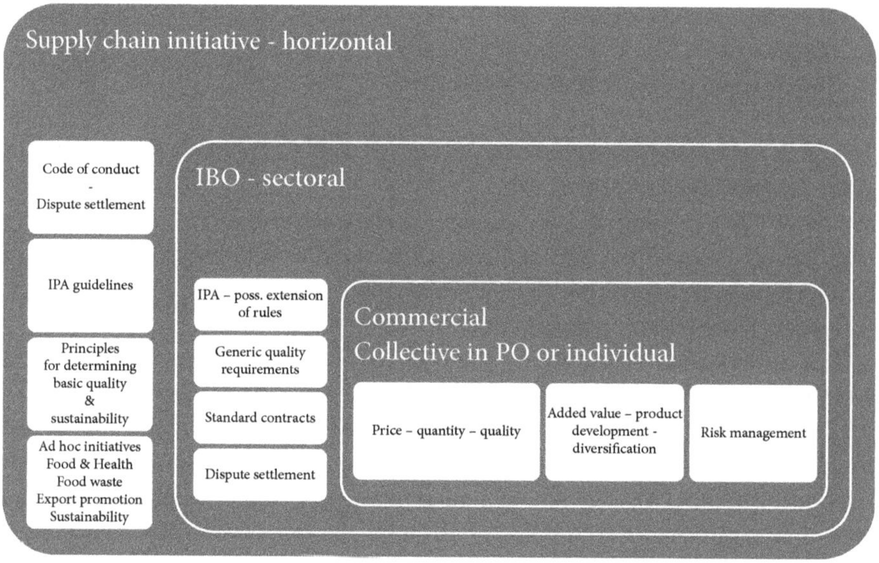

2.3.1.1. Code of conduct

Already in an early stage, the BE SCI has developed a code of conduct for fair relationships between suppliers and purchasers in the agri-food chain (see Box 1). The code was signed on 20th May 2010. To bring it in line with the European code, signed by the EU SCI in November 2011, the Belgian code was adjusted and fully aligned with the EU code in June 2014 allowing full mutual recognition between the BE and EU SCI.

The code applies to all links in the chain and to all operators (both on the side of purchasers and of suppliers) and governs relations between purchasers and suppliers. The code is used as reference within the agro food chain. In case of relations between farmers and their purchasers and/or suppliers, this code is to be considered as a guide to the inter-professional agreements in the various sectors.

Box 1. The code of conduct: 11 principles of good practice

1. In strict compliance with competition and other applicable laws, purchasers and suppliers exchange general information on markets and consumer trends, to enable the supplier to match supply and demand, and-if necessary-to diversify or adapt.
2. Purchasers and suppliers behave as partners towards a sustainable development of the whole agro-food chain taking into account the consumers interests. To this end, the three dimensions
   a. 'Society' (a decent income for both the employee and employer)
   b. 'Environment' (an activity that has minimal impact on the ecological system for future generations)
   c. 'Economy'(a sufficient economic return guaranteeing the continuity of all links of the chain)

   are considered together and approached in a balanced manner.
3. Purchasers guarantee a careful handling of food products, to value to a maximum the efforts of suppliers.
4. Purchasers and suppliers and in particular the agreements they conclude, should comply with all contractually agreed clauses. They should comply with the payment delays parties agreed upon or, in absence of such an agreement, the legal payment delay of thirty calendar days. The payment delay depends on the moment of transfer of the property which is specific to the sector or product.
5. Purchasers source local products where these are competitively positioned (both in terms of price and quality) and where they fit the commercial strategy.
6. Purchasers and suppliers establish a written agreement with clear conditions (possibly with the way of remuneration) of which both parties can take prior knowledge.
7. Purchasers and suppliers do not impose unilateral changes to contract conditions.
8. Purchasers and suppliers will only exchange information in strict compliance with competition and other applicable laws, and they should take reasonable care to ensure that the information supplied is correct and not misleading.
9. Purchasers and suppliers must respect confidentiality of information unless the information is already made public or has been independently obtained by the receiving party lawfully and in good faith. Confidential information shall be used by the recipient party only for the purpose for which it was communicated
10. All contracting parties in the supply chain will bear their own appropriate entrepreneurial risks.
11. A contracting party shall not apply threats in order to obtain an unjustified advantage or to transfer an unjustified cost.

Adherence to the code is voluntary but must be transparent, e.g. by a public "declaration of fair relationships between suppliers and buyers" with reference to the code. Furthermore and although adherence is done individually, the federations will communicate which members respect the code (e.g. via their website). By this individual act of adhesion of the operators the recommendations of the code of conduct become binding.

To date 261 individual companies subscribed to the code: 42 companies from the feed sector, 203 companies from the food industry and 16 companies from the retail sector.

However, the members of ABS, Boerenbond, FWA, UNIZO and UCM joined collectively by means of the signature of the presidents of these associations. The number of operators represented by these organizations, who can make use of the dispute settlement procedure of the code of conduct, is hence substantially larger than the 261 large companies who had to subscribe on an individual basis. This gives the code of conduct a broad support base.

Given the declaration of mutual recognition of the Belgian code of conduct of June 2014, and the European Supply Chain Initiative, memberships are simultaneous at both levels.

The code addresses several of the issues flagged by farmers (see 1.2.1) although only in broad and general terms. Principle 7 tackles the unilaterality, which is an important element in UTPs. Principle 4 handles with post deal changes, another root cause of UTPs, insisting on full respect of contractual agreements, backed by principle 6 insisting on written agreements so that at least agreements are clear. Principles 3, 10, 11 are rough approaches to a fair distribution of risks, costs and benefits. Also the issue of transparency, balanced information and confidentiality of that information is roughly addressed in principles 1, 8 and 9.

The code is instrumental as a guidance document towards fairer dealings in the agri-food chain. However, its broad and general nature makes it harder to use in specific disputes. Therefore more detail is often needed, which is furthermore sector specific.

2.3.1.2. Dispute settlement

The BE SCI organises the codes enforceability through a dispute settlement mechanism (see Figure 5) managed by a governance committee composed of official representatives appointed by the sector organizations involved in the agri-food chain. To ensure independence and anonymity the governance committee is presided over by an independent president from outside the agri-food chain. The latter moderates the discussions, monitors the agreed dispute procedure and the 'comply or explain' principle and assures anonymity of the process and the parties involved, both complainant and defendant.

In principle the committee only acts on aggregated disputes, meaning disputes affecting several companies or a returning complaint or issue. Companies that signed the code and that are affected by alleged breaches of the code inform their professional organisation that can initiate an aggregated dispute on their behalf and assure the anonymity of the complainant. Companies that signed the code but are not affiliated to one of the federations member of the BE SCI can address their complaints directly to the independent president of the committee.

Purchasers and suppliers signing the code are dedicated to the consultation model as a strategy to resolve disputes in their relations. Hence, alleged breaches of the code on an individual level must be first handled bilaterally following an escalation procedure, as complainants are expected to engage all reasonable efforts to resort first to the procedures that are easier, faster and at lower cost to resolve their disputes. The complainant may choose the method for the settlement of disputes. Following modes, in ascending order of complexity, rapidness and cost, can be envisaged:

- Commercial track
- Contract options
- Internal dispute resolution
- Mediation/arbitration which require the consent of both parties
- Jurisdictional methods.

Also in an aggregated dispute the committee shall ask the parties involved in a dispute to demonstrate that they followed this escalation procedure.

Companies that deviate from the recommendations of the code of conduct must clarify or 'explain' their policy on the matter. If, given the context, the explanation is not satisfactory they eventually have to comply with the recommendations of the code. This methodology takes into account that assessing the fairness of a trading practice must consider the specific context that, among others, differs from sector to sector. It acknowledges the fact that trading practices are hard to qualify as black or white as it is all about the right balance given the specific context.

If a dispute raised at sectoral level cannot be solved, the governance committee can invite the parties to appoint a certified mediator in order to start a conciliation procedure (the cost of which will be borne by the parties involved).

In derogation to the general rule, the Committee can act on individual complaints, upon request of both parties, after exhausting the bilateral steps in the escalation procedure or if the necessary contacts in the framework of the bilateral escalation procedure are lacking. The committee in a first instance invites the involved parties to set up a bilateral dialogue and can act as a de facto mediator in the dispute, providing guidance on the way forward and eventually draw lessons from the case that may lead to adjustments to the code or proposals for more specific self-regulation.

Figure 5. BE SCI dispute settlement procedure – individual versus aggregated complaints

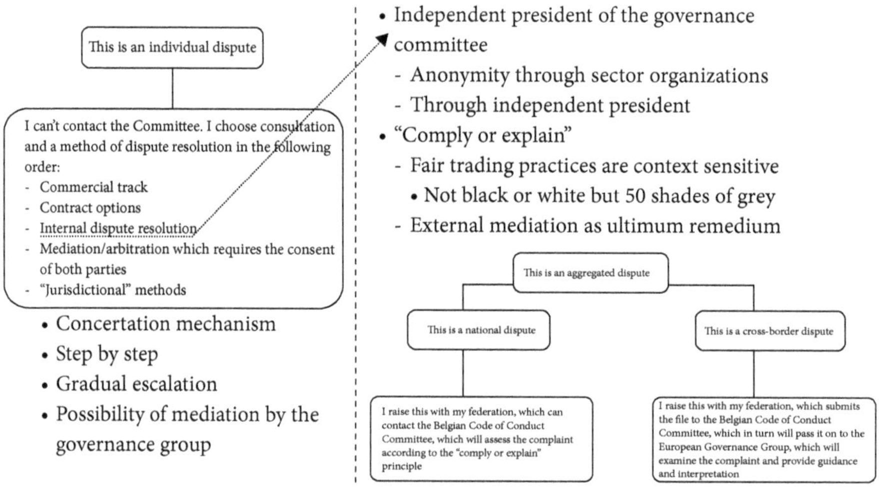

The Belgian Committee can only act on complaints between Belgian companies. However, given the mutual recognition cross-border disputes initiated at Belgian level will be forwarded to the European committee who will investigate and give guidance and interpretation.

The horizontal and abstract level of the code makes it hard to implement it in practice. No formal complaints have been logged. However, a culture of pre-notification of issues that could eventually lead to a formal complaint has grown throughout the years between the actors in the BE SCI. 3 to 5 issues a year on average were discussed over the years in an informal manner, bringing the involved actors back around the table with guidance on how to proceed the discussion further in a constructive matter. Some discussions continued at the sectoral level and resulted in specific inter-professional agreements settling the matter in generic terms.

Furthermore, the BE SCI encourages interbranch organisations to incorporate this dispute settlement methodology in their own inter-professional agreements. The idea is to bring dispute settlement as close as possible to the appropriate level of expertise, in terms of more detailed self-regulation and in terms of assessment of the specific context (see Figure 4).

2.3.1.3. Guidelines for inter-professional agreements

The code is horizontal and general in nature. Hence, to resolve commercial disputes, often arising from lacking, unclear or biased interpretation of contractual terms that are very sector specific, more sector specific depth and details are needed. It is not the ambition of the BE SCI to develop more sector specific inter-professional agreements. Nevertheless, the BE SCI encourages sectors to go further. To facilitate the next steps at sectoral level, the BE SCI developed a set of guidelines for sectoral inter-professional agreements (see Box 2).

The main issue when initiating concertation at sectoral level is how far discussions can go without conflicting with competition law. What is the pre-competitive playing field? The reasons to have this discussions range from reasonable concern to willingly delaying any progress in the discussion. The developed guidelines for sectoral IPA's already set the agenda and allow to go directly to the real content of the discussion. The building blocks identified, are broadly in line with the elements listed in the CMO Regulation Art. 175 §1 c) on inter professional organisations, where they are more specific and detailed.

Box 2. Guidelines for inter-professional agreements

- Measurement & control of delivered quality
- Production requirements (see also 2.3.1.4)
- Delivery conditions
- Obligation of delivery, obligation of purchase, duration and staggering in time, early & late deliveries, place of delivery, transport modalities, …
- Elements and principals of price setting
- Payment conditions
- Agreements on how to handle excess or under supply
- Agreements on the valorisation of co-products
- Risk analysis, responsibility and "force majeure"
- Dispute settlement procedures

Eventually, if an IPA can be reached and how detailed it will be, still depends on the willingness of the parties around the table. As it is all about rebalancing powers and reducing variables or uncertainties that could be used by one of the parties to their advantage and to the detriment of the other, this remains the area of tough negotiations, taking time and yielding only incremental progress. However, any result is always instrumental in reducing the risk of unfair trading practices.

2.3.1.4. Inter-professional market access

A third element discussed in the BE SCI is the demarcation between generic requirements and specific requirements as laid down in specifications. In a commercial discussion the requesting party tends to argue that the specific requirements they ask for are rather common requests from the market at large and should not be remunerated above regular market price. The discussion does not arise from legal food safety, quality or environmental requirements but from requirements going beyond the legal framework. They are often linked with the specific implementation of legal requirements, elements anticipating upcoming legal requirements or elements in response to specific societal expectations.

To rebalance these commercial negotiations a methodology was developed to determine in concertation the inter-professional agreed access to the market demarcation line. The methodology consist of a thorough screening of commercial specifications on the Belgian market to identity the common requirements across all those commercial specifications. The legal requirements, combined with the extra legal requirements found in all relevant Belgian commercial specifications establish the inter-professional market access (see Figure 6). Any requirements going beyond this line justify and require commercial negotiations to agree on a surplus to be paid above the regular market price. This sets the scene for a more balanced discussion on the relation between requested quality and received price, where the imbalance between both is seen by farmers as the main injustice in the agri-food chain and which is strongly associated by them with unfair trading practices. The methodology can not only be applied to food safety and quality requirements but to sustainability and animal welfare requirements as well.

Eventually, it is up to interbranch organisations to define the generic requirements for their sector.

Figure 6. Demarcation of inter-professional market access

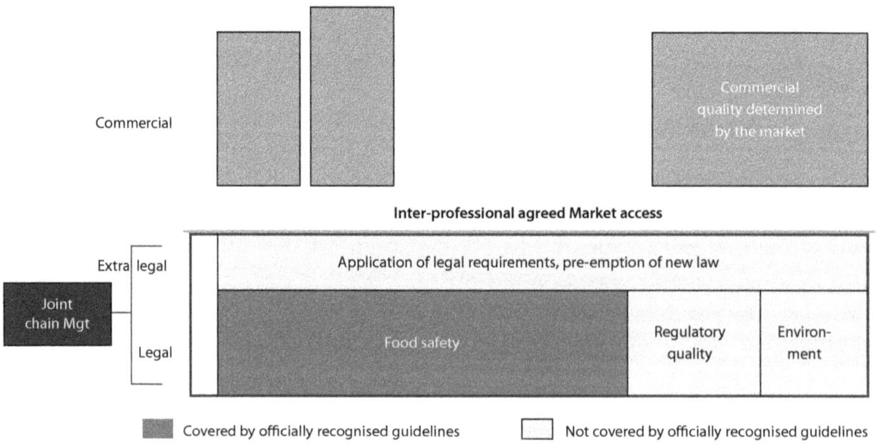

2.3.2. Farmers assessment of the Belgian Supply Chain Initiative

In the survey Boerenbond conducted among its members, they were also asked to assess how useful they think the BE SCI is and what they expect from the BE SCI.

The BE SCI is fairly well known by farmers. 43% already read something about it. 26% talked about it. The importance of the BE SCI is well understood by farmers. 77% strongly agrees with the quote that it is useful that the feed sector, agriculture sector, food industry, traders and retailers meet on a regular basis to discuss common issues and to develop common proposals, with another 16% agreeing with the quote. The support for the concept of a BE SCI among farmers does not mean they would go for a less activist approach as a majority (56%) agrees that farmers' interest are best served by a stern union approach against the other links in the food chain.

Farmers have high expectations towards the BE SCI. Nine out of ten expect that the BE SCI reaches binding agreements on right and fair trading practices. Good three quarters even expects firm price agreements, although this would violate EU legislation. Finally they support a European approach to unfair trading practices rather than an approach at national level. (see Table 7)

Table 7. Expectations toward the BE SCI

	--	-	+	++	NO	Tot.
Boerenbond must reach binding agreements on right and fair trading practices with our suppliers and distributors	2%	5%	23%	66%	4%	100%
The BE SCI must come to firm price agreements	4%	13%	27%	50%	6%	100%
Unfair trading practices are preferably tackled on a European level, rather than on the Belgian level	9%	16%	26%	45%	5%	100%

Farmers see one clear priority for the BE SCI: transparent and fair pricing. This is the number one priority for 44% of farmers. Fair trading practices come in as second priority. Only 18% of farmers see it as the first priority but it is often indicated as second or third priority. But it is clear that both topics are seen as the top priorities as other topic follow way behind. Combating abuses and managing complaints completes the top three priorities (see Table 8).

Table 8. Priorities for the BE SCI

	1ste	2de	3de	Top3
Set up and enforce rules on transparent and faire pricing	44%	15%	9%	67%
Establish and monitor fair trading practices between buyers and sellers	18%	26%	16%	60%
Combat abuses and manage complaints	8%	12%	13%	33%
Mitigate risks within the chain and take measures in the event of crises	4%	8%	10%	21%
Agree on generic and specific quality requirements	4%	7%	7%	18%
Set up and manage a fund to compensate farmers in the event of market crises	6%	7%	4%	17%
Promote Belgian agri-food products at national, European and third country markets	4%	7%	4%	16%
Work on a more sustainable agri-food chain	4%	5%	4%	13%
Adopt common positions on societal topics	2%	1%	3%	6%
Others	2%	1%	2%	5%

2.4. TO REGULATION ON UNFAIR TRADING PRACTICES

After a long political debate the European Commission made a proposal for a Directive (EU) 2019/633 on unfair trading practices in the agricultural and food supply chain in April 2018. It was adopted in March 2019. It complements already existing rules at the level of Member States as well as voluntary initiatives of the industry, such as the BE SCI.

The directive draws a clear bottom line at EU level, indispensable within the common European market. It is important that authorities clearly indicate where the limits of freedom of contract lay as they are used to the detriment of others beyond that point. The Commission rightly recognised the need for flexibility, allowing for stricter rules or going beyond its scope. In this perspective, opting for a Directive instead of a Regulation is reasonable. On the other hand, transposing the Directive in national law takes time, a delay you can miss when you are confronted with UTPs on a regular basis.

Some elements from the code of conduct are covered by the directive, often in more detail, while it adds others. Table 9 compares the black list of the UTP directive with the code of conduct. The most practical elements from the code of conduct are now covered by the UTP directive. Where the code's principle 10 states in general terms that all parties have to bear their own appropriate entrepreneurial risks, the UTP directive seems to make this general principal more tangible and concrete, especially in the grey list. Principles 1 and 8 of the code, about the exchange of information that is correct and not misleading, is covered by other initiatives by the European Commission in its efforts to increase market transparency, instrumental in reducing the risk of UTPs linked to information bias. Principal 2 of the code on the partnership towards sustainable development of the whole agri-food chain, is at the heart and soul of the UTP debate. However, as such it is hard to implement. All other elements can be seen as proxies to that and eventually contributing to the goal set out in principal 2 of the code.

Table 9. Comparison the UTP directive black list and the Code of conduct

UTP Directive	Code of conduct
Late payments	Principle 4
Short-notice cancellations	≈ principle 10
Unilateral contract changes	Principle 7
Not related payments	-
Transfer of risk of loss and deterioration	Principle 3 Principle 10
Refusal of written confirmation	Principle 6
Misuse of trade secrets	Principle 9
Commercial retaliation	Principle 11
Transfer of costs of complaints	≈ principle 10
Grey list	≈ principle 10

The Directive is clear on state supervision, enforcement and sanctioning but limits it clearly to the 16 listed UTPs. Hence, it seems to come in place of the BE SCI for elements covered by the Directive, bypassing any escalation, the basic principle in the codes dispute settlement. Furthermore, the Directive does not strengthen self-regulation as it did not set up the authority to be designated to enforce the Directive as an arbitrator of last resort in any discussion on alleged UTPs.

However, article 7 of the UTP directive on alternative dispute resolution, does not rule out that the governance committee of the BE SCI can still play a role if the designated enforcement authority opts to position itself somewhere in an escalation procedure instead of positioning itself as a third road between voluntary dispute settlements and the jurisdictional road.

The UTP Directive (EU) 2019/633 eventually draws a much needed clear bottom line at EU level. Although it supersedes quite some elements of the industry led code of conduct and even goes beyond that, it leaves enough room for complementarity.

3. CONCLUSION

Farmers are often confronted with unfair trading practices. Imbalance in bargaining power and lack of detailed agreements are at the root of many

UTPs. This results in an eventual imbalance between price received and quality required at the farmers' end.

For decades, strong market regulation at EU level assured a fair price to farmers, hence UTPs were not an issue in itself. But consecutive reforms of the common agricultural policy brought the discussion on UTPs back to the forefront.

Although deregulating, the EU developed a toolbox allowing the farmers to organise themselves and to come to collective agreements with other actors in the agri-food chain, answering the imbalance in bargaining power and bringing in more detail in agreements, already at a higher and supposedly more balanced level. The latter is eventually a kind of self-regulation. Both elements are instrumental in addressing unfair trading practices.

At Belgian level, the representative organisations in the agri-food chain took up this toolbox and developed a horizontal agenda and framework for this self-regulation. However, much needed sectoral specification must be developed at sectoral level, outside the scope of the horizontal BE SCI. This remains the area of tough negotiations taking time and yielding only incremental progress, that however is always instrumental in reducing UTPs.

That's why it is important that there is still regulation drawing a clear bottom line at EU level. This is the aim of the UTP Directive (EU) 2019/633. This bottom line is not fixed and might evolve over time, taking into account national regulation in an effort to level the playing field, and the effectiveness of self-regulation if it is unable to answer manifest UTPs. It is important to notice that the Directive leaves enough room for complementarity with self-regulation initiatives.

Giving the experience that specific trading practices are hard to qualify as black or white as it is all about the right balance given the specific context, hard regulation cannot address all UTPs. Self-regulation and its dispute settlement based on 'comply or explain' are well equipped to add sectoral specificities and details and to take into account the specific context when assessing trading practices on their fairness. Furthermore, a sector led dispute settlement keeps the dialogue open and allows for building on lessons learned. A pure government dispute settlement may break any future dialogue.

However, regulation could also strengthen self-regulation by setting up an arbiter of last resort in the event that industry led dispute settlement does not come to resolution. This angle unfortunately lacks in the UTP directive.

CHAPTER 10

UNFAIR B2B TRADING PRACTICES: GENERAL OUTLOOK AND PRELIMINARY CONCLUSIONS

Jules Stuyck
em. professor KU Leuven

1. INTRODUCTION

This short paper is based on the 'General Outlook and Preliminary Conclusions' presented at the Second UTP Round Table in Leuven on 21 June 2018. It is the fruit of reflections that came up during recent years when studying the subject as well as during the round table.

In terms of scholarly research the subject of unfair B2B trading practices is rather recent, certainly at the EU level. This paper consists of questions rather than answers.

My questions are not confined to the EU proposal that was the main subject matter of the June 2018 round table: B2B unfair trading practices in the food supply chain, but relate to the broader subject of the increasing concern by legislatures with certain practices in the supply chain where the weaker business is unfairly treated by its stronger counterparty (supplier or, and more often, purchaser, *i.e.* large retail chain).

The first series of questions are about the history and nature of UTP regulations: where do we come from and which is the place of UTPs in the law? Does it fill a gap (between antitrust law and unfair competition law)? What do we want: regulation, self-regulation or general contract law, or all of it?

The second series of questions relate to the consequences of UTP regulations. What are the effects of such regulations on competition and market structures, on costs and prices? What is left of the freedom to contract? Can national rules be frustrated by the rules of private international law? Will heavily protected and regulated business in Europe survive in the global economy? And finally: is this the end of the responsible entrepreneur?

2. THE NATURE OF UTP REGULATIONS

2.1. WHERE DO WE COME FROM?

2.1.1. Fairness in commercial behaviour

The involvement of the law in unfair business practices started with the law of unfair competition.

Historically, the law of unfair competition originates in the Paris Convention on Industrial Property of 1883 (PUC), as amended in 1900 in Brussels. Article 10*bis* introduced the principle of domestic treatment of all citizens of Member States of the Paris Union with regard to unfair competition. The Hague revision of the Convention added the obligation for the Member States to provide each other's citizens effective protection against acts of unfair competition ("concurrence déloyale").[1] At the same time unfair competition was defined as acts which are contrary to honest business practices ("*actes contraires aux usages honnêtes en matière commerciale et industrielle*"). The creation of confusion and misleading the public by false statements about competitors are listed as acts of unfair competition.[2] This can be explained in that the initial objective of unfair competition law was the protection of business goodwill ("*le fonds de commerce*"), more precisely the protection of those elements of a business that were not specifically protected by intellectual property rights (such as trademarks and patents). In many countries the law of unfair competition is still closely linked to the law of intellectual property.[3]

Historically, as can *i.a.* be seen in the examples given in Article 10*bis* (3)[4] of the PUC, the law of unfair competition was a derivative of industrial property law: the trader should be protected not only against acts of competitors

---

1 See A. Bakardjieva – Engelbrekt, *Fair Trading Law in Flux*, ph.d. Stockholm University, 2003, at p. 13 et seq.

2 Harte-Bavendamm/Henning-Bodewig, *Gesetz gegen den unlauteren Wettbewerb (UWG)*, 4e ed., Münich, Beck, 2016, p. 46.

3 The TRIPS 1994 Agreement contains a partial reference to unfair competition and to the Paris Convention. Pursuant to Article 39(1) Members shall, in the course of ensuring effective protection against unfair competition as provided in Article 10*bis* of the Paris Union Convention (1967), protect undisclosed information in accordance with paragraph 2 and data submitted to governments or governmental agencies in accordance with paragraph 3. The significance of the reference to unfair competition law in TRIPS remains highly controversial; does it refer to more than the protection of the commercial name? see: M. Pflüger, *Reichweite internationalrechtlicher Vorgaben*, in R. Hilty –F. Henning-Bodewig, *Lauterskeitsrecht und Acquis communautaire*, Berlin, Springer, 2009, p. 72.

4 The following in particular shall be prohibited:
1. all acts of such a nature as to create confusion by any means whatever with the establishment, the goods, or the industrial or commercial activities, of a competitor;
2. false allegations in the course of trade of such a nature as to discredit the establishment, the goods, or the industrial or commercial activities, of a competitor;

infringing on his intellectual property rights, but also against acts that in any other way unfairly diminished his competition capacity, in particular acts that affected other elements of his goodwill, such as his reputation and distinctive features that are not protected by intellectual property laws.

Later, the law of unfair competition evolved so as to include relations between non competitors, such as manufacturers and distributors. Also new forms of unfair competition were recognized, such as industrial espionage, complicity in someone else's breach of contract, boycott, etc. The objectives of unfair competition law also evolved. Gradually the courts took into consideration the interest of consumers and the general interest. In that sense the law of unfair competition was the cradle of the law of B2C unfair commercial practices that first developed in the Nordic countries around 1970 and further spread in many EU countries and culminated in the B2C Unfair Commercial Practices Directive 2005/29 (UCPD). The idea of a general cause prohibiting unfair behaviour (see Article 5 UCPD) is definitely borrowed from unfair competition law.

The law of unfair competition is essentially of an extra-contractual nature. The exploitation of the position of weakness of a contract partner has not (or hardly) been dealt with in unfair competition law. But yes, over the years, the law of unfair competition has mainly been an instrument of protection of small shopkeepers against new entrants that threatened their vested position, such as ambulant traders, emerging large retails shops, discounters. This function of unfair competition law also explains that in countries where it exists the general clause on unfair competition was and is also often supplemented by *per se* prohibitions of specific practices, in particular certain forms of sales promotions, some of which (such as the prohibition of premium offers or restrictions on the announcement of price reductions) have been declared contrary to the UCPD, by the CJEU, in that they were presented by national legislatures as aiming *i.a.* at the protection of consumers. The Court confirmed that the UCPD is a full harmonisation Directive. Hence practices, such as the methods of sales promotions mentioned above, that are not blacklisted by the Directive (see the Annex), cannot be prohibited *per se*, i.e. without examination case by case (by the judge or the administration) of its unfair character, in the circumstances of the case, and its influence on the consumer's transactional decision.[5]

As such, the law of unfair competition in the EU remains purely national, with the exception of (i) protection against misleading advertising, (ii) the authorisation, under certain conditions, of comparative advertising, and (iii) the

3. indications or allegations the use of which in the course of trade is liable to mislead the public as to the nature, the manufacturing process, the characteristics, the suitability for their purpose, or the quantity, of the goods.

5 See J. Stuyck, "The Court of Justice and the Unfair Commercial Practices Directive", *CMLRev.* 2015, 721 et seq.

protection of know-how. This last field has traditionally often been considered as a part of unfair competition law, in the absence of specific protection as an IP-right. Recently, however, as a result of the TRIPS Agreement (1994) the EU adopted a Know-How Directive.[6] Much earlier, in 1984, the EU adopted a minimum harmonisation directive on misleading advertising, both in B2B and B2C relations (Directive 84/450). This Directive was amended in 1997 (by Directive 97/55) to authorise, under certain conditions, comparative advertising.[7] In 2005 the EU legislature harmonised the law of unfair commercial practices by businesses vis-à-vis consumers (Directive 2005/29 or UCPD). In B2B relations the harmonisation remains limited to misleading advertising (minimum harmonisation) and comparative advertising (full harmonisation). This harmonisation was consolidated in the Misleading and Comparative Advertising Directive (MCAD) (Directive 2006/114).

The UCPD is also basically about extra-contractual, or rather pre-contractual, relations.

2.1.2. Fairness in contractual relations

Consumers are protected against unfair behaviour of businesses in contractual relations by national laws that implement the Unfair Contract Terms Directive 93/13 (UCTD). According to Article 3(1) of that Directive "*A contractual term which has not been individually negotiated shall be regarded as unfair if, contrary to the requirement of good faith, it causes a significant imbalance in the parties' rights and obligations arising under the contract, to the detriment of the consumer.*"

The Member States have implemented this Directive, some by adding a black list of clauses that are deemed to be unfair (the Directive is a minimum harmonisation Directive).[8]

Pursuant to Article 4(2) of the UCTD the assessment of the unfair nature of the terms shall relate neither to the definition of the main subject matter of the contract nor to the adequacy of the price and remuneration, on the one hand, as against the services or goods supplies in exchange, on the other, in so far as these terms are in plain intelligible language. Again, in view of the minimum harmonisation character of the Directive, Member States can extend the protection to so called 'core terms', including price control (see e.g. Spain).[9]

---

6 Directive (EU) 2016/943 of the European Parliament and of the Council of 8 June 2016 on the protection of undisclosed know-how and business information (trade secrets) against their unlawful acquisition, use and disclosure, (2016) OJ L 157/1.

7 In the past comparative advertising was prohibited or severely restricted in a certain number of Member States, because it was considered to be a form of unfair competition.

8 See P. Nebbia, *Unfair Contracts Terms in EU aw*, Oxford, Hart, 2007, 126–127; H.-W. Micklitz – N. Reich, "The Court and *Sleeping Beauty*: The revival of the Unfair Contract Terms Directive (UCTD)" (2014), *CMLRev.* 2014, 771 et seq.

9 Judgment of 3 June 2010, *Caja de Ahorros*, C-484/08, EU:C:2010:309.

Some Member States, like Germany, have extended the general protection of consumers against unfair contract terms to businesses.[10]

2.1.3. *Competition*

Competition (or antitrust) law in Europe is much younger than unfair competition law. It started in the late 1950s in Germany and in the EU (effectively in 1962 with Regulation 17/62, providing for the necessary implementing powers, later replaced by Regulation 1/2003).

The aim of competition law is to guarantee effective competition by combatting restrictions of competition: restrictive agreements and abuse of a dominant position (Article 101 and 102 Treaty on the Functioning of the European Union) (TFEU). Strict prohibitions of unfair competition can lead to a restriction of the competitive process. Hence there is an inherent tension between competition law and the law of unfair competition. If conduct is declared unfair because it runs counter to the values cherished by "honest" competitors – who may be inclined to prefer little competition – the outcome will be anticompetitive.

In recent years the official discourse of the Commission relating to competition policy also refers to fairness, but, in all fairness, this is rather rhetoric than reality. It has been submitted that fairness is not a standard of competition law (Articles 101 and 102 TFEU), but of other branches of the law, such as indeed the law of unfair trading practices.[11]

In this context it should be remembered that Article 3(1) of Regulation 1/2003 contains an obligation on the Member States not only to apply national competition rules but also Article 101 or 102 TFEU where they are applicable. This rule *de facto* forces the Member States towards convergence of their national competition laws. Second, there is the rule of Article 3(2) of the Regulation that the application of national competition law may not lead to the prohibition of agreements which may affect trade between Member States but which do not restrict competition within the meaning of Article 101(1), or which fulfil the conditions of Article 101(3). However the latter provision does not preclude Member States from adopting and applying on their territory stricter national laws which prohibit or sanction unilateral conduct engaged in by undertakings (Article 3(2)). Finally, Article 3(3) of Regulation 1/2003 provides expressly that the two principles (mentioned in Article 3(1) and 3(2)) do not preclude the application of provisions of national law that *predominantly pursue an objective*

---

10 Recently Belgium followed, see Act of 4 April 2019 (*Official Gazette* 24 May 2019) on the abuse of economic dependency, unfair contract terms and unfair practices in relations between undertakings.

11 See J. Stuyck, "Unfair Commercial Practices and Fair Competition", in *Fairness in Competition Law Enforcement: Significance and Implications*, 13th Annual Conference of the GCLC (Brussels 25–26 January 2018), in press.

different from that pursued by Articles 101 and 102 TFEU. With the first exception the EU legislature had laws in mind that prohibit UTPs, discussed in section V below. With the second exception, the EU legislature had the law of unfair competition in mind.

In other words the EU competition rules are expressly neutral vis-à-vis the application of national laws on unfair trading practices or unfair competition.

However, the application of unfair competition law to conduct that falls within the scope of competition law may have undesirable consequences in that it can lead to the prohibition of conduct that is deemed to be harmless under competition law standards (such as a refusal to sell by a non-dominant undertaking or a (non-hard core) *de minimis* agreement). The Belgian Supreme Court ruled that restrictive conduct that is permissible pursuant to the competition rules cannot as such be qualified as unfair competition.[12]

2.2. THE PLACE OF UTPS IN THE LAW

It is against the background described in the preceding section (A) that UTP law emerged in Europe.

Some Member States started to prohibit certain forms of unilateral conduct beyond Article 102 TFEU (abuse of a dominant position)[13], i.e. practices by non-dominant businesses that are qualified as abusive in relation to weaker business partners. Examples are Article 20(1) German Competition Act (GWB) and Articles L-420–2 and 442–6 (now: Article L-442–1) French Commercial Code (Code de Commerce). The German provision is rather limited, while French law is very broad in scope.[14] Other Member States introduced legislation in more recent years. According to the Commission already 24 Member States adopted legislation in the field of UTPs.[15]

Interestingly UTP provisions are often integrated in the statutory instrument that relates to the domestic equivalent of Articles 101 and 102 TFEU. This is notably the case in France and Germany (and recently Belgium). One of the consequences is that the sanctions and enforcement tools of competition law apply. It also shows that in these countries the prohibition of UTPs is related, i.e. complementary, to the prohibition of abuse of a dominant position. In that sense

12 Cass. 7 January 2000, *Revue critique de Jurisprudence belge*, 2001, p. 249, note J. Stuyck.
13 The legality of which is recognized by Article 3(2) Regulation 1/2003 (see above).
14 See the contributions of respectively J. Glöckner and D. Voinot to this publication.
15 Explanatory Memorandum Proposal Directive on unfair trading practices in business-to-business relationships in the supply chain, COM(2018)173 def. For an analysis of the laws of Member States that had such legislation in 2013, see A. Renda e.a., *Study on the Legal Framework covering Business-to-Busines Unfair Trading Practices in the Retail Supply Chain, Final Report*, 26 February 2014, ^prepared for the European Commission, DG Internal Market DG MARKT/2012/049/E.

a prohibition of UTPs can be seen as imposing on non-dominant undertakings a special responsibility, which the Court of Justice has put on dominant undertakings[16], here not because of their absolute market power, but because of a kind of relative market power vis-à-vis certain commercial partners (suppliers or clients).

As to the effects of such legislation it is interesting to quote a Study presented in 2012 to the European Commission[17]:

> "Most national rules that are stricter than Article 102 TFEU appear to be harmful to consumers. This is due to reduced product variety created by the lack of a Single Market; but also to the fact that many of the stricter rules on unilateral conduct are meant to protect smaller competitors, rather than the competitive process, most often leading to price increases for end consumers. This is particularly the case for national rules on abuse of economic dependence/ superior bargaining power, as well as rules on sales below costs, which –as we estimated through an economic analysis – lead to artificial price increases up to 3%."

Since competition law does not address unilateral conduct by non-dominant undertakings and unfair competition law does not address contract terms or practices that relate to the conditions of supply, UTP law obviously fills a gap, at least in so far as one considers that the phenomenon of UTPs should be regulated. Because of the effects of such regulation on prices and/or the possibility to tackle the most obvious forms of abuse of relative market power with existing legal instruments or less intrusive legislation (such as a general prohibition of unfair contracts terms in B2B contracts or a per se prohibition of very specific practices), legislatures might be well advised to refrain from introducing UTP legislation like the one that e.g. exists in France.

Yet, legislatures of most of the Member States have adopted legislation to prohibit B2B UTPs, or are in the process of doing so. The EU has recently adopted a Directive on unfair business-to-business trade practices in the food supply chain.[18] In some Member States there is, so far, only self-regulation, as promoted by the European Commission, until recently, as the best way to tackle UTPs. At the EU level there is the voluntary Supply Chain Initiative. Regulation takes very different forms: short or long black lists, a general clause, or a combination of both. Eventually general contract law also plays a role here.[19]

---

16 Constant case law of the European courts.

17 *The Impact of national rules on unilateral conduct that diverge from Article 102 TFEU (Final report)*, p. 182.

18 Directive (EU) 2019/633 of the European Parliament and of the Council of 17 April 2019 on unfair trading practices in business-to-business relationships in the agricultural and food supply chain, OJ L 111, 25.4.2019, p. 59–72.

19 See e.g. France, the paper by D. Voinot.

There is a risk that an accumulation of norms of a different kind lead to confusion and to a stifling effect on competition and normal commercial practice.

Generally speaking, there is not one answer in Europe about what we want: the prohibition of specific practices (black list), a general clause, or both, self-regulation, protection of businesses against unfair contract terms, reliance on general contract law (probably not the latter), a mix of it, or all of it.

The law of UTPs is like the *platanus hispanica* in my garden. It blossoms very late in the season and then branches and leaves begin to spread intensely and in all directions. After trimming the next year the branches come back in full glory.

3. THE EFFECTS OF UTP LAW

3.1. WHAT ARE THE EFFECTS OF SUCH REGULATIONS ON COMPETITION AND MARKET STRUCTURES, ON COSTS AND PRICES?

It would seem that the introduction of regulations on UTPs in the Member States was not always preceded by an impact assessment.

In an Annex to the Impact Assessment of the Proposal for a European Directive on UTPs in the Food Supply Chain[20], called "Economic Impact of unfair trading practices regulations in the food supply chain" and presented by the Chief Economist of DG Comp, the risks of regulating unfair trading practices are pinpointed. Richard Sexton, who has written a technical report for the Joint Research Centre of DG Agri, warns that such a regulation could prevent efficiency-enhancing behaviours and commercial practices from taking place.[21] There can even be unintended negative consequences of regulating practices in the food supply chain. This concerns notably the trading relationships between (mostly brand) manufacturers holding a significant share of the market of the sales of food products in a particular product category in a given Member State. Regulation could reduce the pressure that large customers can exert on large manufacturers to reduce their margins (although this may not be the case where the rules only relate to UTPS of large retailers against SME suppliers, as was originally proposed by the Commission). The Chief Economist also refers to the fact that the French "loi Galland" that was supposed to protect small firms resulted in *de facto* industry-wide price floors to the detriment of consumers.[22]

20 SWD(2018)91 final.
21 P. 261–262.
22 P. 262.

3.2. WHAT IS LEFT OF THE FREEDOM TO CONTRACT?

The freedom to contract, one of the basic principles of liberal legal orders, is constantly under pressure. Where freedom to contract is discussed in literature it is generally to emphasise how in practice it is limited or should be further limited in the general interest: the protection of employees, tenants, consumers, and other parties in a weak position.[23] There is a tension between freedom (of contract) and social justice.[24]

Basedow has emphasised that the freedom to contract, which is a fundamental principle of European Union law, has to be seen in connection with the protection of competition. In this context freedom to contract is not a mere individualistic legal concept but an "Ordnungspolitische" one. As long as competition limits the excessive exercise of economic power, private autonomy and freedom to contract are in the general interest. Where market imperfections do not lead to competitive relationships, state intervention in the freedom to contract is legitimate.[25]

The contractual protection of consumers, in particular with regard to unfair standard terms, is based, according to the Court of Justice of the EU, on the idea that the consumer is in a weak position vis-à-vis the seller or supplier, as regards both his bargaining power and his level of knowledge. This leads to the consumer agreeing to terms drawn up in advance by the seller or supplier without being able to influence the content of those terms.[26]

It is often submitted that SME may be equally vulnerable as consumers when it comes to "lack of information, inexperience and dependence".[27]That may be so, but does not answer the question whether this is a sufficient legitimation to limit the freedom to contract in B2B relations (albeit limited to large versus small businesses) in a similar way as in B2C relationships. In business relationships contractual protection may lead to inefficiencies, e.g. the maintenance in the market of inefficient businesses.

3.3. CAN NATIONAL RULES BE FRUSTRATED BY THE RULES OF PRIVATE INTERNATIONAL LAW?

UTPs are contractual arrangements. UTP laws are national. Some are stricter than others and some Member States do not have a law on UTPs.

23 See e.g. F.H. Bucley (ed.) *The Fall and Rise of Freedom of Contract*, Duke University Press, Durham, 1999.

24 See M. Hesselink, *CFR and Social Justice*, Sellier, München, 2008.

25 J. Basedow, Die Europäische Union zwischen Marktfreiheit und Überregulierung – Das Schicksal der Vertragsfreiheit". *Bitburger Gespräche* München: C.H. Beck, p. 102.

26 Constant case law since Judgment of 27 June 2000, *Océano Grupo Editorial and Salvat Editores*, Joined Cases C-240/98 to C-244/98, EU:C:2000:346, at paragraph 25.

27 See *i.a.* M. Hesselink, footnote 24, at p. 36.

Looking at the EU UTP Directive it must be stressed that it is a minimum harmonisation instrument, meaning that Member States can take or maintain more protective measures. Hence, there will be disparities between national laws. According to the Rome I Regulation[28], parties can freely choose the law applicable. Article 3(1) reads: "*A contract shall be governed by the law chosen by the parties. The choice shall be made expressly or clearly demonstrated by the terms of the contract or the circumstances of the case. By their choice the parties can select the law applicable to the whole or to part only of the contract.*"

Pursant to Article 3(4) of the Directive Member States shall ensure hat the prohobitions of the Directive constitute "overriding mandatory provisions". Article 9 of Rome I[29] provides that nothing in this Regulation contains an exception. Nothing in the Regulation shall restrict the application of the "overriding mandatory provisions" of the law of the forum. "Overriding mandatory provisions" are provisions the respect for which is regarded as crucial by a country for safeguarding its public interests, such as its political, social or economic organisation, to such an extent that they are applicable to any situation falling within their scope, irrespective of the law otherwise applicable to the contract under this Regulation.

The concept of overriding mandatory provisions remains unclear.[30] It remains to be seen whether it applies to UTP laws. If not, parties can circumvent the stricter law of the forum by choosing the less strict law of another Member State.

But even if Article 9 applies, the application of the stricter law of the forum can perhaps be avoided by a jurisdiction clause. Pursuant to Article 25(1) of the Brussels I*bis* Regulation[31] parties can, by an express provision in their contract, confer jurisdiction on the courts of the Member State of their choice. Where a foreign judge is competent that may, often, despite the mandatory character of the provisions of the country of the abuse, *de facto* lead to non-application of the latter provisions.

It has been argued in France[32] that the prohibition of UTPs, which indeed is a provision of the section on competition law of the Commercial Code, is governed by Rome II on non-contractual obligations. Article 6(3) of that Regulation provides that the law applicable to a non-contractual obligation arising out of a restriction of competition shall be the law of the country where the market is, or is likely to be, affected, i.e. where a French distributor abuses his

---

28 Regulation 593/2008 on the law applicable to contractual obligations.

29 See also Article 16 of Rome II: Regulation 864/20007 on the law applicable to non-contractual obligations.

30 See Judgment of 17 October 2013, *Unamar*, C-184/12, EU:C:2013:663.

31 Regulation 1215/2012 on jurisdiction and the recognition and enforcement of judgments in civil and commercial matters.

32 M. Béhar-Touchais, "*Abus de puissance économique et droit international*", *Rev. Int. De dr. écon.*, 2010, 142 et seq.

market power vis-à-vis a supplier (established in France or elsewhere) that will be France. Hence French law applies. But again, the Regulation recognises the freedom of choice (Article 14(1)). However where all the elements relevant to the situation at the time when the event giving rise to the damage occurs are located in a country other than the country whose law has been chosen, the choice of the parties shall not prejudice the application of provisions of the law of that other country which cannot be derogated from by agreement (Art. 14(2)).

Eventually parties, or: the stronger party, can avoid the application of mandatory provisions of the country of the abuse (under Rome I or II) by an arbitration clause. The case law, notably in France on the enforceability of such an arbitration clause in this matter, is unclear, to say the least.[33]

3.4. WILL HEAVILY PROTECTED AND REGULATED BUSINESS IN EUROPE SURVIVE IN THE GLOBAL ECONOMY?

The EU is notoriously stricter than its trade partners in the regulation of B2B contracts, above many other matters (consumer protection, environmental protection, labour relations) and rightly so, where a general interest is at stake.

Protection of a weaker party has its cost. Where the weaker party is a business the extra cost of regulation may not always be justified by its benefits. Protecting small European suppliers against mighty retailers established in the EU may not directly harm the competiveness of EU businesses but it may lead to the survival of the less fit and weaken in general the responsiveness of SME-suppliers to market changes. It may weaken them where they want to export to third countries where they will not encounter the same protection.

3.5. IS THIS THE END OF THE RESPONSIBLE ENTREPRENEUR?

In the line of the foregoing observation the regulation of UTPs may be just the one bridge too far in protecting businesses against the risks of operating in evolving markets. A question that legislatures should also ask themselves is: why protect small entrepreneurs? There would seem to be some good reasons for such protection, namely to avoid the concentration of market power to the detriment of consumers – which is the role of competition law – or to guarantee the self-sufficiency of a country in foodstuffs, and hence measures to protect agriculture (although protection against UTPs may not be the most adequate tool). But

33 *Ibid.*

protecting existing business against market forces may lead to inefficiencies, like impeding the entry of more efficient suppliers.

4. GENERAL CONCLUSION

The introduction of laws against UTPs is in "l'air du temps." Most member States have now enacted some sort of prohibition of UTPs and there is now the EU Directive on UTPS in the food supply chain.

The idea is that small businesses, in particular, small suppliers, are at the mercy of their mighty commercial partners, in particular large retailers.

The regulation of UTPs seems sympathetic, but it is questionable whether the, sometimes far-reaching, protection that is offered, is desirable and, if it is, whether it is efficient. The consequences of regulating UPTs have generally not been sufficiently examined or at least not been taken sufficiently serious.

Eventually, if on the face of it, certain conditions imposed by the stronger party on the weaker one seem blatantly unfair and should therefore not be tolerated, their prohibition may fail to take into account the economic reality as well as the inhibiting effect of such prohibitions on dynamic competition and self-reliance of businesses.

The case for a comprehensive regulation of UTPs still has to be made.

CONSUMER COMPETITION MARKET SERIES

The books in the CONSUMER COMPETITION MARKET SERIES bundle the results of research activities of the CONSUMER COMPETITION MARKET (CCM) institute of the KU Leuven, co-directed by Wouter Devroe, Bert Keirsbilck and Evelyne Terryn.

The series focuses on the legal infrastructure of the internal market of the European Union in the broadest sense. Like CCM itself, the series deals in an integrated way with consumer law, B2B and B2C commercial practices law, sectoral market regulation, the four freedoms (free movement of persons, goods, services and capital) and competition (including EU and national antitrust law, EU merger control and EU state aid law).

www.ingramcontent.com/pod-product-compliance
Ingram Content Group UK Ltd.
Pitfield, Milton Keynes, MK11 3LW, UK
UKHW051847100926
8556IPUK00005B/499

9 781780 689807